Changes in Soviet Policy
Towards the West

D1282463

Changes in Soviet Policy Towards the West

Gerhard Wettig
*Federal Institute for Soviet
and International Studies,
Cologne*

Pinter Publishers
London

Westview Press
Boulder & San Francisco

DK
289
·W478
1991

© Gerhard Wettig, 1991

First published in Great Britain in 1991 by
Pinter Publishers Limited
25 Floral Street, London WC2E 9DS

All rights reserved. No part of this publication may be
reproduced, stored in a retrieval system, or transmitted by
any other means without the prior written permission of the
copyright holder. Please direct all enquiries to the publishers.

British Library Cataloguing in Publication Data

A CIP catalogue record for this book is available from the
British Library

ISBN 0 86187 158 8 (hb)

Typeset by Witwell Ltd.
Printed and bound in Great Britain by SRP Ltd.

Published in 1991 in the United States of America by
Westview Press, Inc., 5500 Central Avenue,
Boulder, Colorado 80301

Library of Congress Cataloging-in-Publication Data
CIP data available upon request. CIP No. 90–072132

ISBN 0-8133-8347-1

Contents

Acknowledgements

To write a book on Soviet foreign policy when events are moving so fast and changes occurring all the time, is certainly not without risk. There is not only the possibility that new factors may come into play tomorrow which disprove, or at the least relativize, what has been correct until today. An even greater danger lies in the individual author's limited capacity to absorb and digest vast quantities of the most divergent source materials, too many of which are both interesting and relevant. I could not have dared to write my study under these conditions if I had not had the chance to talk about the events and the related problems with a great number of colleagues, particularly at the Federal Institute for Soviet and International Studies in Cologne where I have the privilege to have worked for a long time. I have also used their knowledge and elicited their advice in fields of study which are not precisely my Soviet foreign policy speciality but which are nonetheless crucial for the more general context in which Soviet foreign policy operates. Some of my colleagues in the Federal Institute, notably Olga Alexandrova, Heinz Brahm, Helmut Dahm, Hans-Hermann Hoehmann, Fred Oldenburg, Heinz Timmermann and Gerhard Simon, have read parts of the emerging book manuscript, and I have greatly benefited from their helpful remarks. Any errors which may be contained in this study are of course mine. I want to express my thanks also to the Director of the Federal Institute, Heinrich Vogel, who has largely contributed to creating the conditions which have allowed me to write the book.

Chapters 4, 5, 6, 8 and the final Conclusions have been written in English. Rosemarie Leusch, the most capable and devoted English-language secretary of the Federal Institute, has written out my taped dictation and patiently inserted my subsequent additions. For technical reasons, the rest of the book – Chapters 1, 2, 3 and 7 – were originally German. Robert Taubman provided good English translations of them. Last but not least, Adéle Linderholm of Pinter Publishers, has thoroughly edited the whole and thereby greatly contributed to what I hope will be good reading.

The study was completed in the early summer of 1990. Thus it has not been possible yet for the author to assess the international implications of increasing disorganization within the USSR.

Gerhard Wettig

1 The domestic sources of Gorbachev's new approach to foreign policy

GORBACHEV'S UNDERLYING CHALLENGE

Gorbachev has on several occasions described the transformation he has prescribed for the Soviet Union as a 'revolution within the [1917] Revolution'. According to Marxist theory, a revolution presupposes a revolutionary situation. Such a situation comprises not only widespread 'grass roots' dissatisfaction with the prevailing conditions, it also implies that those 'up top' are no longer able to preserve the existing order. The Soviet leader admitted that this was indeed the case when, at the Plenum of the Central Committee of the Communist Party of the Soviet Union (CPSU) in January 1987, he first spoke of a 'pre-crisis situation', thereby indicating that preventive measures would have to be taken to avoid full-scale crisis.

The crucial factor giving rise to this reference was the explicity voiced recognition that 'real socialism' had been 'lagging behind capitalism in terms of the standard of technological development' attained. In particular, there was concern that the Soviet Union was in danger of missing out on the incipient 'new technological stage in the scientific and technological revolution' with its as yet inestimable impacts and, as a consequence, being relegated to the ranks of the underdeveloped countries. The revolution from above that Gorbachev prescribed for the Soviet Union was expressly intended to create propitious 'conditions for overcoming this dropback'.[1]

The circumstances that initially attracted the greatest attention from the Soviet leadership was the country's weak economic and technological performance. In the past decades, as Soviet economists are now free to point out in public, the Soviet Union had plummeted in the world development ranking tables, and this downward trend was continuing. It was already affecting the material basis of Soviet power in the international system. A shortage of resources had for a long time been seriously restricting the Kremlin's foreign-policy options. A glance into the increasingly gloomy future made it apparent that the Soviet Union would shortly be unable to preserve its military might as the crucial basis for its international status unless there were a change for the better. These concerns were further heightened by the realization that the socio-political structure of the Soviet Union was also exhibiting worsening symptoms of weakness. The leadership was beginning to lose control of the bureaucracies, of the production process and of the proceeds of the economy.[2]

One of the most serious aspects of the situation was that it was becoming more and more difficult to remedy the multifarious deficits with the aid of the accustomed administrative tools. For example, the Soviet leadership had, despite the weak economic and technological performance of the country as a whole, been able to keep up arms production by concentrating all available resources on the arms sector and by procuring Western blueprints, often by illicit means. As the rampant 'shadow economy' made the economic process less and less susceptible to reliable control from above, and as technological progress came to depend more and more on all-round development of the country rather than on selective successes, the traditional remedies became ineffective.

At the same time, the life nerve of the regime was being pinched by a loss of party control over public morality. The terror of the Stalin era, which had largely dissuaded the bureaucrats and producers from pursuing their own interests when these were frustrated by the existing command structures, was by now a thing of the distant past. Accordingly, plan compliance was decreasing, while the misappropriation of state authority and goods for private purposes was becoming more and more widespread. The *apparatchiki* had set up their own feudal system and were covering up their unauthorized activities with the aid of a mutually arranged reporting network which prevented higher-level authorities from reviewing or intervening in what was going on below. For instance, those involved in the production and distribution process were not only able to fake the plan fulfilment reports but also to divert from the goods to which they had access everything needed for themselves and their dependents for barter for other commodities and for 'gifts' to persons thought to be useful some day. The scale on which the products of the economic process were being sidetracked in this way had in the course of time become enormous.

According to authoritative Soviet reports, the pressure on resources as a result of the Brezhnev leadership's imperially expansionist policies had also become unbearable. The scale of the arms effort was ruining the country's economy. This already strained situation was aggravated still further when, in the late seventies, the United States began to step up its own arms effort in response to the Soviet challenge. The Kremlin was particularly worried by the qualitative innovations envisaged by the rival superpower in the context of its 'Strategic Defense Initiative' (SDI). Critical Soviet observers had come to see Brezhnev and his aides as the true originators of the dreaded arms race against the economically and technologically superior Americans. In the latter half of the eighties, the old regime was accused in retrospect of having, with its over-zealous arms build-up, added impetus to the Reagan administration's efforts to embroil the Soviet Union in an arms race in order to ruin the country completely.

In Gorbachev's overall diagnosis, the Soviet Union had already dropped almost to the level of an underdeveloped Third World country and was in danger of lagging further and further behind even in those sectors — such as arms production and space technology — on which the Soviet Union had always based its claim to superpower status. If this trend were not reversed, the country would one day be an 'Upper Volta with missiles'. But this — coupled with the signs of incipient decay in domestic order — could not fail to have repercussions for the authority of the party, and especially of the top-line rulers within the CPSU. The first general secretary to have become fully aware of the problems and their potential impact appears to have been Andropov. But during his short period of rule, and beset by his failing health, Andropov had had no opportunity to draw effective practical conclusions from this new awareness. It was only after Gorbachev came to office in March 1985 — following the Chernenko interlude — that the task of renovating the country was placed on the CPSU's political agenda.

PHASES IN THE EFFORTS TOWARDS REFORM

From the very beginning, criticism of the old Brezhnev regime centred around the charge that it had been inefficient and had blocked progress. This was reflected for instance in the retrospective description of the years under Brezhnev as a 'period of stagnation' (period *zastoia*). Gorbachev's ideas about the remedies required at first circled within traditional terms of reference. His initial approach was to attempt to get the country's development moving again solely by means of corrective actions in the economy and technology. 'Acceleration) (*uskorenie*) was what was needed. This unequivocally implied that the conventional systemic orientation was essentially correct and that everything could be solved merely by giving new impetus to development. As in earlier attempts to remedy systemic deficiencies, the present difficulties were to be eliminated by means of corrections to the existing framework — for example by improving labour discipline and performance incentives and by rationalizing the steering mechanisms. An anti-alcohol campaign — which gained Gorbachev the nickname 'Mineral Secretary' — was launched with the aim of improving the performance of the workforce.

It soon became apparent, however, that the deficiencies in the system of administrative socialism could not be eliminated without fundamental changes to the system itself. The new ideas that gained acceptance in the Kremlin in the winter of 1986/87 envisaged the centrally administered economy adopting some market economy elements, with a view to attaining a productivity level comparable with that in the West. Efforts were to be directed towards the 'restoration and evolution of the principles of democratic centralism in the steering of the economy', ie towards revitalizing the existing system. The 'borrowing of capitalist methods' was expressly intended not to culminate in an emulation of Western models. On the contrary, the intention was to carry out changes 'in keeping with the socialist choice' already made once and for all in the Soviet Union. Anybody who was counting on a departure from the socialist path was in for a 'bitter disappointment'. The objective was not less but 'more socialism'.[3] The reasoning behind this was that the system of administrative socialism imposed by Stalin was merely a perversion of an intrinsically good and correct system. The elimination of a number of misguided practices was thus going to lead back to true socialism.

But even at this stage, Gorbachev and his advisers were beginning to realize that their goal of adding 'more dynamism' to socialism could not be achieved by changes to the economic system alone. As of 1987, this viewpoint gained more and more acceptance. The aim was now to change society as well as the economy, for instance by introducing wide-scale publicity (*glasnost*). The political system was also in need of new impetus, which was to be imparted by 'more democracy'. A new understanding of the socialist system was proclaimed. 'We want more socialism and therefore more democracy.' The difficulties under which the Soviet Union was suffering were 'by no means a crisis of socialism as a socio-political system, but just the opposite, the result of not adequately consistent application of socialist principles, of departure from them and even their distortion.' Precise adherence to the social system and a planned economy would put the Soviet Union in a particularly good position to carry out the necessary changes.[4] This last claim was based on the conviction, still widely held at the time, that the command structure of the socialist system was inherently superior to the West in that it enabled the leadership to establish priorities and to give precedence to their implementation.

The change of approach was reflected in a change of terminology. Instead of the 'acceleration' of the economy that had been propagated in the first two years under Gorbachev, in 1987, talk focused on 'restructuring' (*perestroika*) of the Soviet Union as a whole. The original reform plan was extended in scope and in the quality of the projected changes. If, at the first session of the Council for Mutual Economic Assistance (CMEA) following his coming to office, Gorbachev was still insisting that he considered even a strictly economic reform along the lines of the modest examples of Yugoslavia or China too drastic, by 1987 he was calling more and more emphatically for a radical transformation — in all aspects of the economy, of society and even politics.

In a third phase, starting in the second half of 1989, the Soviet leadership began to move more and more apparently towards the idea of a new style of socialism, to be implemented with the aid of market-economy tools. This change of direction reached its climax first in Bonn on 10 April 1990 with the Soviet consent to the Conference for Security and Cooperation in Europe (CSCE) countries' adoption of market economy principles[5] and then with the announcement on 26 May 1990 that the Soviet Union would make the transition to a market economy.[6]

PROBLEMS IN THE IMPLEMENTATION OF *PERESTROIKA*

The ideas guiding the Soviet leaders in their re-orientation were not, however, so clearly defined and detailed as the public announcements suggested. The practical steps undertaken were still based on not very clear conceptions of the concrete consequences of their programmatic ideals. This was particularly apparent with regard to public-order issues. The 1987/88 attempt to adopt Western market economy elements to increase productivity while adhering to the principles of a centrally administered economy and a socialist system of ownership was by its very nature doomed to failure. But even later, the Kremlin continued to succumb to illusions: when it professed its commitment to a market economy but at the same time was unable to detach itself from old socialist notions such as the ownership of the means of production. Also, the anti-capitalist prejudice prevalent among the population and in the bureaucracy as a result of decades of indoctrination (expressed, for example, in the indignation over the profits made by the new private cooperatives, and the subsequent restrictions imposed on them) constituted another major psychological resistance potential. Insecurity by the Gorbachev leadership itself — revealed in its procrastination over the introduction of essential price reforms because of their potential social and political repercussions — is yet another factor casting doubt on whether the proclaimed transition to a market economy can actually be put into practice.

In principle, though, Gorbachev and his aides gradually concluded that radical changes were imperative and that the long overdue reforms must be more than mere corrections to the existing system. The social and political conditions in the country were in need of a wide scale *perestroika*. The patterns of behavior instilled in the people in the past were a constant barrier to improving the country's performance. If society was to perform well, it required leaders able and willing to bear responsibility in its key positions. But the bureaucracy, in whose hands the decisions lay, had grown accustomed to a logic of mutual complicity which ruled out any form of individual responsibility. This collectivization of responsibility had previously been the only possible way to evade the unfair and intolerable personal risk that arose with the need to ignore established procedures.

Administrative socialism was continually producing instructions and bottlenecks which could not be handled without departing from the bounds of legality. The workforce and the *apparatchiki* alike were in constant danger of being reprimanded for having violated regulations that simply could not be obeyed. The only way to alleviate this risk was to involve as many colleagues and supervisors as possible as accomplices and allies; these would then have a vested interest in warding off any investigations. In this way, responsibility for impending decisions in the Soviet bureaucracies became so widely distributed that in the end no personal accountability could be discerned at all, and evey action taken was defended tooth and nail by a multitude of implicated individuals. As long as this pattern of behaviour persisted, nobody could be made personally responsible for the success or failure of any particular action.

But willingness to bear personal responsibility is essential if any real performance is to be achieved. The performance-based society envisaged by Gorbachev requires self-confident citizens — and not timid underlings anxious to avoid anything that could expose them to criticism. The Soviet leadership thus made political emancipation its motto. *Glasnost* was one of the means to this end; the introduction of elections involving true decisionmaking another.

As of the summer of 1988, proliferating disruptions in the country's economy made it doubtful whether the measures introduced up to then were going to have the desired effect. This was not surprising. The workforces' efforts to fulfil the established planning targets slackened still further, with the result that the old steering mechanisms lost even more of whatever effectiveness they still commanded. But no new, consistent steering mechanisms were created in their place. The supply situation deteriorated still further. Two contrary interpretations of the ensuing predicament emerged. One claimed that the changes had not gone far enough or had not been consistent enough to fulfil their purpose; the other line of argument maintained that it was precisely the departure from long-standing practices that had been the cause of all the difficulties. But for Gorbachev and his aides there was no going back along the path on which they had embarked; otherwise they would have forfeited all credibility. The decisionmakers in the Kremlin were also well aware that a return to administrative socialism offered the country no perspective for the future. There was thus no alternative to a continuation of *perestroika*. However, Gorbachev also attempted to allay the growing dissatisfaction among the population, suffering more and more from supply shortages, by looking for strategems with an immediate relieving effect. One such expedient was to divert funds urgently needed for investment to improve the supply of consumer goods. This, however, did no more than plug a few gaps.

On the whole, the Soviet leadership's record up to now is one of hesitancy. Though it insists it has abandoned administrative socialism, it has taken no clear steps towards creating a new system. It is important that this half-heartedness be recognized despite Gorbachev having, in the autumn of 1989, accepted the countries of Eastern Europe's transition to a market economy system and despite his having, in the spring of the following year, himself vociferously proclaimed his endorsement of the market economy system.[7] Decisions on crucial questions have been put off again and again — with the inevitable result that the problems have grown even more serious; Gorbachev has been forced more and more into the role of a defender of domestic status quo interests in opposition to reformist forces that have been drifting ever further away from him. If the reforms have nevertheless made some progress, this is due to the pressure exerted on the president by groups such as the Democratic Platform.

THE POLITICAL WRESTLING OVER *PERESTROIKA*

From the very beginning, Gorbachev was more successful than any of his predecessors at filling the crucial posts in the central power apparatus with men of his own choosing. However, the results of his team selection were marred by the fact that he had had less opportunity than previous general secretaries to build up a reliable clientele of followers before coming to office. For this reason he had to fall back on some people inherited as followers of deceased politicians such as Kirilenko and Andropov and who did not always follow him on his new course. This meant that he soon had to make replacements, for instance when he dismissed Chebrikov, whom he had himself made chairman of the KGB.

Greater still were the difficulties encountered as a result of the instinctive opposition to *perestroika* from broad sections of the middle- and lower-level *apparat*. Though the Soviet leader at no time needed to fear for his own position, the conservative trends especially predominant in the party hierarchy nevertheless constituted a political burden. As long as Gorbachev was an active reformer, he had to reckon with the possibility of being outvoted, particularly in the Central Committee of the CPSU; he had to find new ways of ensuring this did no happen, for instance by launching a surprise coup to send a number of the Central Committee members packing or by diverting the decision about the future political orientation of the country — normally a matter for the Central Committee — to a hastily convened *ad hoc* party conference, over the composition of which, however, he had only limited control.

Such abrasive antagonisms were certainly a major factor in a personal performance trend in which Gorbachev has gradually — and especially in the course of 1989 — lost his reformist verve, reverting more and more to conservative positions. Another factor may have been that the Soviet leader was worried about the long-term prospect of a coalition emerging among the *apparatchiki*, the military and the national conservatives. Such a political combination might conceivably count on support from the lower social strata who have been in need since time immemorial, afflicted by still further privations in recent years and faced with at least temporary further pauperization in the wake of a future economic reform. The right's weakness, of course, was that it had no plausible alternative to offer, neither in terms of policy nor personalities. In the winter of 1989–90, the displeasure that had been building up for a long time among broad circles of the high-level military over unwelcome domestic and foreign-policy developments displayed itself in a demonstrative warning addressed to the president.[8] Gorbachev tried to take the wind out of the opposition's sails by making equally demonstrative concessions on a number of points. But when the democratic and market-oriented radicals elected Boris Ieltsin president of the crucial Russian republic, which then proceeded to proclaim Russia's independence from Union legislation, the associated loss of important power positions meant that Gorbachev now has to make allowance for even more particularist interests.

Gorbachev attempted to counter his domestic opponents not only by means of power-policy tactics (including close liaison with prominent members of the KGB) but also by mobilizing the general public (such tactics, however, have proved effective only against the conservatives). *Glasnost* was used with some success against the bureaucracy. Critics both from within and outside were encouraged to expose the activities of the functionaries to the public spotlight. One of the main objectives pursued by the top-level leaders in promoting *glasnost* was to ensure that they would no longer have to rely on reports from their subordinate agencies as the sole basis for assessing those agencies' performance. An information source not manipulated by those concerned was essential if the top-level authorities were to gain a more accurate picture of the activities and omissions of their subordinates. In this respect, *glasnost* was an instrument that was intended to make it more difficult for local bureaucrats, in the tradition of the feudal lords of the middle ages, to evade control by the central powers.

There was another reason Gorbachev considered it important to break the bureaucracy's monopoly on information enabling it to influence the leadership in its own interest. As publicly discussed in Moscow as of 1987/88, many of the political errors of the past had been committed because the competent experts had not been consulted. A fatal decision such as the go-ahead for military intervention in Afghanistan were alleged to have been taken because Brezhnev had relied almost exclusively on a biased recommendation from one agency. Many of the obvious repercussions had been overlooked out of pure ignorance and had later cost the Soviet Union dearly. If the arguments for and against had been discussed in public, it was mooted, events would have taken a more propitious course. The practical conclusion was that official secretiveness had been harmful in the past and must not be allowed to recur in the future. *Glasnost* was required in the political issues hitherto reserved for the bureaucracy. Public discussion of public policy must be invented, if it did not exist already. Despite such professions of openness, however, there was still no question of the Kremlin allowing its policies to be shaped by public participation. The leadership continued to take its decisions without preparatory opinion-forming in society as a whole. There were, however, other cases in which *glasnost* gave the politicians an idea of the sentiment within important sectors of public opinion on which to base their decisions.

Gorbachev also used 'democratization' to curb the influence of the apparatuses. He instituted a quasi-parliament to be a third political force alongside the party and state bureaucracy structures. Although the Supreme Soviet had always existed, it had hitherto exercised no real power. It had neither been legitimated by real elections, nor put in an appearance as a working body with standing committees. At the general secretary's instigation, both these deficits were discussed and eventually remedied in 1988/89. Following general elections in the spring of 1989, the People's Deputies met in the middle of the year to appoint from their ranks the members of the new Supreme Soviet, which was also given significant powers of consultation and ratification on domestic and foreign policy affairs. Gorbachev was voted chairman and filled the most important parliamentary positions with his own confidants. Thus a new power centre was created, curtailing the competences of the party apparatus. Furthermore, the new option of nominating competing candidates, first introduced for the election of the People's Deputies meant — even if not exercised everywhere — that conservative party functionaries ran the risk of being voted out of office. This freedom of choice was also intended to pave the way for the removal of unsuccessful candidates from their functions within the party.

The calculation that the conversion of the Supreme Soviet and of the regional and local soviets into something resembling real parliaments would solve Gorbachev's domestic power problems did not entirely work out. Although the Soviet leader succeeded with the help of the Supreme Soviet in adding the office of president of the Soviet Union to his former function as general secretary of the CPSU, thus extending his power on a scale unparalleled since Stalin's day, and although there was a significant shift of political weight from the party to the renovated hierarchy of the soviets, the power of the state and of the KGB remained undiminished and in many cases it proved impossible to remove the party establishment from the Supreme Soviet and the lower-level soviets. Many conservative functionaries either did not stand for election or, like Gorbachev himself, gained their seats via the blocks reserved for the various organizations. Nor did failure to gain election to a soviet necessarily result in loss of party functions, if the unsuccesful candidate still enjoyed enough support within the party. Nevertheless, the progressive forces managed to gain a strong backing in the Supreme Soviet and in the soviets of many Republics (to which elections have been held since the beginning of 1990). However, this loss of influence by the old cadres benefited Gorbachev less and less: the more the president himself withdrew to more conservative positions, the more the progressive forces in the soviets formed up without — and in some cases even against — him.

In the wake of the landslide towards democracy and market economy in Eastern Europe in the autumn of 1989, the criticism that had originally been directed only against Gorbachev's domestic policy was extended to encompass his foreign and security policy. One of the most prominent right-wingers in the Politburo, Ligachev, speaking at the February 1990 plenum of the Central Committee, cast a negative spotlight on the 'occurrences in Europe', identifying an 'approaching danger'. He raised a warning finger about the 'precipitation of the reunification of Germany' in which West Germany threatened to swallow up the German Democratic Republic. The 'massive economic and military potential' which a unified Germany would have at its disposal gave grounds to expect it to exert pressure for a 'revision of the post-war boundaries' and to fear a repeat of 'pre-war Munich' along the lines of 1938. The time had come 'to recognize this new peril of our age and to inform the party and the people' before it was 'too late'.[9]

The second secretary of the Kazakhstan Central Committee, V. G. Anufriev, blamed Gorbachev for 'the disintegration of the unity of the party', for the 'ideological breakdowns', and for the 'occurrences in Eastern Europe'.

They have destroyed our buffer zone. God be with them, may they live as they see fit. But if even today they are advancing territorial and material claims, threatening consulates, and defiling the graves of our soldiers and our shrines, then they are humiliating a great country.

The Soviet Union, Anufriev continued, was prepared to extend its hospitality to the new masters of Poland and their like, but must take care not to feed other countries so that these could have it better than the Soviets themselves.[10] The Soviet ambassador to Warsaw, Brovikov, also criticized his country's official policy towards Eastern Europe, albeit in more moderate tones. And from the general public more and more voices were heard to complain vehemently and bitterly that the Soviet empire and the ideology that had been its cornerstone were being abandoned. In the late spring, a number of high-ranking military personnel cast off the reserve they had been exercising up to that time and publicly vented their critical opinions.[11]

CHANGING PRIORITIES IN FOREIGN AND SECURITY POLICY

The developments within the Soviet Union had significant consequences for the country's conduct towards the outside world. Under Brezhnev, foreign-policy interests had always taken priority; the exigencies of foreign policy had had to be fulfilled unconditionally. The satisfaction of necessities within the country itself had been relegated to second place. Accordingly, expenditure on arms and on the 'countries of socialist orientation' in the Third World had taken on enormous proportions. Defence spending at that time, the precise amount of which was probably unknown even to the Kremlin because of arbitrary pricing for the development and production of its weapons, is nowadays estimated by Soviet economists to have accounted for 20 to 25 per cent, if not more, of the gross national product.[12]

Among the Third World countries which had been entitled to Soviet support and maintenance by virtue of their leaderships' profession of Marxism–Leninism, Cuba was the most costly. But other countries also devoured high and constantly escalating subsidies. The most expensive country in Africa — though still ranking far behind Cuba on the money-drain scale — was Angola, which according to Foreign Minister Shevardnadze, accounted for nearly three billion roubles per year.[13] In the light of a budget deficit now publicly admitted to have amounted to more than 100 billion roubles in 1989, the Gorbachev leadership came to the conclusion that it could no longer afford its interminably high expenditure on client states. However, this was a decision in principle from which exceptions could be made in special cases. For instance, military *matériel* aid to the pro-Soviet regime in Afghanistan continued on a massive scale even after the withdrawal of the Soviet armed forces in 1988/89, and Castro continued to enjoy enormous subsidies from the Soviet Union despite his rejection of urgent recommendations from Moscow that it was time for *perestroika* in Cuba, too.

In general, however, the Kremlin considered its costly material commitment to the 'countries of socialist orientation' to be no longer justified. The recipients had failed to fulfil the political expectations made of them. The Brezhnev leadership had hoped that its subsidized clients would serve as points of attraction for other developing countries. Instead, just the contrary had been the case. Its nurselings had become poorer and poorer despite all the Soviet aid, becoming caveats for their neighbours. Besides, more and more of the Soviet-supported regimes were being challenged by guerrilla movements from within — a clear indication of how unpopular they were or had become among their own populations. Thus from Moscow's perspective the aid hitherto granted appeared in the majority of cases to be unwarranted in terms of political advantage. For this reason, Soviet foreign-policymakers looked around for possible ways of extricating their country from its commitments without losing face and without leaving their former friends completely in the lurch. This was the background to the need for an 'economization of foreign policy' voiced as of 1987/88.

In the field of security and arms policy, too, domestic exigencies brought about a change of strategy. The Gorbachev leadership adhered to the view that defence was the 'principal priority of the State',[14] but it changed the practical conclusions it drew from this statement of principle. Until the early eighties it had been taken for granted that the security of the Soviet Union was directly proportional to the numbers of soldiers and weapons at the Kremlin's disposal. Gorbachev and his aides had challenged this blind assumption as early as in the summer of 1984, even before Gorbachev had come to office. In the course of an altercation with Marshal Ogarkov, who was calling for the arms build-up to be increased, the Gorbachev team had pointed out that excessive exploitation of Soviet research, development and production capacities for the benefit of the armed forces could in the long term impair the country's ability to meet the military's requirements both in quantitative and especially in qualitative terms. To dedicate too much effort to satisfying present-day wishes involved the risk that not enough resources would be left over for the modernization of the economy and of technology, on which the ability to meet future arms requirements depended. Thus an enlightened military interest was used as an argument against excessive expansion in the arms sector.

Soon after Gorbachev came to office, he backed up this approach by pushing more and more emphatically for mutual reductions in the armed forces making up the East–West balance with a view to reducing military demand at home. The further the arms level could be reduced on both sides, the better the Soviet prospects for preserving the existing correlation of military forces at lower cost. This consideration explains the urgency with which Gorbachev has, from his very beginning, pursued the cause of arms control.

In the new general secretary's first years in office, economic necessities increasingly dominated the Soviet public's attention. This trend was reflected in a growing reluctance to give priority to the demands put forward by the military and paralleled by a significant loss of their influence, also attributable to the fact that Gorbachev was consulting civilian advisers and thus breaking the military experts' decisionmaking monopoly on defence issues. The recommendations of the civilian advisers boiled down to the opinion that the Soviet Union could hold its own in the outside world with a lower level of military resources than had been demanded in the past. This assessment found widespread acclaim in the Soviet media which, in the light of the country's unsatisfactory economic situation, supported the conclusion that much less weaponry would still be adequate.

In official circles, too, there were new tones to be heard. As early as July 1987 one prominent social scientist from Gorbachev's entourage spoke of the need to bring about an 'optimization of the ratio between productive and military expenditure'.[15] A year later, the Soviet foreign minister drew attention to the 'economic aspect of national security' and put a different perspective on the traditional notion that security was best assured by the 'presence of properly prepared and equipped armed forces'. 'More than ever before, the ability of the armed forces to fulfil their mission [depended] directly and principally on a powerful economy and highly developed science.' What was important to the security of any country was 'not so much its arsenals as its ability to create and to produce new things'. Accordingly, defence efforts counted less than 'reserves of scientific ideas, reserves of technological capabilities, reserves of production potential, and reserves of qualified cadres' capable of creating all that.[16] In the field of the economy, Shevardnadze regarded 'scientific self-sufficiency and technological independence as the most important guarantees for a future without worries about the existence and the fortunes of socialism'.[17]

The pressure emanating from the domestic situation was so strong that not even the military could close their ears to the economic line of argumentation. In December 1988, a spokesman of the General Staff endorsed the viewpoint that 'in the age of nuclear weapons and missiles' security could not be assured 'by endless accumulation of weapons'.[18] From semi-official circles came even more sceptical assessments of the importance of arsenals. A power that had 'concentrated fully on the problem of the foreign threat' was in reality precipitating the 'deterioration of its national security'. The extraction of 'massive resources' for military deployment could lead to the emergence and intensification of 'economic, social, national, and other problems' in society.[19]

According to the judgement expressed by one Soviet colonel in the journal of the Main Political Directorate of the Soviet Army and Navy in early 1989, past concentration on efforts towards establishing a military counterweight to the West had resulted in the Soviet Union having lost parity 'in the economic and scientific/technological sectors'. This had given rise to a catastrophic situation. 'Since the mid-seventies we have started to drop behind the US in the growth rate of the gross national product and in recent years also in the growth of labour productivity.' Experts estimated that the Soviet standard of living ranked fifty to sixty in the world. 'Neither in material nor in intellectual terms does this match our possibilities and our needs.' For this reason it was essential to place less emphasis on weaponry and to invest more resources in the development of the country.[20]

When, in the course of 1988, the Soviet supply situation deteriorated still further and the leadership was faced with growing public discontent, discussion turned more and more to the 'social dimension' of external security. What this meant was that it was essential to dedicate adequate resources to the consumption sector; otherwise there was a risk of a public reaction that would jeopardize external security and integrity. In the light of all the above considerations, Gorbachev came to the conclusion that it was necessary to 'review expenditure on defence' and voiced his conviction that it would be possible to make cuts 'without impairing security and defence capability'.[21]

CHANGES IN DECISIONMAKING IN FOREIGN POLICY

The Gorbachev leadership's endeavours to curtail the influence of the bureaucracies had its effects on foreign policy, too. The point of departure was the public criticism, referred to earlier, of the autocratic decisions taken by Brezhnev with just a small inner circle of advisers. To preclude any such decisions ever again being taken without adequate debate, what was needed was public discussion of political issues. This public discussion should serve as input for in-depth consultation between decisionmakers and experts. In this context, Shevardnadze made it clear that in his view those systems that closed themselves off to the 'influx of fresh ideas' were 'doomed'. For that reason, his ministry was open to advice from experts from the Soviet Union and the whole world.[22] What the foreign ministry had in mind was more than just a non-committal exchange of opinions. The public must participate to a certain extent in decision-making. That was an imperative of *perestroika*, which necessitated a 'democratization of social life', *glasnost*, a 'fight against bureaucracy', and 'legalism' throughout the country. The goal was the 'renovation of the political system of socialism', which presupposed the elimination of the distortions in the legal sphere and guarantees for an irreversible democratic evolution. These conceptions were linked with the idea of a state based on law and order in which everybody could rely on established legal procedures.[23]

According to official declarations, such state legalism also implied 'public and democratic discussion of foreign-policy problems and decisionmaking in accordance with procedures strictly defined in law'.[24] The pertinent legislation, another purpose of which was to improve the Soviet Union's international reputation, was modelled on Western parliamentary principles and prescribed that foreign-policy initiatives be submitted to the Supreme Soviet for approval. A committee was set up for preliminary deliberation on the foreign-policy bills to be submitted to the Supreme Soviet. Of course, the introduction of this new procedure in mid-1989 did not necessarily mean that all the fundamental issues of foreign and security policy were thereafter made the subject of public discussion. Gorbachev continued in the old Soviet habit of taking his decisions behind closed doors, even if certain projects now had to be debated and approved by the Supreme Soviet. The real effect of the new procedure was to deprive the party cadres of their traditional influence over foreign affairs.

The principal formulator of foreign policy in the Soviet Union is the foreign ministry which, in addition to its own highly qualified specialists, can draw upon the expertise of an advisory board and various pertinent Institutes of the Academy of Sciences. It may also be assumed that the propaganda apparatus of the Central Committee continues to exercise some considerable influence on foreign policy, not least because, as it admits itself, Moscow attaches major importance to the aspect of courting sympathy abroad in its foreign- and security-policy decisionmaking. In this context, Shevardnadze has stressed the need 'to correlate public opinion [in the West] with the foreign-policy actions planned [by the Soviet Union]' and at the same time 'to foster and to form' Western public opinion. He also advanced the principle that 'every diplomat [must be] a mediaman' and 'every mediaman a diplomat'. What was needed was an 'alliance between diplomacy and journalism' that would be 'unique as regards its means and possibilities for bringing influence to bear on public opinion' and that would have to be accepted as 'indispensable and highly effective'.[25]

Since 1987/88 at the latest, the International Department of the Central Committee of the CPSU has hardly been in a position to bring direct influence to bear on state foreign policy any more. Its domain was the establishment and cultivation of relations with political parties and other social groups abroad. However, it retained its membership — alongside the foreign ministry, the propaganda apparatus of the Central Committee and the foreign department of the KGB — in the International Commission, which was responsible for formulating the basic lines of Soviet policy towards the rest of the world.

CHANGES IN FUNDAMENTAL RELATIONS WITH THE COUNTRIES OF THE WEST

The 1956 CPSU party congress proclaimed the binding principle of 'peaceful coexistence' (*mirnoe sosushchestvovanie*). This principle reflected the Soviet desire to prevent war between the East and the West and superseded the previously valid theory that in its final stage the replacement of capitalism by socialism would have to be consummated by military action against an opponent that was in its death throes but fighting tooth and nail to defend its existence. The main motive for reviewing that earlier doctrine had been the realization that a military conflict between the Soviet Union and NATO entailed the danger of nuclear escalation and thus incalculable destruction. The change of doctrine did not, however, imply that the principle of antagonism with the West had been abandoned altogether. Both Khrushchev and Brezhnev had adhered to the earlier notions of a fundamental antagonism between socialism and capitalism. Thus, from 1956 to the early years of Gorbachev, 'peaceful coexistence' merely meant carrying on the ideological struggle against the West in forms other than war in direct East–West relations. The official doctrine formulated at the Twentieth Party Congress and thereafter held open options for armed conflict outside the sphere of direct relations between the two sides and also options for hostile behaviour by other than military means. The 'principles of peaceful coexistence', ie the renunciation of the use of armed force, referred solely to 'relations between states with different social orders'. All other international relations which were not of a state-to-state nature and did not affect the direct relationship between the major powers in East and West were excluded from the no-war imperative. Any other conflicts that might break out within individual states or within either bloc were regarded as essentially open to the use of military coercion — evidently because they gave no grounds to fear devastating nuclear escalation.

In those areas which did not affect the balance of mutual nuclear deterrence between the two world powers, an inexorable 'anti-imperialist struggle' with 'ideological' means was proclaimed. Accordingly, Moscow defined 'peaceful coexistence' as a 'form of the international class struggle' against the West that took into account the conditions of the nuclear age. The *détente* policy slogans of the seventies did not change this basic interpretation in the least. *Détente* was based on the 'principles of peaceful coexistence' and was thus to be played by the same rules.

The Gorbachev leadership's endeavours to reverse the process of Soviet fallback behind the West made it difficult to continue applying the old 'coexistence' principle. Could the Soviet Union still afford to maintain a posture of principled hostility towards the countries of the West? The difficulty was not just that upholding the principle of an irreconcilable antagonism with the West meant continuing that military confrontation which, as of 1987–88, the Kremlin wanted to eliminate because it was putting an intolerable military burden on the economy and on society. At least just as important was the fact that the Soviet leadership urgently needed across-the-board cooperation with the advanced Western industrialized nations as part of its efforts, as of 1986–87, to expedite the scientific and technological development of its own country.

Thus, from 1986–87 on, there was talk of increasing global 'intermeshing' and 'interdependence'. The replacement of the old 'stereotypes' of antagonism by the desire for cooperation was an historical imperative. These new proclamations were at first still closely related to the traditional class struggle doctrine. But this link-up was progressively loosened until by the end of 1989 it had disappeared altogether, an open admission of the fact that the Kremlin was dependent upon non-confrontative relations with the countries of the West in its endeavours to improve the Soviet Union's scientific and technological capability. The Kremlin realized that it had no option but to recruit Western experience if it wanted to reorganize its productive forces and to establish market mechanisms. At the same time, the envisaged technological modernization would be impossible without the transfer of know-how from the West. The Soviet leadership was also demanding that NATO should abolish or at least drastically shorten the COCOM list which prohibited the export of strategically important items to the countries of the Warsaw Pact. There was no chance of the West accommodating these wishes as long as Moscow stuck to the principle of irreconcilable antagonism.

In the first years of Gorbachev's period in office, anti-Western tones predominated in official Soviet statements. Only as of 1987 did any clear relaxation of the traditional thinking in rigid antagonisms become apparent — at first only vaguely and only gradually emerging. One major indication of the incipient modification of Soviet attitudes was the changing public assessment of the prospects of a war with the countries of NATO. If initially the theme had been that there was still a serious military threat from the West, by the summer of 1988 this theory had become subject to substantial qualifications. The Soviet foreign minister declared that it had been possible 'to avert the threat of war', but that that threat was 'not yet eliminated'.[26] When Gorbachev reported to the Supreme Soviet one year later on the successes of his policy on Europe, the prospect of war had been relegated to remote perspectives. Relations with the countries of the West, the president declared, were governed by the desire for wide-scale cooperation.[27]

It was also at this time that the Kremlin revealed its intention to open Soviet society to outside influences. The seclusion policy pursued since Stalin's day was condemned as having been detrimental to the interests of the country. It had not only damaged the Soviet Union's reputation abroad but, even worse, it had prevented that exchange of goods, people and ideas that the Soviet Union needed if it was to develop to the full and to attain world standards. In this context reference was made to the need to rise to the level of the advanced industrial nations in the area of human rights, too. These aspirations, which were of course still a far cry from Soviet reality, are also to be seen in connection with endeavours to win over the countries of the West to the idea of a pan-European economic, legal, security and cultural homeland.

CONCLUSIONS

The Gorbachev leadership's policy can be characterized by a growing emphasis on Soviet domestic interests and needs. The cardinal motive behind this change initiated from above is concern that the Soviet Union could fall even farther behind in its economic and technological performance capability, thus calling into doubt the material basis of its world superpower status. To reverse this decline is the declared aim of all endeavours. One of the conclusions drawn in terms of foreign policy has been to discontinue costly commitments abroad.

The Soviet Union's relations with other countries are now viewed very much from the aspect of economic effectiveness: foreign policy must serve the country and not vice versa. The priority given to domestic policy in practice is nowadays so high that even long-standing principles — such as that of irreconcilable antagonism with Western capitalism — are being abandoned if they impede progress towards the new objectives. Even the country's external security, previously predominant over and in a separate class from all other political necessities is now seen largely as a function of the exigencies of domestic scientific and technological development.

The argument advanced in justification of this new view of things is that, in the long term, the Soviet Union can maintain its power in the international theatre only as long as the requisite material foundations are present. It must therefore reduce its overcommitments in order to have the strength to defend the essential components of its power status.

By now, realities have overtaken the theoretical considerations on which they were originally based. In the light of the many unforeseen factors that have emerged, both in Eastern Europe and in the Soviet Union itself to cast doubt on the future of the Soviet empire, hope of being able to gain strength by casting off inherited burdens and consolidating new frontiers is dwindling — a sore spot which serves Gorbachev's opponents as a point of attack. But there is no going back along the path that has now been taken. If the Kremlin were to attempt to return to the old imperial power policies of the Brezhnev era, it would sacrifice the opportunities afforded by the new policy without being able to regain the positions it has already abandoned. There is no obvious alternative to continuing a policy which seeks cooperation with the developed industrialized nations of the West and which has as its objective that modernization of the country which, arduous and lengthy as the road may be, ultimately constitutes the only conceivable solution to the Soviet Union's problems. A backward-looking imperialist regime might, for a limited period and at the cost of great human sacrifice, be able to bring the country some apparent stability, but it would only intensify the unsolved problems of underdevelopment and would necessarily entail an antagonization with and isolation from the outside world that could pose a danger to the Soviet Union.

NOTES

1. Argument of Gorbachev during a discussion with representatives of the world communist movement on 4 November 1987, *Pravda*, 5 November 1987.
2. Cf. the analysis by Françoise Thom, *The Gorbachev Phenomenon*, London, Pinter, 1989.
3. M. S. Gorbachev, 'Perestroika i novoe myshlenie dlia nashei strany i vsego mira', Moscow, Izdatel'stvo politicheskoi literatury 1987, pp. 30–3.
4. Ibid., pp. 32–3.
5. *Pravda*, 11 April 1990.
6. *Pravda*, 28 May 1990.
7. For the state of the economic reform see Hans-Hermann Hoehmann, 'Die sowjetische Wirtschaft am Beginn der neunziger Jahre: Krisenlage und Reformperspektiven (unpublished paper); John Tedstrom, 'What to Export in the New Stage of Economic Reform', *Report on the USSR*, 6/90, 20 April 1990, pp. 1–3.
8. Andrew McEwen, Troops 'Handed Arms in Warning to Gorbachev', *The Times*, 4 May 1990.
9. *Pravda*, 7 February 1990.
10. *Pravda*, 8 February 1990.
11. An author particularly close to the military is A. Prokhanov, who started the polemic: see Aleksandr Prokhanov, 'Tragediia tsentralizma' *Literaturnaia Rossiia*, no. 1, 5 January 1990, pp. 4–5. For the political context and other related comments see Vera Tolz and Elizabeth Teague, 'Prokhanov Warns of Collapse of Soviet Empire', *Report on the USSR*, no. 6, 1990, pp. 1–3; Olga Alexandrova, 'Konservative Opposition gegen das "neue politische Denken" ', *Aktuelle Analysen des Bundesinstituts fuer ostwissenschaftliche und internationale Studien*, Cologne, no. 22, 21 March 1990.
12. For reports of the scientific conference at which the Soviet participants presented these and other related data see Vladimir Gurevich, 'Kakogo my rosta', *Moskovskie novosti*, 20 May 1990; 'Die Sowjetunion am Rande des Abgrunds', *Neue Zuercher Zeitung*, 26 April 1990.
13. M. Iusin, 'Novyi vzgliad na Afriku', *Izvestiia*, 30 March 1990.
14. Statements by Foreign Minister Shevardnadze at the scientific and political conference of his ministry on 25 July 1988 in *Mezhdunarodnaia zhizn'*, no. 9, p. 16.
15. E. Primakov, 'Novaia filosofiia vneshnei politiki', *Pravda*, 10 July 1987.
16. Shevardnadze 25 July 1988, op. cit., p. 19.
17. Ibid., p. 22.
18. General V. Lobov in an interview in *Pravda*, 17 December 1988.
19. I. Malashenko, 'Bezopasnost — nevoennye aspekty', *Mezhdunarodnaia zhizn'*, no. 12, 1988, p. 45. The article served to prepare the public for Gorbachev's initiative of 7 December 1988 on unilateral forces reduction.
20. Colonel V. Strebkov, 'Voennyi paritet vchera i segodnia', *Krasnaia zvezda*, 3 January 1989.
21. Gorbachev's speech to scientists and cultural workers of the Soviet Union on 6 January 1989 in *Pravda*, 7 January 1989.
22. Shevardnadze, op. cit., pp. 26–7.
23. Statements by the director of the Institute of State and Law of the

USSR Academy of Sciences, V. N. Kudriavtsev, at the scientific and practical conference of the foreign ministry, 25–7 July 1988 *Mezhdunarodnaia zhizn'*, no. 10, pp. 47–9.
24. Deputy Foreign Minister A. L. Adamishin at the scientific and practical conference of the foreign ministry, 25–7 July 1988, *Mezhdunarodnaia zhizn'*, no. 9, pp. 49–50.
25. Shevardnadze, op. cit., p. 30.
26. Ibid., p. 16.
27. *Pravda,* 2 August 1989.

2 Changing patterns of foreign policy

THE TRADITIONAL PATTERN OF SOVIET POLICY TOWARDS THE WEST

The revolution that Lenin inaugurated in Russia was intended to eliminate capitalism as a world system of oppression and exploitation and to liberate mankind by the creation of a socialist order. That implied two things. An unrelenting battle was launched against the 'old world'. And the new system was to be established not just in one country but throughout the world. Thus from the very beginning the aim was the universal overthrow of the existing political, economic and social conditions. The founder of the Soviet state acted on the conviction that the socialist revolution would rapidly spread from Russia to encompass the other developed industrial nations. In all of Europe — at that time the only other important region of civilized progress besides the United States — the proletariat would rise to free itself from the old order and carry socialism to triumph. This conception of a world-wide revolution governed Soviet thinking and actions in the early years of the socialist regime. By the mid-twenties at the latest, however, it had become apparent that socialism was going to remain only 'in one country' for a long time to come. Even when eleven other socialist countries joined the fold after World War II, the division of the world into two, and thus the opposition to the countries of the West, remained.

The Soviet leaders from Lenin to Brezhnev responded to this systemic bisection of the world, not provided for in the original doctrine, by developing the premise of an ideological antagonism. The idea of the class struggle was extended from the domestic situation to international relations. Policy towards the countries of the West took on the semblance of a permanent contest that was defined largely in military terms, even if the correlation of forces made it expedient to forego the use of military force. International politics became the continuation of war by other means, described as 'peaceful'. Up to the Twentieth Party Congress of the CPSU in 1956, the notion was upheld in principle that the final phase in the transition from capitalism to socialism would necessarily involve the use of armed force. In the stages leading up to that ultimate showdown, the objective was to use every means short of actual warfare to debilitate the other side, which was stigmatized as capitalist and imperialist, while at the same time strengthening the socialist side as far as possible. One of the principal strategies to this end was to foment conflict between the countries of the West, and if possible to aggravate it to the point of mutually suicidal war. It was this formula that induced Stalin to conclude a non-aggression pact with Hitler in 1939 to enable Nazi Germany to concentrate on its war against Poland, France and Great Britain.

The 'Cold War' that broke out into the open in 1947 did not suit Soviet intentions. The last thing the Soviet Union wanted was for the countries of Western Europe to join forces with each other and with the United States under a perceived threat from the Soviet bloc, thereby leaving the Soviet side little scope for playing off one against the other. That the awareness of an antagonism to the Soviet Union had now started to govern thinking and actions on the other side, too, was essentially the result of a misjudgement on Stalin's part. Roosevelt had remarked at the Conference of Yalta that the American troops would soon be withdrawing from Europe. The Soviet leader had misinterpreted this remark as an expression of a complete lack of interest by the United States in European affairs and had accordingly felt free to engage in reckless policies that offended Western interests in every conceivable way. Thus it was Stalin himself who created the basis for anti-Soviet coalescence in the West, a process which included Washington's decision to maintain a long-term political, economic and military commitment in Europe.

In the years following World War II, nuclear weapons changed the foundations of international relations. The prospect of total destruction that nuclear weapons opened up called the feasibility of war as such into doubt for the first time in human history. As the practical consequence to be drawn from this new situation, Stalin's successor Khrushchev proclaimed 'peaceful coexistence' (*mirnoe sosush-chestvovanie*) as the new guideline for relations with the West. Western public opinion welcomed this revision of the traditional doctrine, though many overlooked the fact that the Soviet leader had by no means abandoned the idea of antagonism. On the contrary, Khrushchev presented 'peaceful coexistence' to the Soviet Union's followers and sympathisers as a 'form of the class struggle' against the West, stating explicitly that his aim remained to 'bury' the Western system.

The intention behind the new doctrine was, in fact, to preserve the premise of antagonism under changing circumstances. The fundamental conflict which, according to the Kremlin's conceptions, had to continue to govern relations with the West had been called into question by the nuclear factor. The Soviet Union could no longer afford to make the struggle against the countries of the West, even to the point of military hostilities, its political imperative if it involved exposing itself to the charge that that could only lead to a nuclear holocaust. For this reason, Khrushchev assured the West that the Soviet side no longer regarded war between East and West as inevitable but was now seeking a transition to socialism in peaceful forms.

At the core of the re-defined doctrine lay the formula that 'war between states of different social orders' should be avoided. This is to be seen as a qualification of the imperative that war must be prevented altogether. War was to be ruled out as a means of settling differences between sovereign states and between East and West. But conversely, wars were permissible provided they were carried on within individual countries and/or outside the sphere of East–West relations. Accordingly, the Soviet leadership declared 'national liberation wars' (*natsional'nye osvoboditel'nye voiny*), ie wars in Western colonial empires and/or in Third World countries, and 'citizens' liberation wars' (*grazhdanskie osvoboditel'nye voiny*), ie civil wars in Western countries, to be fundamentally desirable. But the new doctrine also allowed a 'progressive function' to be attributed to wars between countries within either of the two blocs — if they served either to weaken the other side (in the postulated event of armed hostilities in the West) or to maintain discipline within the Soviet sphere of hegemony (military intervention in allied countries to restore a regime conforming to Soviet specifications).

It also allowed for all options beneath the threshold of the use of armed force to be exploited in the struggle against the West. The logic behind a 'peaceful coexistence' thus interpreted was clear: armed conflict was to be restricted to sectors that were outside the terms of reference of the mutual nuclear deterrent balance and thus held no threat of nuclear escalation. The antagonistic stance towards the West was to be upheld by eliminating the contingencies of unacceptable nuclear risk.

In other ways, too, Soviet politics revealed the intention not to encroach upon the element of antagonism. The Cuba crisis in 1962 opened the eyes of the governments in East and West to the fact that the policy of confrontation up to the brink of war that they had been practising up to that time was just too risky. Both sides came to the conclusion that it was no longer sufficient to back down just in time to prevent an escalating conflict turning into an open war. There had to be some sort of conflict de-escalation mechanism to stop situations arising in the first place that could eventually lead to war. This realization became a major motive force in the East–West *détente* that began in the ensuing period and that matured in the early seventies. Another sphere in which the two sides discovered inter-dependencies was arms control. And finally, as of the late sixties, the Soviet leadership found itself relying more and more on economic and technological cooperation with Western countries. But the Kremlin was resolved not to allow any general political convergence to develop out of these points of community in detail. Accordingly, *détente* could be no more than a partial collusion that did not invalidate the fundamental antagonism.

The more time passed, the more the practical consequences of this new doctrine became apparent. The Brezhnev leadership launched a political offensive in the Third World, backed up more and more by military resources. Client regimes were set up in countries such as Angola, Ethiopia, in various South American states and finally in Nicaragua. The creation of such 'states of socialist orientation' served to extend Soviet influence to encompass the developing countries, to set up model societies that recommended themselves for imitation and gradually to rob the countries of the West of their political backyards. All this was intended to promote the gradual weakening and eventual overthrow of the capitalist system. At the same time, the Soviet decisionmakers continued to take every opportunity to kindle differences and tensions between the Western countries. For instance they appealed to Western European interests that differed from those of the United States. And on the other side of the coin, the Soviet side used bilateralism with the United States to prevail upon Washington to disregard the wishes and needs of its Western European allies.

Soviet calls for intensive economic and technological cooperation — frequently heeded especially by the Western Europeans — did not prevent the Kremlin from pursuing a security policy geared towards military superiority on the European continent, at the same time using slogans of 'military *détente*' to incite public opinion in the countries of the West against their own governments. The result was new, escalating tensions between East and West, culminating in the controversy in 1979–83 over the deployment of American missiles in Western Europe.[1] Another circumstance typical of the antagonistic approach of Soviet policy towards the West was that, parallel with its economic and technological cooperation with the West, the Soviet leadership elaborated plans which the KGB was to follow in procuring blueprints and specimens of militarily relevant technology in the West — an enterprise that was undertaken on a scale that defies imagination.[2]

Traditionally, the Western countries as perceived antagonists — and among them the United States as the 'chief power of imperialism' — were always the focal point of the Kremlin's foreign-policy interest. The Soviet assessment of the international situation proceeded on the following basis: the first question to be asked was whether American policy was currently being determined by the 'extremist' or by the 'moderate' or 'realistically thinking' opponents of Soviet power; this would indicate the magnitude of the tensions to be anticipated overall. The other countries of the West were judged by whether they followed the American lead and, if not, by whether they exhibited a tougher or a softer line.

The standard argument, emphasized to a greater or lesser extent depending on the prevailing assessment of the situation, was the 'imperialistic' and 'militaristic' nature of Western policy. That is to say, the Western countries and in particular the United States were alleged to be aggressively intent on the subjugation and/or oppression of other peoples, taking recourse to military power not only in pursuit of these targets but also to preserve their own existence. This was based on the conception that only the possession of military resources, including nuclear weapons, had enabled the West to defend itself against the people's will and against the course of history. Seen from this perspective, it was only logical for the Soviet Union to evaluate the countries outside the Western sphere of influence by their behaviour towards the United States, their allies and other Western nations.

THE BEGINNINGS OF GORBACHEV'S POLICY TOWARDS THE WEST

In the first year or two Gorbachev showed hardly any significant departures from the traditional Soviet policy towards the West. The statements delivered and resolutions passed at the April 1985 Plenum of the Central Committee,[3] the anti-nuclear campaign launched on 15 January 1986,[4] and the documents from the Twenty-seventh Party Congress of the CPSU held in February–March 1985[5] reveal the familiar tones of anti-Western animosity. A call for the elimination of nuclear weapons was directed at NATO on the grounds that this would deprive the Atlantic alliance of one of its principal instruments for preserving the 'social status quo'.[6] This was just a new version of the old notion that the Western system was able to hold its own against the forces of revolutionary transformation only because it had adequate military resources at its disposal. The continued political existence of the West thus rested on the Atlantic Alliance, which itself was able to exist only by virtue of a military factor, namely the nuclear deterrent. The practical consequences to be drawn from this was that the socialist countries must direct their efforts against NATO's deterrent strategy and against the nuclear weapons which NATO needed to pursue that strategy as the

foundation for the continued existence of the capitalist system.
At first, the Gorbachev leadership used traditional means to these ends. As had been the case especially between 1969 and 1979, arms control talks were aimed primarily at weakening the security positions of the countries of the West wherever possible. A first step had already been taken while the languishing Chernenko was still in office but Gorbachev was already performing the chairman's duties. In the summer of 1984 the decision was taken to resume the talks that had been broken off following the deployment of the American missiles in Western Europe. The Soviet–American talks that ensued on the subject of strategic and intermediate-range nuclear weapons and anti-missile defence got under way just as the new general secretary of the CPSU came into office in March 1985. Gorbachev lost no time in launching a course of hectic activism, characterized essentially by a deluge of propaganda-style proclamations and initiatives intended to impress Western public opinion, in the hope that it would put pressure on the Western governments. The schedule for the phased elimination of nuclear weapons by the year 2000, introduced into the discussion by Gorbachev on 15 January 1986, marked the first culmination of this propaganda strategy and also established a style which was to be continued for several years thereafter.

It would appear that Gorbachev recognized from the very beginning that the old standards and procedures held little prospect of success if they continued to be applied in the traditional manner. After having come off second best in the 1979–83 missile controversy, he was particularly concerned to improve the Soviet Union's political and moral credibility in the West. For this reason, the new Soviet leaders ceased making vociferous demands. Even as early as 1985, special importance was being attached to visibly demonstrating Soviet goodwill. The Kremlin backed up its campaign for a ban on nuclear weapons' testing with a unilateral limited-term moratorium, which it subsequently extended several times. To the initiated, though not to the general public, the underlying bias was evident: the Soviet Union had just completed a large-scale test series, while the United States which were being called upon to reciprocate, were only just starting their own tests.

The more time passed, the more Soviet endeavours were dedicated to stopping the Strategic Defense Initiative (SDI). Following the 1972 Anti-Ballistic Missile (ABM) treaty, the Soviet Union had made full use of its right to develop ABM systems and to deploy them within a limited region. The United States, however, had refrained from similar action. Thus SDI confronted the Soviet leadership with the prospect of losing a monopoly it had hitherto enjoyed. Though the effectiveness of the Soviet ABM capabilities appeared to be rather limited, the Kremlin was evidently very proud of its achievement. But even more dire than the prospect of losing its monopoly was, from Moscow's point of view, the probability that the Americans could create a highly efficient system if they decided to turn their attentions to it. It appeared urgently necessary to prevent them from doing so.

The Soviet attempts to mobilize Western, and especially West German, public opinion against SDI were not very successful. This was not because SDI was very popular in Western Europe and in West Germany; on the contrary, SDI met with disapproval not only from wide sections of the public but also from the experts and government confidants. If the majority of the Western capitals, and especially Bonn, nevertheless assured President Reagan of their support, this was much less out of enthusiasm for the SDI programme itself but rather the desire to demonstrate political solidarity with their American allies.

The low level of public response to the Soviet anti-SDI appeals can be attributed to the fact that there was no gut feeling in the Western European societies to motivate militant protest. Unlike at the time of the anti-missile movement of the early eighties, the Europeans did not feel essentially threatened by the prospects opened up by SDI. There were no fears comparable to the anxiety that had been aroused by the notion that the deployment of American missiles in their own backyard could attract the other side's deadly counterparts. The peace movement's argument that SDI was intended to spark off a new arms race that would increase the danger of war was of a largely intellectual nature and did not stir up an emotive response in the public at large. Furthermore, the failure of the anti-missile campaign had spread frustration among potential protesters. The lasting impression that even the unprecedented mobilization and activity of that earlier campaign had achieved nothing had paralysed the *élan* of popular opposition. The Soviet leadership found itself forced to adapt to this public sentiment. Though it did not drop its anti-SDI slogans, for the summer of 1986 it stressed that the supreme cause was to 'liberate mankind from nuclear weapons'.

THE REYKJAVIK SUMMIT AND ITS WAKE

Gorbachev's anti-nuclear endeavours were much abetted by the fact that his American counterpart Ronald Reagan likewise had his reservations about the notion of using nuclear weapons to preserve peace. The American President was impressed by the moral protest, endorsed also by prominent clergymen, which argued that it was not ethical to rely on weapons that threatened the very existence of all of mankind. His proclamation of the Strategic Defense Initiative in March 1983 was in response to these objections. As Reagan explained, the aim of the programme was to build up an invincibly strong guard mechanism so as to render nuclear missiles ineffective and thus to neutralize the nuclear instrument.

This justification, the impact of which the American administration later attempted, with good reason, to nullify, ran completely contrary to NATO's security policy — one of the main reasons for the lack of enthusiasm on the part of the allies. Consensus on the strategy of using the nuclear option to prevent war by deterring the Soviet adversary from military adventures was the very cornerstone of the Atlantic Alliance. President Reagan, however, like Gorbachev, was convinced that peace and security could not be built on the potential for total annihilation. Being aware of this community of sentiment enabled and induced the Soviet leader to take advantage of Reagan's moral attitude for his own anti-NATO purposes.

Having got to know each other at their first summit conference, discussion arose between the leaders of the two superpowers of a second meeting which, it was hoped, would bring concrete steps towards *rapprochement*. Public opinion in the United States and other Western countries pushed for the meeting to be held as soon as possible in the hope that the coolness and stagnation persisting in East–West relations could be overcome. President Reagan was thus cast in the role of the supplicant. Gorbachev cleverly took advantage of this situation by at first displaying reserve while at the same time secretly preparing for a summit and then making the American side a proposal for a venue at quite short notice. This enabled him to establish the formalities to suit his own convenience and to gain a considerable time lead in terms of preparations. He further loaded the bias by leaving the American administration in the dark about his intended agenda. All this enabled him to pull off a surprise coup when the summit meeting was held in Reykjavik on 12 and 13 October 1986.

Reagan had concentrated his hasty preparations on an attempt to convince the Soviet leader of the advantages to be gained for his country, too, from a security relationship on the basis of SDI. This approach was to centre around the assurance that the United States intended to share SDI technology with the Soviet Union so that both sides could apply the envisaged protection against the nuclear risk. Though Gorbachev listened to Reagan's ideas, he did not enter into a discussion on them. Instead, he advanced anti-nuclear arguments in an attempt to persuade his counterpart to renounce the instruments of nuclear deterrence. Above all, he postulated that all intermediate-range missiles must be eliminated.

This implied that the United States would have to scrap all those nuclear assets it had so laboriously deployed since the missile controversy of 1979–83. In return, Gorbachev was prepared, in contrast with his predecessors, to scrap the equivalent Soviet weapons systems. Deep cuts were proposed for strategic, ie intercontinental missiles, amounting to a reduction by half in the first phase. A further gradual reduction down to zero was also *envisaged* in vaguely postulated terms. Reagan was impressed by this new Soviet willingness to reciprocate, found himself in fundamental agreement with the Soviet Union and was happy to consent to the proposals. That was apparently the reaction Gorbachev had been waiting for. He even had concrete suggestions at hand as to how these general conceptions could be put into actual practice. On the basis of this exchange of ideas, instructions were formulated that were to serve both sets of negotiators as guidelines for the specific arrangements they were to work out.[7]

The principal item, an agreement on intermediate-range missiles (in Western terminology the INF systems), appeared balanced because both sides were to do away with a specific class of weapon. It even gave the impression of being a deal to the West's advantage because the Soviet Union would have to scrap far more systems than the United States. The Kremlin, however, proceeding on the basis of a different assessment, had worked out that only the American side would really be losing a military option. NATO would no longer have any missiles it could use to deliver a nuclear first strike on Soviet territory, whereas the Soviet Union would still be in a position, using other launchers, to carry out nuclear strikes against Western Europe. In the light of such considerations, it was immaterial that the Soviet side would be making the greater sacrifice in terms of pure numbers.[8]

However, in October 1986 Gorbachev was not yet prepared to conclude a treaty with the United States for the sake of this advantage. When the instructions to the negotiators in Geneva had already been implemented in full detail, Gorbachev stated that such an agreement would be acceptable to the Soviet Union only if the United States abandoned SDI simultaneously. This supplementary condition caught Reagan and his advisers completely by surprise. Since the Soviet negotiators in Geneva had long ceased insisting on the abandonment of SDI, and Gorbachev had made no mention of this point in Reykjavik, the Americans had taken it for granted that the nuclear missiles problem was to be treated as a separate issue from the SDI dispute. They now felt cheated and refused to accede to the demand.[9]

Judging by his response, Gorbachev had expected this all along. He accepted the American rejection without a word of regret and immediately went before the press with the message that the president of the United States had been willing to make an anti-nuclear commitment but had refused to put that commitment into practice, instead continuing to pursue his SDI plans which constituted a threat to humanity. The general secretary of the CPSU hoped to gain a twofold propaganda advantage from this version of the proceedings. The most important man in NATO had on the one hand forsworn the Alliance's nuclear philosophy and on the other had failed to embrace the 'liberation of mankind from nuclear weapons'.[10]

After the Reykjavik meeting, the Soviet propaganda machinery worked overtime to convince public opinion that the idea of a nuclear-free world was no longer just a remote vision. The agreement reached but subsequently torpedoed by the Americans was irrefutable proof of the realistic nature of the proposed de-nuclearization. As one prominent personality from Gorbachev's entourage in Moscow explained in public, nuclear disarmament had in the past been a 'task of supreme mathematical complexity'. But the proposals formulated in Reykjavik had 'extremely simplified' it. The entire problem could now be 'jotted down on a single sheet of paper, and everybody in the world can see what can and must be done'. This was of decisive importance, for 'not only the politicians but all mankind' wanted to know 'on which decisions their fate depends'.[11]

A high-ranking official of the Soviet foreign ministry quoted Gorbachev in pointing out that US rejection of the Soviet package was unacceptable given the need to make substantial progress in demilitarization for the sake of mankind's survival. Writers and journalists must 'learn to think in keeping with the nuclear age and teach others to do so, too'. Accordingly, an appeal was addressed to the Western press 'to participate in the process of peaceful negotiations'.[12]

But Soviet hopes of a propaganda success were disappointed. Not only among the governments but also among the journalists of Western Europe, the predominant sentiment was one of relief that the Reykjavik agreements had been revoked. Otherwise, the general tone ran, Western European security would have been dangerously compromised. Of course, the spokesmen for the peace movement voiced the opposite opinion, but since they met with little response from the general public that did not matter much anyway.

The longer they waited, the more Gorbachev and Shevardnadze were forced to realize that their post-Reykjavik propaganda strategy was getting them nowhere. For this reason, the general secretary of the CPSU eventually dropped the linkage between the mutual elimination of the INF systems and American abandonment of SDI and on 28 February 1987 declared himself willing to authorize negotiations on the former point.[13] As was to be expected, President

Reagan agreed to this proposal. The Western European governments, which would have preferred low ceilings on both sides, reluctantly gave their approval. With NATO having committed itself in 1981 to the objective of a mutual zero option for the INF systems, which at the time had appeared expedient in the light of the domestic pressures being exerted by the peace movement. It was also at the time regarded as an inconsequential gesture that, given the intransigent Soviet stance, would never have to be consummated. Now the countries of Western Europe felt they had no other choice but to stand by their earlier undertaking.

The following nine months were packed with talks to work out the details of the reciprocal liquidation of the land-based INF missiles. The only serious point of contention to arise was the question of seventy-two non-nuclear West German Pershing IA missiles. Because these missiles did not belong to the Americans and were not armed with nuclear warheads, they did not fall within the scope of the planned treaty. Nevertheless, the Soviet leadership declared that the continued existence of these systems would be contrary to the spirit of the agreement. It launched a propaganda campaign against the Federal Republic of Germany which succeeded in pressurizing Bonn to give up the missiles. By the same logic, the comparable missiles the Soviet Union had supplied to East Germany and other allies should have been subjected to a similar ban; they were not because the Western side was not aware of their existence. Indeed, they did not come to light until 1990, when the Kremlin, having seen the signs of the impending unification of Germany, demanded the return of the missiles it had put at the disposal of its ally.

A decisive factor in the American decision to accede to an INF treaty was Soviet consent to a comprehensive verification programme — an arrangement which the Kremlin had hitherto consistently rejected as constituting the establishment of an unacceptable 'espionage' system. The INF Treaty was signed on 8 December 1987.[14] Both in Moscow and in Washington, the treaty was celebrated as a decisive milestone in arms control. For the first time, whole categories of weapons were being eliminated. The Soviet leadership added that the first step had been taken in the 'liberation of mankind from nuclear weapons'.

The Kremlin gave a contradictory appraisal of the Western policies that had led to the INF Treaty. One political scientist with close links to the leadership, and who in the next year and a half was to assume important functions within that leadership, claimed there had been a 'breakthrough in Washington'.[15] Gorbachev himself declared that the agreement 'reflected the level that peace potential [in the world] has attained'. The success achieved should not be ascribed to a change of mind on the other side. The Soviet leader also indicated that the power of circumstances alone had brought about the about-turn in Western policy. In particular, the 'growth of the role of the masses and of the all-democratic factor in domestic and global politics' had had an effect. But further efforts were still necessary if the requisite progress was to be made. The signing of the INF Treaty, the general secretary expressly added, had opened up a new 'phase in the struggle for disarmament and peace, including the ideological struggle'. In this context it was still necessary to ward off Western attempts to make ideological breakthroughs in the Soviet hemisphere. There were good opportunities for doing so, now that NATO's ideological foundations and its picture of its adversary were in a state of progressive disintegration.[16] Gorbachev's message was clear: credit for the INF Treaty was due exclusively to the Soviet Union; the United States were still the adversary, from which every little progress in the interest of international peace still had to be wrested.

This continuing antagonistic view of the world was matched by the appraisal given to the success achieved in the INF Treaty. In Moscow's interpretation, the Treaty eliminated a military option on the part of NATO without the Soviet Union for its part having had to renounce any such option.[17] This shift in the correlation of military forces in the Soviet Union's favour was considered significant. Without its 500–5,500 kilometre range land-based missiles, the Atlantic Alliance had lost the most important part of the instrument that had constituted its crucial nuclear first-strike capability and thus the ability to extend the American nuclear deterrent to Europe. For the Soviet leadership, this was the real breakthrough on the way to the elimination of the Western nuclear deterrent in the European theatre, the true objective concealed behind the call for the 'liberation of mankind from nuclear weapons'.

This Soviet intention was clearly revealed in the manner in which Moscow conducted the Strategic Arms Reduction Talks (START). As early as in the first half of 1986, the two superpowers had agreed in principle to reduce their strategic missiles by half. Despite vigorous American endeavours to come to a concrete arrangement, however, by mid-1990, an agreement was still unconcluded: the Soviet interest in such a treaty extending only to the degree that it limited land and air-based systems, and especially the highly sophisticated cruise missiles. By contrast, the second major point of contention, the American Strategic Defense Initiative, was given diminishing importance as it became increasingly apparent that the Americans themselves were less and less inclined to invest major efforts in the mammoth programme.

CHANGES IN SOVIET POLICY TOWARDS THE THIRD WORLD

Alongside arms control policy, Soviet activities in the Third World have long been a factor of major importance to relations between the Soviet Union and the United States. American disillusionment over Soviet *détente* policy from the mid-seventies onwards was attributable to two factors: Soviet endeavours to gain military superiority and Soviet expansion as of 1974–5 in black Africa, Western Asia and subsequently Central America. Angola, Ethiopia and South Yemen were the first and most prominent examples of a new Soviet policy that used large-scale financial and military aid to bring Marxist–Leninist-orientated client regimes to power and to keep them there, even if, as in the first two cases, this involved carrying on a protracted civil war in the countries concerned. The MPLA leadership in Angola especially came to rely for its existence on Cuban troops that were equipped by the Soviet Union assisted by Soviet military advisers and occasionally also by Soviet specialists (for instance pilots) intervening directly in combat actions. Experts from various Warsaw Pact countries organized the secret police and security apparatus, established a single ruling party and administration and in many cases assumed direct steering functions. This model was applied in many 'states of socialist orientation' in the Third World.

Soviet expansion culminated in 1979–80 with the military intervention in Afghanistan in late 1979 and with support for the victorious Sandinistas in Nicaragua. In the course of time, however, this foreign policy proved more and more clearly counterproductive. Not only in the case of Afghanistan, where the Soviet armed forces became more and more deeply involved, at enormous cost in terms of *matériel* and manpower, in a civil war that offered no positive perspective, but elsewhere, too, costly commitments led to unwelcome consequences. In numerous countries, military resistance to the Soviet client regimes intensified or — as in the case of Nicaragua — was sparked off in the first place by the extremist and brutal policies pursued by those regimes. Despite all the financial aid poured in by the Soviet Union, the 'states of socialist orientation' became poorer and poorer because the Soviet economic system they had imported did not work. The end result was that its client regimes not only cost the Kremlin a fortune but also served as a warning to other countries.

The Gorbachev leadership appears to have decided at a relatively early stage that the policy it had inherited from its predecessors needed to be revised. The existing commitments were reviewed, with the result that, from 1987 onwards, a trend towards disengagement in the Third World became more and more evident. Moscow's reasoning was that its own scarce resources should be invested only for purposes yielding some reasonable return. And as material need in the Soviet Union itself became progressively worse in the course of time, this was increasingly taken to mean reasonable economic return. The new leadership criticized past practices by suggesting that the Brezhnev leadership had allowed Western imperialism to seduce it into squandering valuable resources on the Third World.

But this new political line did not mean that the Soviet Union retired from its commitments to its client regimes immediately and across the board. The Soviet disengagement took place gradually and on the basis of a differentiating assessment of local circumstances in each particular country. While countries considered to be of only secondary importance, for instance Mozambique, were quick to feel the full effect of the new Soviet reserve, aid to countries deemed to be of major significance was at first reduced only negligibly or not at all, and in some specific cases — for instance the Sandinista regime, at times under serious pressure from the American-funded Contras — aid was even stepped up. Apparently, the Kremlin was attempting to stabilize its more important client regimes at least to the extent that they would not have to fear losing power. Soviet endeavours to compromise were also motivated by the desire not to leave its client regimes completely in the lurch. Typical of such endeavours was the case of Angola, where the prospect of the withdrawal of Cuban troops was opened only after it became certain that the Western-orientated rebel movement UNITA was going to lose its own source of aid.

Afghanistan presented a particularly tricky problem. The decision to withdraw the Soviet troops was made especially difficult by the fact that it would mean abandoning important military and political positions on their own periphery. On the other hand, military disengagement appeared imperative by the winter of 1986–7. The Soviet involvement in Afghanistan was placing a material, political and psychological burden on *perestroika* in the Soviet Union; worse still, the supply of American 'Stinger' missiles to the Mujahedin, which began in the autumn of 1986, meant that the Soviet forces had lost their previously unchallenged control of the skies. As a result victory by the Soviet occupation forces had become inconceivable without a massive escalation of military effort. The Kremlin was aware that it could not afford to step up its commitment to the extent that would be required to put a military end to the war. Thus, for the long term, it had no alternative but to cut back its involvement to the level of merely supplying arms to the Najibullah regime.

In these dire straits, the Gorbachev leadership cleverly managed to make a virtue out of necessity. When it entered into talks with the United States and other countries in an attempt to escape from its dilemma, it succeeded in passing off its already inevitable military withdrawal as a voluntary offer and a sign of goodwill. In this way — combined with a temporary step-up of its military efforts — it was able to achieve favourable conditions for its withdrawal. Though it did not manage to obtain for the Soviet Union the unilateral right to continue supplying its clientele within Afghanistan, nevertheless the Geneva Agreement signed on 14 April 1988 did not rule out continued military support for the Najibullah regime, even after the planned withdrawal of the Soviet occupation forces — and it was relatively propitious in some of its other conditions, too[18]. It was not until after the Soviet armed forces had left Afghanistan on schedule by 28 February 1989 that the asymmetric effects of the Soviet right to continue supplying weapons to its clients became apparent. The Soviet leadership carried on supporting its protégés in Afghanistan on a much larger scale than the American assistance to its own favourites. As a result the Mujahedin, who up to then had been on the advance, were unable to gain victory after all and even suffered some setbacks. The civil war continued with no end, one way or the other, in sight.

In Washington, the impression that the Soviet Union was cutting back on its global commitments was a major factor in the decision by Congress to overrule President Reagan and withdraw support for the Contras in Nicaragua. Nevertheless, an international solution to the problems in Central America, and especially free elections in Nicaragua, remained matters of prime concern in the United States. The members of the European Community also appealed to Moscow to push for a compromise settlement. In response to these approaches, the Kremlin agreed to bring its influence to bear on Managua to exercise military restraint towards the guerrillas in El Salvador and to allow free elections in Nicaragua which, it was felt at the time, would bring a liberalization of the political situation but would not fundamentally challenge the Sandinista regime. The endeavours undertaken by various interested parties to tone down the situation in Central America were eventually successful. Free elections were held in Nicaragua from which, to everybody's surprise, the national opposition union's candidate emerged victorious. The Sandinistas retired from the government but retained some influential positions of power in the country.

Cuba presented the Kremlin with a particularly difficult case. The Castro regime relied for its political and economic survival on massive Soviet subsidies introduced by the Brezhnev leadership with the aim of preserving Cuba as a Soviet outpost on America's doorstep. The new leadership in Moscow was loath to continue this policy both because of the drain it was placing on its resources and also because of the orthodox orientation of the Castro regime; at the same time it was reluctant to give up its strategic foothold in the

Caribbean. Its advice to Havana to relax its confrontation with the United States in order to improve its economic situation (which would have relieved the economic burden on the Soviet Union) had little effect: Washington saw no reason to help its old adversary Castro and his communist regime to survive. The Cuba problem remained, and by mid-1990 the Kremlin had still found no way to cast off the associated burden without profoundly prejudicing its power interests in the Western hemisphere.

The new Soviet policy towards the Third World was also decisively shaped by the realization that the hopes harboured under Brezhnev — that it would be possible to destabilize the Western world via Africa, Asia and Latin America — had not been fulfilled and were not going to be fulfilled. Gorbachev and his aides were no longer able to evade the fact that the Soviet large-scale investment in its client regimes was increasingly having the adverse effect of convincing the governments of other underdeveloped countries that they would be better off with western ties. Thus, the costly Soviet efforts to court the developing countries had been strengthening the West in the Third World rather than weakening it. For this reason, it appeared time for a general cut-back in the Soviet commitment. As already pointed out, this did not rule out the Soviet leadership maintaining its interest in certain key countries such as Afghanistan, Angola, Nicaragua and Cuba. In the first two of these instances, the Kremlin even managed to design its withdrawal from direct involvement so as to produce a more cost-effective policy variant. Its reduction of its own commitment was paralleled — as was the case for some time in Nicaragua, too — by a corresponding reduction of American interest. However, post-election Nicaragua and the recalcitrant Cuba made it clear, each in its own way, that this logic was not applicable everywhere.

THE IDEA OF NEW THINKING IN FOREIGN POLICY

The Soviet leadership placed its revised policy towards the Third World in the context of new thinking (*novoe myshlenie*) in foreign policy. The fundamental concept of this new thinking was that the human race was confronted with global challenges to which it had to find a joint response. As the logical conclusion, serious tensions had to be avoided and mutual solutions found to any problems arising. On the pragmatic level, new thinking formulated standards for a more intelligent power policy than that pursued by Stalin and Khrushchev. To attempt to assert one's own interests without regard for the needs and desires of other countries was necessarily counter-productive.

A Soviet Union striving for expansion, especially when military resources are seen to be supplied or even used, gave the outside world the impression of being threatened and induced it to render resistance and to join forces against the Soviet Union. The more obvious the attempts to exercise power over others, the stronger were the obstacles that were put up. This reasoning, expressed in ever plainer terms in Moscow since 1987, also allows a converse conclusion: if one reduces one's own pressure in the face of growing resistance, a relaxation of the other side's counterpressure can likewise be expected. These considerations were generated primarily with a view to Soviet arms policy, but they have also had a pronounced influence on Soviet foreign policy in general. The realization has also gained ground that, in the age of *perestroika*, the Soviet Union was compelled more and more to cut back on the overcommitment of its resources abroad and to concentrate on its problems at home.

This 'new thinking' in Soviet foreign policy has always — and especially in its early period — been of an ambivalent nature. The notions of a common challenge and of mutual dependence or interdependence (*vzaimnaia zavisimost, vzaimozavisimost*) without regard to political conviction and class membership could certainly imply willingness to engage in true and comprehensive cooperation. However, these key terms can also be defined along the lines of an Orwellian newspeak to portray the Soviet Union with its policies as the sole champion of the class-transcending all-human interest. In this case, any Western thinking or action that does not coincide with the Soviet standards must necessarily be directed against the alleged true interest of humankind and must therefore be vehemently and remorselessly combatted. Understood in this way 'new thinking' thus becomes an instrument of antagonistic policy directed against the West.

This is not just an abstract theoretical consideration. The concept of a 'new thinking' was first formulated along these lines by two Soviet hardliners as the controversy between the East and the West over the deployment of the American missiles in Western Europe reached its peak. At this stage, 'new thinking' was unmistakably only a new label for the old policy of the anti-Western struggle. The objective was to assert the cause of peace, as championed by the Soviet Union in the 'true' interest of all mankind, including the capitalists themselves, against the opposition of intransigent Western leaders.[19]

When the Gorbachev leadership first adopted the concept of 'new thinking', it was as yet unclear to what extent any thought was given to its cooperative and/or antagonistic implications. For a long time, the antagonistic aspects predominated, but gradually, as awareness grew among the Soviet public under the aegis of *glasnost*, more emphasis came to be placed on the cooperative aspect — although in many cases it was difficult to decide what, in concrete terms, was in fact intended. If, for instance, there was talk of a 'de-ideologization of relations between states' this could just as well be equated with an affirmation of ideology-free politics as with the traditional ideological reservation with respect to the societal sphere as the truly relevant one.

The fact that the Soviet leadership ceased to define 'peaceful coexistence' as a 'form of the international class struggle' on the grounds that this would cancel out all the Western goodwill gained by the proclamation of peaceful relations can likewise be interpreted in two completely different ways. It can be argued that the Gorbachev leadership had now set its sights on unconditional peaceful coexistence with the West, but neither can it be ruled out that it was only the counterproductive effects alluded to in the reasoning that made it inexpedient to adhere to the old *wording*, despite continued endorsement of the old spirit.

Since 1988, the cooperative interpretation of 'new thinking' has been stressed more and more in official statements. The antagonistic notes have become increasingly restricted to persons and circles that are in one way or another critical of Gorbachev's policy towards the West. This shift in the officially proclaimed interpretation can be explained as the consequence of a changing interest situation. The more Gorbachev found himself confronted with economic difficulties, challenges to his authority and ethnic and national separatist problems within the Soviet Union, the less he could afford to antagonize the countries of the West. He came to rely upon those countries more and more not to exploit his domestic weaknesses but instead to come to his assistance with material and other aid.

And in fact the Western governments showed much sympathy for the Soviet leader's straits. In the capitals of the West, Gorbachev slowly but surely came to be seen as the guarantor of a Soviet policy that made a continuing improvement in mutal relations appear possible. One of the functions of the more friendly official communications from the Kremlin was to preserve and enhance this accumulation of political capital in the West. Furthermore, Gorbachev appears to have been personally impressed by the warm welcome given to him on the occasion of various visits to the West, in distinct contrast with the indifference and indeed disapproval he was familiar with at home.[20]

In addition, the Soviet leadership found itself faced more and more frequently with foreign-policy problems which it could not solve to its satisfaction without goodwill on the part of the West. A prime example of this has been the question of German unification. It was thus no coincidence that, on the way back from Ottawa, where the representatives of NATO and the Warsaw Pact had reached agreement on procedures for the handling of the German question, Soviet Foreign Minister Shevardnadze expressly dismissed the topic of antagonism with the United States. The Soviet Union, he added, was now shaping its relations with the other superpower 'in a different way'.[21] The Gorbachev leadership had thus come a long way since its early statements of 1985 and 1986 in which it had upheld the theory of a radical and irrevocable antagonism with the 'imperialist' camp led by the United States. This reconfiguration of Soviet relations with the countries of the West and in particular with the United States implied an immeasurable relief for Soviet foreign and security policy, making it possible both to dispel perceptions of threat and also to reduce the demand for valuable resources.

In this context, improved relations with the United States as the foremost power in the Western alliance system are of decisive importance. But the new Soviet foreign policy also makes possible a change in relations with the countries of Western Europe, a change which may be capable of relieving the Soviet Union of more than external pressure. The Western Europeans are also the Soviet Union's most important prospective partners in the broad-scale economic and scientific cooperation that Moscow intends should make a decisive contribution to the reconstruction of its dilapidated country. Thus Gorbachev and his aides are also interested in a radical restructuring of the system of Soviet relations in Europe. In this respect, too, the Western Europeans are the prime addressees of Soviet attempts to court international favour.

NOTES

1. See Gerhard Wettig, *High Road, Low Road: Diplomacy and Public Action in Soviet Foreign Policy*, Washington, Pergamon-Brassey's, 1989, pp. 73–129.
2. See, for example, Thierry Wolton, *Le KGB en France*, Paris, Editions Grasset, 1986.
3. *Pravda*, 24 April 1985.
4. Gorbachev's speech of 15 January 1986: *Pravda*, 16 January 1986; Iurii Zhukov, 'Ot slov k deistviiam', *Pravda*, 13 February 1986.
5. See, in particular, Gorbachev's speech of 25 February 1986: *Pravda*, 26 February 1986; Shevardnadze's speech of 1 March 1986: *Pravda*, 2 March 1986.
6. Ibid.
7. Cf. the detailed statements by Gorbachev in *Pravda*, 13, 14, and 15 October 1986.
8. This statement was expressly contained in the Russian version of a quasi-official article on the subsequently concluded INF Treaty: 'Pervyi rezul'tat perestroiki', *Mezhdunarodnaia zhizn*, 2/1988, pp. 2–4.
9. For the underlying events see the sources mentioned in note 7 and the

following press reports: Fritz Wirth, 'Einen Meter vor dem Traumziel blieben sie stehen', *Die Welt*, 14 October 1986; Michel Tatu, 'Les ambiguités de l'après-Reykjavik, *Le Monde*, 6 November 1986.
10. Ibid.
11. 'Vremia i novoe myshlenie': statement by G. Kh. Shakhnazarov at a round table session inaugurated by APN, the Soviet news agency which specializes in preparing and disseminating information for foreign audiences, *Izvestiia*, 1 November 1986.
12. Ibid. (statement by A. M. Adamovich).
13. *Pravda*, 1 March 1987.
14. Text: *U.S. Policy Information and Texts*, United States Information Service (ed), Special Edition, 10 December 1987.
15. 'Proryv v Vashingtone' (interview with E. M. Primakov) *Mirovaia ekonomika i mezhdunarodnye otnosheniia*, 2/1988, pp. 3–7.
16. Address to the PSU Central Committee on 18 February 1988, *Pravda*, 19 February 1988.
17. See note 8.
18. Text: *United Nations Information Service*, 15 April 1988.
19. Anatolii Gromyko and Vladimir Lomeiko, 'Novoe myshlenie v iadernyi vek', Moscow: Mezhdunarodnye otnosheniia, 1984.
20. For Gorbachev's response to his welcome in the West see his report to the Supreme Soviet on 1 August 1989, *Pravda*, 2 August 1989. For an assessment of his relative popularity at home and abroad see Shevardnadze's hints in his 25 July 1988 address, *Mezdunarodnaia zhizn*, 9/1988, p. 25.
21. Interview with Shevardnadze, *Izvestiia*, 19 February 1990.

3 The societal level of foreign policy

The Soviet Union's traditional 'revolutionary' self-image as a power antagonistic to the West has its counterpart in a specific Soviet approach to the conduct of foreign policy. Usually foreign policy is concerned with the shaping of relations between states, that is to say between governments and the state apparatuses under their control, while the societies living within those states are given an autonomous status, and the cross-border links between them are independent and affected only indirectly by their respective states. The traditional Soviet conception of foreign policy, however, encompasses both interstate (*mezhgosudarstvennye*) and societal (*obshchestvennye*) relations. Since, in a traditional Soviet-style regime, the leadership claims for itself not only control over the state but also full control over society, its relations with the outside world are similarly governed by a universally controlled approach, but pursued at different levels: one, at the level of interaction with other governments and two, the societal level by bringing influence to bear on the autonomous social forces in other countries. A leadership which uses these two diverse channels does not have to rely solely on the results of its intercourse with other governments but can, if expedient, directly address other societies in an attempt to undermine their governments' foreign policy activities.

In the latter days of the Brezhnev and Andropov era, the Soviet leaders launched a large-scale campaign along these lines by endeavouring to persuade public opinion in the major NATO countries, in particular the Federal Republic of Germany, to thwart the deployment of American missiles in Western Europe even though the governments and parliaments concerned had already given their approval.[1] This example serves to illustrate how the specific approach to foreign policy employed by the Soviet Union in the past can have far-reaching practical consequences.

The evolution of these two distinct levels of foreign policy was directly linked with the development of the revolutionary conceptions followed by Lenin and his companions. In 1917, the Bolshevik leaders were concerned only with gaining power in the country in which they were politically active. They gave no thought to formulating a foreign policy because they were convinced that the 'proletarian revolution' was about to break out in the other major countries of Europe, too. Thus, the first Soviet foreign policy spokesman, Trotsky, thought that his activities would entail no more than making revolutionary calls to the oppressed workers abroad in order to accelerate the process of international upheaval that was supposedly already under way. It was not until these expectations failed to materialize that the new holders of power initiated a diplomatic corps. At the same time, they continued their appeal to the exploited and oppressed in other countries to encourage them to rise and join forces with the Bolsheviks.

The pattern of action of the 'struggle for peace' in the NATO countries instigated by the Soviet leadership in the late seventies and early eighties against the official government policies continued to reveal clear evidence of these revolutionary origins. Although the Soviet appeals were not this time directed towards overthrowing foreign governments with the aim of extending the Soviet order, they nevertheless were a continuation of the tradition of attempting to mobilize political forces in other societies to take action against their respective governments, in this case with the declared objective of imposing a specific foreign and security policy. The approach was the same: the stimulation and propagation of a policy directed against the country's government from below.

At the interstate level, Soviet foreign policy is, as in other countries, the responsibility of the Ministry for Foreign Affairs. Since the dissolution of the Comintern in 1943, responsibility for the societal level of international affairs, for which there is no parallel in non-Soviet-style states, has rested with an organ of the Central Committee of the CPSU: this has long been the International Department. Traditionally, the principal duty of this organization has been to guide and instruct the communist parties in the West and in the Third World, to coordinate their political activities and to employ them for the purposes of Soviet policy. Until the late sixties, no other political forces counted in the Soviet concept of a societal struggle to be carried on at the international level. It was only at this time that the Kremlin started to cast about for links with non-communist parties and groups — first with the social democrats and then with the bourgeois left. This was also a time when, originally incited by the Soviet–Chinese schism, parts of the world-wide communist movement were starting to cast off Soviet control and/or break away from the Soviet-dominated Internationale. From then on, the Soviet Union was no longer able to rely on having communist cadres at its beck and call everywhere. Nevertheless, in those countries in which strong Soviet influence could still be brought to bear on society, communist forces remained as the main transmission belts for Soviet foreign policy.

Traditionally the International Department's main means of exercising control over those parties and groups which accept its leadership is via the formulation of a binding political strategy. It designates concrete objectives to be attained in the current phase of the political struggle and specifies the attitudes to be adopted towards the other political forces in the society of the country concerned — in particular who is to be courted as an 'ally' and who is to be regarded as the principal opponent. These assessments, objectives, alliance precepts and slogans are embodied in ideological statements which are by no means merely abstract theory. On the contrary, the ideological form is used to transmit instructions for concrete political activity in the West. For this reason, any attempt to discern the political intentions being pursued by the Kremlin in the societies of non-communist countries must start with an analysis of these ideological statements.

Under Gorbachev the Soviet Union claims to be a normal state without quasi-revolutionary ambitions. There is much talk of the 'de-ideologization' (*deideologizatsiia*) of interstate and international relations. If this claim is to be credible, the Soviet Union must abandon its traditional practice of carrying on its foreign policy at two distinct levels. Whether and to what extent this is actually the case is the subject of the present chapter.

THE THEORY OF INTERDEPENDENCE IN INTERNATIONAL RELATIONS

The Gorbachev leadership prides itself on its 'new thinking', on its departure from antiquated dogmas and clichés. One of the major aspects of this re-think is that the Kremlin no longer stresses the antagonism and confrontation between the systems but now talks of the 'mutual dependence' (*vzaimnaia zavisimost*) or 'interdependence' (*vzaimozavisimost*) between all countries and peoples, irrespective of their political or ideological stance. Though the world will still be divided by 'contradictions' (ie conflicts), it nevertheless forms a global unit of manifold interrelations. For this reason, one must not focus on the existing differences but must also recognize and appreciate that, even where its various components are engaged in conflict with each other, the world as a whole is closely related and thus is dependent upon mutual cooperation. Its community, not its division, should be stressed. The practical imperative derived from this theory is that 'all-human' interests and values (*obshchechelove-*

cheskie interesy, obshchechelovecheskie tsennosti) must be given priority over class interests (*klassovye interesy*).

Gorbachev has likened the peoples of the world to a 'roped party of mountaineers on a mountain face': 'They can either climb up to the top with each other or plummet to the depths together.'[2] This 'concept of a mutually linked and mutually dependent, contradictory and yet by nature universal world of our times' does not, of course mean departing from the 'basic arithmetic of Marxism', that is from the 'importance of the class approach' to political problems. Instead, a distinction must be made. 'The class struggle was and still is the cardinal point of social development in states with divided classes. Nevertheless, the appearance of weapons of mass destruction has imposed an objective limit on class confrontation in the international arena.[3]

According to the official reading, it is more than anything else the possibility of mutual nuclear destruction that makes it imperative to exercise mutual reserve in the conflict between the systems. Warfare involving the use of nuclear weapons, Gorbachev stressed, could not be 'a means for attaining political, economic, ideological, or any other objectives'. In such a conflict there would be 'neither victors nor vanquished', 'but inevitably world civilization will go to its doom'. This was 'a completely new situation' — with the consequence that the old rules for the settlement of conflicts were no longer valid.[4]

The Soviet leader, who likes to paint a picture of himself as a communist reformer in the spirit of Lenin, expressly traced his conceptions of interdependence back to the founder of the Soviet state. In both his and Lenin's opinion, he claimed, it is 'mutual dependence and the closest, indivisible correlation of *all* sides of any phenomenon' that constitute the dialectic correlation of historical phenomena.[5] The class struggle theory brings law and order into the apparent chaos of historical events. The antagonistic classes, as Engels had explained, are engaged in 'an unbroken, sometimes hidden, sometimes open struggle, a struggle which each time [ends in] a revolutionary reorganization of all of society or in the communal demise of the struggling classes'.[6]

Lenin was cited as witness in evidence of the pragmatic conclusion that mutual dependence dictates the need to give priority to 'all-human' interests. The founder of the Soviet state had once pointed out that a 'war between advanced countries' would lead to 'the undermining of the existential conditions for human society'.[7] Another time he had given voice to the idea that one day war would 'take on such destructive power as to become completely impossible'.[8]

Gorbachev also referred to Lenin as having spoken explicitly of the 'priority of the interests of social development and all-human values over the interests of one or other class'.[9] However, this statement was taken from a completely different context, in which Lenin as the leader of a then still tiny splinter group was trying to make his goal of overthrowing the czarist regime attractive to other groups by basing his demands on the 'interests of social development', which were 'higher than the interests of the proletariat' alone, and thus deserved the support of other opposition groups.[10]

THE BASIC PORTRAYAL OF INTERDEPENDENCE AND THE CLASS ASPECT

The official conception of 'all-human' and class interests in a dialectic mutual relationship implied a fundamental adherence to the traditional class perspective. The crucial point was the theory, borrowed from Lenin, that the two classes — or, in present-day terms, the protagonists of the two systems — despite being engaged in a fierce struggle against each other, must not physically annihilate each other and, in this respect, had to consider themselves mutually dependent. Thus the confrontation between the systems remained essentially unchanged. What was considered important was to make allowance for the 'mutual dependence' by carrying on the struggle in a more cautious manner. However, there was no intention to eliminate the fronts themselves.

As the dialectic interaction of community and diversity changed, so too, as Shevardnadze made clear, did the objectives associated with the struggle. The Soviet Union was emblazoning 'all-human values', the 'all-human ideal' on its banners and was proclaiming the 'fight for the survival of mankind'. This introduced a change in the 'character of the class struggle, its forms'. The declared goal of 'all-human' interests became at the same time the 'supreme class interest' which the Soviet Union was advocating against NATO policies. The Soviet foreign minister unmistakably pointed out in this context that the 'problems of competition and rivalry between the two systems' by all means continue to exist. The systemic antagonism was merely being put into the perspective of the 'growing trend towards the mutual dependence of the states of the world community' which is the 'real dialectics of contemporary development'. In concrete terms, what mattered was to 'save the world'. If these endeavours were successful, this was portrayed as the fulfilment of 'the supreme class mission of socialism' which would indeed 'bring about a world revolution'. 'The — by the way, growing — force of this class interest lies in its complete coincidence with the all-human interests.'[11]

Elsewhere, Shevardnadze stressed that there must be 'no dividing borders between the proletarian and the all-human'. The Soviet concept had to 'give expression to the unity of interests of mankind, the community of its goals and ideals: survival, prevention of nuclear disaster, and the salvation of world civilization — ideals of which socialism is the champion'. The reasoning went: 'Our class interests determine the struggle for the all-human ideals.'[12] One of the concrete expressions of this conception was the Soviet quest for a nuclear-free world, which it had to carry on against the 'policy of nuclear blackmail' being pursued by NATO. Against this background, an almost Manichean picture of the world was occasionally construed:

The class antagonisms of the contemporary world and the ideo-political watershed in the capitalist countries run above all between the 'Party of Peace' and the 'Party of War', between the forces of militarism and the vast majority of the population that is represented by various social groups which are united in calling for the prevention of catastrophe and [for] disarmament.[13]

The reason cited for the transition from the old class-specific to the new 'all-human' line of rhetoric was that the ongoing techno-scientific revolution and the economic and social changes it was generating had 'also affected the character of the class struggle and its forms'. The struggle for the survival of mankind had, for the Soviet Union and socialism, become the 'supreme class interest'.[14] As it was explicitly explained, this did not imply any change in the Soviet negative 'appraisal of imperialism [ie the United States and its allies] and its policies'. Seen from this point of view, 'neither the reality of the historic contraposition of the two systems nor the ideological irreconcilability of socialism and capitalism' could be forgotten.[15] The important thing was to direct one's actions towards the conception 'that socialism can and must save mankind'. This conception, which was portrayed to be 'through and through and by nature Marxist—Leninist', provided 'convincing class arguments' for the validity of the 'all-human' orientation towards peace as advocated by the Soviet Union.[16]

There were two noteworthy aspects to this new line of argument. First, the traditional concept was 'undergoing a *perestroika*' in that the two economic systems were now regarded as being inter-dependent and that 'all-human' interests were given priority over class interests and second that not a word was spoken in favour of the Soviet Union moving closer to the West. On the contrary, 'all-human' interests were cited as necessary for maintaining the struggle against the United States and its allies or at least against certain aspects of their policies. In practical as opposed to theoretical considerations, the Kremlin set itself up as the defender of the 'all-human' interest in survival, which, it was claimed, was threatened by the West's 'policy of strength', and especially by nuclear deterrence. Early in the Gorbachev era, it was also intimated that the West's capability to uphold the 'social status quo', especially in the European theatre, was dependent upon its ability to wield military and nuclear options, without which the Western system would be defenseless.[17] This implied that the cornerstones of the West's status quo were irreconcilable with 'all-human values'. And this, in turn, appeared to corroborate the Soviet claim that it was necessary to 'limit the scope of the destructive effects of the egocentric, strictly class-related inherent laws of the capitalist system', 'as expressed in NATO's nuclear policies'.[18]

THE DIALECTICS OF 'ALL-HUMAN' VERSUS CLASS ORIENTATION

It would thus appear that a commitment to anti-Western policies 'in the interest of all-human values' had taken the place of the 'international class struggle'. The deputy head of the CPSU International Department Zagladin whose views can be seen to reflect the ideas of Gorbachev spoke in this connection of the 'historical mission (*istoricheskaia missiia*) of the working class' to promote, by means of its class struggle, 'the liberation of all of mankind'. The close link-up between the two was based on the fact that, as Engels had recognized, 'the interests of the working class coincide with the "interests of mankind as a whole" '.[19]

By fighting against war with its inherent threat of universal destruction and instead committing itself to less devastating, dialectic forms of conflict not associated with the threat of nuclear disaster, the 'working class' was transcending its class interests and giving priority to 'all-human' interests. This, however, by no means implied a 'renunciation of our class interests, more specifically: of the assurance of the interests of socialism. Indeed, *only* such an approach [to the problem] is really able to assure the interests of socialism — its survival and its healthy development.' But socialism could not 'detach its fortunes from those of humankind'. The interests of both classes (ie the systems of socialism and capitalism), the theory continues, were on the one hand 'antagonistic' but on the other identical with each other, in that the people on the capitalist side were also interested in their physical survival and were thus in unison with Soviet policy. (ibid.)

Here the Soviet theory identified a fundamental dilemma for the adherents of capitalism: for them — unlike for the people living under socialism:

the position of class egoism is dangerous. This is linked with a crucial asymmetry in respect to the historic trend of the contemporary period. Objectively, it must be easy for the working class and its party to appreciate: its historic mission (of which we spoke earlier) has not only a class-specific but also an all-human dimension (in which consists, one may say, the capital distinction of the proletariat from all classes that have preceded it). For a capitalist, the situation is more difficult: that portion of his interest which coincides with all-human interest comes into contradiction with those parts of his interest which are dictated by his class egoism and which emerge as the irreconcilable enemy of all-human progress. (ibid.)

Thus, the West was portrayed as characterized by a conflict of motivation between interest in self-preservation and interest in political self-assertion. The Soviet Union, as Zagladin made it clear, was able and obliged to draw benefit from this situation by appealing to the West's fears for survival in contrast to its political interests, thus advocating the 'theory of the priority of all-human interests' was not a 'renunciation of the struggle for class interests'. Accordingly, 'the struggle for all-human interests [is] currently coinciding with the struggle for class interests'. (ibid.)

This analysis was based on two cardinal premises. First, the Soviet construct took it for granted that the threat of an all-devastating war emanated from NATO's nuclear escalation and could be averted only by the mobilization of all political forces against the West's security policy. This line of argument, in turn, could be traced back to Moscow's theory that NATO's deterrent did not serve, as its Western originators claimed, to prevent a conventional war but instead itself inevitably moved the world closer to nuclear conflict. Second, the assertion that only the spread of socialism afforded an alternative to nuclear disaster was based on the traditional Marxist–Leninist doctrine of historical materialism, according to which capitalism and socialism were linked in a merciless life-and-death battle, in which victory by the capitalist side was ruled out *a priori* by the unalterable historical trend towards socialism. Thus the Western system was inherently devoid of any possibility of opening up positive prospects for humanity. It could only act destructively.[20]

This theory was used to substantiate the claim that the West's policy of deterrence constituted a threat to all mankind. According to this theory, capitalism, as the system historically destined to die out — in contrast with socialism, whose victory was likewise pre-ordained — was not capable of gaining the upper hand in the conflict. If, contrary to the course of history, capitalism should nevertheless become strong enough to stand in the way of socialism, this could only — the conclusion drawn from Lenin's reference to the possibility of the mutual destruction of the combating classes — lead to the common annihilation of all mankind. This theory was the sole basis for the

Soviet claim, propagated by Moscow's followers in the countries of the West, that the Soviet Union was defending the survival of the human race against the policies of NATO.

THE SOVIET INTERDEPENDENCE DOCTRINE: A CONCEPTUAL WORLD *SUI GENERIS*

The above definitions and lines of argument reveal a conception of interdependence and 'all-human' interest completely different from what the Western observer would suspect on the basis of his own understanding of the terms used. Artificial semantic synthesis was used to create a newspeak which was comprehensible only against the background of Soviet doctrine. According to the official terminology, the semantic unit 'interdependence' referred to the cardinal postulations of an antagonistic conflict between the systems and a socialist perspective for the future. The interest of mankind, of which the Kremlin was the self-declared champion, was coupled with the objective of the implantation of the socialist system.

Until mid-1989, related Soviet statements of principle occasionally spoke of the 'socialist world perspective', ie of the goal of supplanting capitalism by socialism, in noteworthy contrast to the incipient political retreat of the Soviet system from many parts of the world. Was this supposed to mean that, regardless of all setbacks, the socialist objective remained valid and would be pursued again as soon as circumstances became more propitious? Soviet officialdom even interpreted the right of self-determination to be enjoyed by all peoples as being the right to choose the Soviet system: the peoples of the world had to be put in a position to decide on their own systems and their own courses of development in line with the historical logic of social evolution.[21] The 'free choice' in the opposite direction made by the Soviet allies in 1989 did not, however, conform to the postulated objective. Since the Soviet leadership later declared itself in agreement with the results of that choice, it would appear in retrospect that the ideological rhetoric cultivated up to then in Moscow was just a relic of days gone by.

This applied also to Politburo member Medvediev's 1988 characterization of the current epoch as an 'epoch of proletarian revolution and of the transition from capitalism to socialism'.[22] Equally outdated was the claim still being made in 1989 by leading political scientists with good contacts in the leadership that capitalism, despite its temporary relative stabilization, was still heading for its 'collapse'. This claim was also linked with the prophesy that the Western system was on the point of 'revolutionary shake-ups and changes'.[23] The working class, as the director of the International Department of the

Central Committee of the CPSU had insisted one year earlier, had taken the mission to establish a 'social alternative' to capitalism.[24] The Twenty-ninth Party Conference of the CPSU in the summer of 1988 passed a resolution which stated that 'only a political approach to the solution of the contradictions of world development and the settlement of conflict situations' afforded 'the USSR the possibility of playing the role assigned to it by history in assuring the survival of mankind and its further [socialist] progress'.[25] As to foreign policy, it was stressed that it was essential not to become bogged down in foreign-policy pragmatism but to preserve a 'principled' orientation.[26]

IDEOLOGY VERSUS GROWING SCEPTICISM REGARDING PRACTICAL OPPORTUNITIES FOR ACTION

The obvious discrepancy between ideology and practical politics that was revealed in the wake of Eastern Europe's abrupt turn away from the traditional conceptions of socialism indicates the need for a time-based analysis. Such an analysis shows that the viewpoints of the Gorbachev leadership have been changing over the years in response to the changing situations with which it has been confronted.

Initially, militant tones against the West predominated, with the traditional ideology typically equating the West's nucleus, the United States and NATO, with 'imperialism'. On 15 January 1986, Gorbachev announced his programme for the abolition of nuclear weapons by the year 2000.[27] This programme was directed against the security policy pursued by the Atlantic Alliance and was intended to mobilize public opinion in NATO countries against their respective governments.[28] In keeping with a doctrine that was only later to be formulated in greater detail and according to which 'all-human' interests and values constituted a suitable basis for alliances between the communists and the broadest possible spectrum of protest and opposition groups in Western societies against the protagonists of official Western policy, the CPSU's new Party Manifesto of March 1986 declared the 'forces of peace' in the West to be the fourth force in the 'anti-imperialist struggle', after the socialist states, the non-ruling communist parties and the liberation fronts in the Third World.[29] Evidently the mass movement of 1980 to 1983 against NATO's projected missile deployment had, despite its eventual failure, made such a strong impression on the Kremlin that it was subsequently seen as the ideal means for combating Western policies in the future.[30] This strategy for foreign-policy activity on the societal level went hand in hand with a strongly anti-Western overall orientation.[31]

Such a bold approach to the foreign-policy issues under dispute succeeded in creating the impression of a pronounced feeling of strength *vis-à-vis* the West. But on closer examination it became apparent that the triumphant gesturing in the Kremlin was beginning to give way to a more cautious appraisal of the situation. As early as at the Twenty-seventh Party Congress of the CPSU, Gorbachev had already questioned the hitherto sacrosanct theory of the constantly worsening 'universal crisis of capitalism' and had pointed out that the West was as much as ever capable of preserving the 'social status quo' and possibly even of regaining lost ground, ie of pushing back socialism.[32] This put an end to the ideologically motivated expectation that the West's ability to uphold the capitalist system would inescapably be soon exhausted. For the first time, scepticism about the scope of the Soviet Union's own freedom of action was voiced, to be intensified in the years that followed.

In early 1988, the Central Committee's Academy for Party Cadres, citing Gorbachev's comments made at the Party Congress, carried out a more detailed analysis of socio-political conditions world-wide. It came to the conclusion that

the capitalist system of production has not lost the ability to work profitably, to adapt to changing circumstances, and to manœuvre in accordance with changing historical realities. This brings us to a further reason for the relative historical stability of capitalism: the ability to practise an effective and flexible social policy. Capitalism has learned to draw conclusions from its own failures and from our victories, to take account of its errors and to use our errors to improve the profitability of planned programmes. Nowadays it can be said that the combination of the capacity for revolutionary changes in technology with flexible social manœuvring is one of the main reasons for the comparative stability of capitalist social structures.[33]

The director of the International Department of the Central Committee of the CPSU spoke out along the same lines. At a communist congress held in Prague on 12 April 1988 he declared that the world was experiencing 'new phenomena in the evolution of capitalism'. These were bringing about changes in 'the character of the mass basis on which the communist movement has traditionally rested'. This was creating 'no simple problems'. While admitting that capitalism had achieved a certain consolidation, this high-level official nevertheless still maintained that socialism continued to be the only alternative to capitalism and that the communists must direct all their efforts towards attaining their goal. Alluding to the Soviet Union, he voiced the opinion that socialism had up to now shown only some of its benefits and had 'to date not supplied any example of a thoroughgoing democratization of society nor of a radical, superior solution to economic problems that was capable of convincing the masses in the countries of the West'. Achievement of this task was an essential prerequisite to further successes abroad.[34] This new appraisal of the situation included the unpleasant admission that a 'conservative wave' had gained the upper hand in the West and was at the same time being accompanied by a 'crisis of the labour movement and the leftist forces'. Some consolation was, however, to be gained from the fact that there was 'widespread discontent with the traditional parliamentary institutions' in the West.[35] The current setback was blamed in part on misguided Soviet courses of action during the Brezhnev era. 'The politics and psychology of "total" confrontation' between the two systems had 'had an adverse effect on the activities of the progressive, democratic forces in the capitalist countries, strengthened the positions of reaction and allowed it to bring about the political isolation of the communist movement'. This had become a 'serious obstacle to the social progress of mankind', ie to mankind's transition to socialism.[36]

PRACTICAL CONSEQUENCES OF THE RE-ASSESSMENT

From its pessimistic assessment of the situation, the Soviet side drew the conclusion that it must stop deluding itself and start to see things as they really were. The CPSU had repeatedly pointed out that capitalism had 'not insignificant reserves' at its disposal. For this reason, what was needed was not 'voluntaristic predictions of its demise' but rather 'concrete historical work on strengthening the world revolutionary process, taking into account the historical realities of capitalism in our time'. This entailed 'difficult problems of global strategy' concerning in particular 'the containment and weakening of the aggressive, egocentric and narrowly class-specific aspirations of world capitalism' and its dependence on militaristic and neo-colonialist trends. The slogan 'Proletarians of the world, unite!' was as valid today as ever before, even if profound changes had taken place within the working class in the West.

Thus the question arose as to new ways of pursuing the revolutionary objective.

Under the characteristics of the current epoch, capitalism's ability to prolong its historical existence and the lack of any notable progress of the labour movement in the developed countries of Western Europe and the United States are attracting attention. This in itself severely complicates the struggle for the realization of the socialist ideal, which is made even more difficult by the growing aggressiveness of imperialism, which has generated a real threat to the global foundations of human civilization.

This challenge could, in the Soviet view, also be turned to advantage.

Everything that is forward-looking and progressive in mankind is uniting to ward off this threat, and this in turn is inevitably having a qualitative effect on the social composition and the structure of the revolutionary forces both in the international and in the national dimension. An essentially new interrelationship is emerging between the fight for peace and the revolutionary struggle of the working class for social liberation.

The socialist side was adopting, as a complement to its traditional interests, 'all progressive objectives of mankind' as its own, with the result that the 'revolutionary process' was becoming an 'effort of will by the majority of the world's population'. In this way, a world-wide unity was arising 'on the basis of Marxist–Leninist intellectual values', which would then be adopted by a broader 'world revolutionary process'. The conflict between capitalism and socialism was not being eliminated but was taking on 'essentially new forms', especially those of 'co-action' instead of 'counteraction'.

Such a transformation, of course, did not come of its own accord. It had to be gradually and carefully orchestrated in order to make allowance for the 'needs of each of the sides' involved. This assumed the ability to 'make concessions and enter into compromises'. The new scheme for the struggle against capitalism also had to be attractive to the non-socialist forces and consequently to be built on the conception of a 'universal, mutually dependent world'. This theoretical concept clearly revealed 'the all-human potential of Marxist–Leninist philosophy'.[37]

In his speech in Prague referred to earlier, the director of the International Department of the Central Committee of the CPSU also called for the urgent 'polishing up' of the Soviet image in the outside world.[38] He also stated that it was necessary to re-define the 'relationship between all-human and class-specific interests and problems'. In this context, he called upon the 'working class', ie the communist cadres, to make the issues of mankind their own. This was 'both a class-specific and an all-human imperative'. It entailed more than just carrying on the old anti-Western struggle under new, 'all-human' slogans. The time sequence of the changes to be brought about internationally must also be amended. 'The first [problem] lies in the fact that while the Marxists were earlier of the opinion that the oppression of the working class had to be eliminated before the problems of an all-human nature could be solved, we today cannot expect to succeed in the class struggle if we do not take up all-human slogans and tasks as our weapons.'[39]

THE ENVISAGED COALITION

The motive for this new political strategy in the spring of 1988 was expressly identified as the fact that 'dwindling voter support for the communist parties in a number of countries, the shrinking of their social basis, the splits in the individual parties and the deterioration of the international links between the parties' had led to an unsatisfactory situation in which the established parties were able to make 'less impact on the international processes'. In many respects, the communists and their activities had fallen behind other political currents and parties such as the social democrats, the greens, the Christian democrats, the conservatives, and the liberals. In the light of the 'favourable atmosphere' currently existing in East–West relations, it was hoped that intensification of broad-based dialogue with other groups, and in particular the improvement of relations with the social democrats, would help alleviate concern that the communists might be relegated to the sidelines by other advancing forces.[40]

One of the reasons for this change in the Soviet attitude was the realization that the Kremlin and the Moscow-orientated communist cadres in Western countries had, in the late seventies and early eighties, alienated many potential sympathizers in Western societies by insisting that they, too, must identify themselves unquestioningly with the policies of the Soviet Union. For this reason, the call now went out to desist from all 'sectarianism' that was obstructing the 'unification of the various classes, of the advocates of different philosophical views and doctrinal lines, of ideological and political currents on the platform of new thinking'. All efforts should be directed towards 'finding a common denominator' — the "all-human" component — 'in the interests and convictions of the most varied categories of people according to ethnic origins, social class etc.' in order to win them over to the Soviet concept. This was the purpose to be served by the guiding slogan of the 'survival of mankind'.[41]

Accordingly, the object of the proclamation of the struggle for 'all-human' interests was to create a platform from which all the forces in the countries of the West could be mobilized in support of Soviet objectives. From Moscow's viewpoint, of course, this formulation was not quite accurate. It would be an '[over-]simplification to equate the struggle for all-human interests with the struggle against the monopolies — especially since the social mass basis of these two lines of struggle, the compositions of the actual and potential participants, do not coincide'. For it was necessary for the purpose of achieving the 'all-human' objectives to form 'very broad alliances between different social and political forces', even including persons and groups that were 'hostile' to the communist cause.[42]

As Gorbachev stressed at the Nineteenth Party Conference in the summer of 1988, the important thing was to establish and maintain 'broad contacts with the representatives of other countries' — 'from the heads of government down to the simple man in the street, with the generally recognized authorities in science and culture, with prominent writers and delegations from parties, social organizations and movements, with trade union and social democratic leaders, with religious protagonists and members of parliament'.[43] These endeavours were evidently directed towards finally emerging from being associated with protest groups and establishing a consensus with as broad a spectrum of social groups as possible. In this context, the most important factor was to include the underlying notion of 'staatstragende Kreise' (in German), ie those leading forces in society which, by their willingness to support the democratic order of the country, and by virtue of their influence on the country as a whole, are the very 'columns' on which the democratic regime rests.

The new communist strategy aimed at hitting the democratic order by seeking to alienate from it the very groups on which it depended most — an acknowledgement of the growing realization that uniting oppositional forces for common action had led into a political ghetto.

To achieve a broad basis of sympathy and approval for Soviet foreign policy would require patience towards the most varied viewpoints. Because of the perceived need to appeal to the most diverse audiences, the effect should not be directed toward socialist class interests. Instead, 'all-human' slogans should be used to create propitious conditions for later efforts to achieve communist goals.

The various appeals made in the name of 'all-human' interests give an insight into which forces Moscow considered likely to have a determining influence on the future and thus eligible as primary target groups. The general theme of all these appeals was that all mankind must, irrespective of its diverse ties and convictions, concentrate on solving the 'global problems' (global'nye problemy) that had to be tackled in unison. The aversion of the nuclear threat was identified as the cardinal problem. The disaster of nuclear war sooner or later was portrayed as inevitable, unless nations and peoples were to unite in eliminating nuclear weapons, ie in putting an end to NATO's nuclear policy.

For a long time, this line of argument easily accounted for the greatest part of all comments on 'global problems'. A second topic of prominence was environmental conservation. Initially attributed little importance, this was given more and more attention after 1987–8. Calls were occasionally also made for a new world economic order, for the alleviation of the debt burden on the Third World, for a campaign against hunger in the underdeveloped countries and for the money being spent on arms to be re-directed into development aid projects. From this summary it is evident that the Soviet leadership regarded the entire package of the new social movement's popular concerns, from anti-nuclearism to commitment to the Third World — but with the exception of women's liberation — as the trend to be carefully observed in the future.

FUNDAMENTAL CHANGES TO THE TRADITIONAL STANDPOINT

Since then, the prevailing conception was that the Soviet Union must make 'global problems' the focal point of its statements in order to achieve a community with non-communist forces under the banner of 'all-human' ideals. At the same time, however, the political context was itself undergoing rapid and sweeping change. Together with its communist sympathizers in the countries of the West, the Kremlin found itself being forced more and more on to the political defensive, especially as it became clear that the Soviet Union's 'pre-crisis situation' as identified by Gorbachev in January 1987 was not improving but becoming progressively worse. Even before the about-turn in Eastern Europe in 1989, the impression was spreading that the communist order was heading up a blind alley. The attraction of Marxist–Leninist models for solving 'all-human' problems was steadily dwindling. The impact of the inner-Soviet discussion unleashed by *glasnost* further helped to sweep aside the traditional ideological clichés. As a result, the Kremlin found itself forced more and more to cease its usurpation of the 'all-human' ideal for its own class purposes and to adopt Western conceptions of 'all-human' activity.

This gradual process was accompanied by a development within the Soviet Union which was making the CPSU's ideologically based claim to exclusive authority and power less and less acceptable. On 5 February 1990, Gorbachev drew his conclusions before his party's Central Committee. These were that the CPSU must abandon not only 'the ideological dogmatism inrooted over decades' and 'the traditional domestic-policy clichés' but also its 'obsolete views on the world revolutionary process'. And he added, all this had led to the 'isolation of the socialist countries from the mainstream of world civilization' and had erroneously made the 'paths of progress' appear to be a 'continuous confrontation with another social world'. At the same time, the general secretary called for a 'political pluralism' and drew up the prospect of the various 'socio-political organizations and movements' currently emerging in the Soviet Union being allowed in future to vie with the CPSU as alternative parties.[44] This constituted the cautious initiation of a departure from the absolutist claims of the communist party on the domestic scenario and also from the call for world revolution in the international dimension.

FUNDAMENTAL CHANGES IN POLITICAL CONDITIONS

The political transformation in Eastern Europe, the first signs of which became noticeable in the spring of 1989 and which spread to all countries of the region in the following autumn, made nonsense of the conceptions based on the doctrine of 'all-human' interests and values. The world public sat by and watched as the purportedly future-orientated model of socialism was challenged and swept aside by the peoples of Eastern Europe, once the Soviet leaders had withdrawn their military shield from the socialist governments. This outcome can hardly have been what the Kremlin had intended. On the contrary, Moscow appears to have expected that the 'demilitarization' of relations with its allies would bring reformist communist forces to power which would restructure their countries along the lines of *perestroika* in the Soviet Union. Gorbachev and his associates were, however, prepared to respect the 'free choice' (*svobodnyi vybor*) of the peoples of Eastern Europe as it became apparent that a strongly West-orientated political dynamism had been generated and become widespread. In doing so, the Soviet leadership not only acceded to the countries of Eastern Europe following a different domestic-policy path, it also recognized that its own potential for influencing Western societies was drastically reduced.

The talk of the impending demise of communism that began to spread in the West was indicative of one aspect of the difficulties that were emerging: the loss of their political homeland by the partisans of communism. This was accompanied by the fact that the cadres backing the Soviet cause in the various countries were losing their drive and capability for effective action. Of course, this process did not start only in 1989. Precisely in those parties which were the Kremlin's most wavering followers, the growing discrepancy between the traditions of orthodox communism imposed internally by the cadres and the unconventional reform policies being pursued by Gorbachev was generating insecurity and conflict. Strategically important parties, particularly the DKP in the Federal Republic of Germany, had fallen into a state of internal tension which, even before the changes in Eastern Europe, was often paralysing political work and making an open split between intra-party groups appear imminent. In the case of the West German communists, it was becoming more and more evident by the summer of 1989 that the majority of party members favoured Gorbachev's reform policies, but the leaders of the party, and with them the party apparatus, were adhering unswervingly to the orthodox course of the regime in East Germany. This was no coincidence: the tiny DKP was dependent on East Berlin for its lavish funds. In August 1989, the party leadership decided that, if need be, it would have to do without the major part of its membership in order to be able to continue its traditional course along the lines dictated by their East German comrades.

The events of the autumn of 1989 in Eastern Europe consummated the ongoing decline of Western European communism. The collapse of 'real existing socialism' persuaded even those parties to abandon their belief in the old system which up to then had taken their bearings exclusively from that system. This not only meant that orthodox communists such as the British and French parties had been proven wrong with their traditional lines; they were also left without a substitute for the long proclaimed ideal. The situation of the reform communist parties was only slightly better. Even those — as for instance in the case of the Italian Communist Party — who had been calling for a different, better socialism long before Gorbachev came along with *perestroika*, the extent of the communist breakdown in the East (including the Soviet Union itself, despite its hitherto not very successful efforts at restructuring) nevertheless were put in an unfavourable light in Western public opinion. Among reform communists, this reinforced an already present trend towards social-democratization, while the orthodox communists tended more to join up with other radical forces to form a united left. This polarization intensified — for instance within the Greek communist party — the trend towards a split in their own ranks: more and more members with leanings towards Gorbachev's course wanted to form a party of their own or at least to join an existing reformist group.

The situation proved fatal to the West German communists. In the wake of the popular upheaval in East Germany they lost the financial support which had been the almost exclusive source of their income. The number of members, sponsors and sympathizers had always been small in the Federal Republic of Germany. Hence Socialist Unity Party (SED) in East Germany had provided large funds, estimated as more than 60 million DM annually, for a wide range of political activities. When this money dried up, the West German communists had to close down most of their publications and front organizations. After late 1989, exertion of Eastern influence through the communist party in the Federal Republic of Germany — which Moscow regards as the most crucial European member of NATO — reached a very low point. Mobilization of social forces in support of Soviet foreign policy like that during the 1979–83 missile controversy is most unlikely to be repeated.

The financial blow not withstanding, the West German communist party sought to continue their activities as best as they could. The leadership was reduced to a small fraction of its previous size; political work was almost completely handed over to honorary personnel. Membership had been reduced by more than half to 20,000. On this modest basis, some reconsolidation was achieved.

A new perspective was opened when top functionaries began to consider the option of operating in the wider spectrum of extremist left-wing groups. Another opportunity presented itself when, against a reluctant communist leadership in East Germany, German unification was put on the international agenda. The SED which had begun to seek a reformist image and had renamed itself the Party of Democratic Socialism (PDS), sought to extend itself into West Germany. The natural cadres to use for the purpose were the activists of the West German communist party. On 16 March 1990, the first local PDS organization in the Federal Republic was founded in Hamburg. This development provided new hope to the West German communists that their situation would improve again. After all, the PDS retained many assets from the time when it held the power monopoly in East Germany, it continued to maintain a sizable if reduced party apparatus and it received 16 per cent of the votes cast in the GDR elections on 18 March 1990 (a fantastic number compared to the less than 0.5 per cent which the West German communists normally collected).

CONCLUSIONS

The Soviet leaders have significantly changed their performance at the societal level of their foreign policy. They have virtually abandoned their former practice of seeking to undermine the policies of Western governments 'from below'. The current situation is clearly not conducive to such action: disintegration of the communist movement offers little, if any, opportunity for the use of communist cadres in the West in the pursuit of Soviet foreign policy goals; and the Kremlin badly needs Western governments' cooperation — not only in economy and technology, but also in policies of security and integration. Accordingly, Soviet efforts at the societal level are limited to normal 'people's diplomacy' (*narodnaia diplomatiia*), ie the projection of a positive Soviet image on Western audiences and a concomitant bid for sympathy to be extended to the Kremlin's policies. All Soviet personnel abroad — diplomats, journalists, traders and others — have been asked to do their best to create a favourable disposition toward the Soviet Union in Western countries. It may be expected that this effort at public diplomacy will both be increased and become more differentiated in the years to come. Gorbachev's positive image in the West will be a principal point of departure. The thrust of the argument will be that the Soviet Union has de-ideologized, abandoned all antagonistic feeling toward Western nations and embarked upon a course of full-fledged cooperation with other countries.

In the new context, the previous instrument for running the communist movement and mobilizing domestic forces against Western governments, the International Department of the CPSU Central Committee, has shifted its attention from the communists and protesters susceptible to Soviet influence to socialist and social democratic parties. Contacts are also sought with 'bourgeois' groups, including those in power. While traditionally the International Department did not deal with Eastern Europe and other areas of Soviet influence (which were the responsibility of another Central Committee department with a specific competence for ruling communist parties), 'de-communization' of Eastern Europe in 1989 has resulted in the ID being entrusted with the establishment and cultivation of relations with the emerging non-communist parties of the region. It is through good relations with the new political forces in Eastern Europe that the Kremlin feels some influence in the region can, and must, be maintained.

Soviet abstention from efforts to undermine Western policies has resulted less from intent than from necessity, if one judges by the Kremlin's own statements. Previous ideological schemes of action and the sequence of successive situation assessments as discussed in the preceding analysis seem to indicate that the Soviet leaders have always taken a keen interest in using all available opportunities for political action in Western societies and that only unfavourable conditions led to abandonment of such activity. There is, however, also a possibility that Gorbachev and his aides accepted the change after it became imperative. If this assumption is correct it would imply that they understood the benefits which *genuine* rather than simply verbal de-ideologization of Soviet foreign policy could offer: a stable relationship of cooperation with the West at all levels promising, *inter alia*, a cost-effective, long-term solution to the Soviet security problem and a durable boost to the country's underdeveloped economy. Only the future will reveal whether the Kremlin currently abstains from subversive action in Western societies for reasons imposed of necessity or internalized principles.

In the light of a progressing debilitation of and subsequent loss of power by the communist parties in most West European countries, particularly where those parties were strongly subservient to Soviet control, Moscow has increasingly shown a keen interest in cooperation with social democratic parties. If the Soviet leaders have really substantially changed their attitude to the West, this shift would also have to be seen as an indication of a fundamentally changed underlying intent. In any case, the Socialist Internationale has become a major factor in the Kremlin's foreign-policy considerations. In some countries — particularly in Germany — there is even a long-term Soviet hope that social democrats and communists will move toward each other and possibly merge, thus providing a basis for pro-Soviet feeling, if in a fashion other than through commitment to communist dogmas.

Soviet institutions continue to reflect the traditional dual character of foreign policy as an activity to be displayed at both diplomatic and societal levels. The ministry of foreign affairs stands side by side with the International Department. Coordination between the two is provided by an International Commission in which, in addition the KGB and — in the light of past experience presumably also — the propaganda apparatus are represented. It remains to be seen whether this pattern of foreign-policymaking will change when the CPSU (which runs both the International Department and the Propaganda Department) ceases to hold the political monopoly in the Soviet Union and to act on behalf of the Soviet state interest.

NOTES

1. For a detailed description of the events see Gerhard Wettig, *High Road: Low Road, Diplomacy and Public Action in Soviet Foreign Policy*, Washington, Pergamon-Brassey's, 1989.
2. M. S. Gorbachev, *Perestroika dlia nashei strany i dlia vsego mira*, Moscow, 1987, pp. 142–3.
3. 'Dialektika novogo myshleniia', (authoritative statements on Gorbachev's book mentioned in note 2), *Kommunist*, 18/1987, p. 4–5.
4. M. S. Gorbachev, op. cit., p. 143.
5. V. I. Lenin, *Polnoe sobranie sochinenii*, 5th ed., vol. 26 Moscow, Gospolitizdat, 1961, p. 55.
6. Ibid., p. 59.
7. Ibid., vol. 36, 1962, p. 396.
8. N. Krupskaia, *O Lenine*, Moscow, Izdatel'stvo politicheskoi literatury 1960, pp. 40–1.
9. M. Gorbachev, 'Vremia trebuet novogo myshleniia', *Kommunist*, 16/1986, pp. 11–12.
10. V. I. Lenin, op. cit., vol. 4, 1958, p. 220.
11. Closing speech of Shevardnadze at the Scientific and Practical Conference of the Soviet ministry of foreign affairs, 27 July 1988, *Mezhdunarodnaia zhizn'*, 9/1988, p. 65.
12. Report by E. A. Shevardnadze to the members of his ministry on 3 May 1987, *Vestnik ministerstva inostrannykh del SSSR*, No. 1, 6 August 1987, p. 19.
13. V. Kortunov, 'Revoliutsionnyi sdvig v soznanii millionov', *Mezhdunarodnaia zhizn'*, 10/1987, pp. 24–5.
14. Closing speech by Shevardnadze on 27 July 1988, op. cit., p. 65.
15. Report by E. A. Shevardnadze on 3 May 1987, op. cit., p. 18.
16. Ibid., p. 19.
17. Statements suggesting this conclusion are, *inter alia*, Gorbachev's and Shevardnadze's remarks on the issue made at the Twenty-seventh Party Congress of the CPSU (*Pravda*, 26 February and 2 March 1986).
18. Report by Gorbachev to the Central Committee, 2 November 1987,

2. Cf. the analysis by Françoise Thom, *The Gorbachev Phenomenon*,

Pravda, 3 November 1987.
19. V. Zagladin, 'Put' ternistyi, no neobkhodimyi', *Mezhdunarodnaia zhizn'*, 8/1988, pp. 19–24. Zagladin was first deputy chief of the International Department of the CPSU Central Committee until autumn 1988 when he became one of the two advisers of the chairman of the Supreme Soviet (Gorbachev) on international affairs.
20. For example Gorbachev at the Twenty-seventh Party Congress of the CPSU (*Pravda*, 26 February 1986).
21. Report by E. A. Shevardnadze at the Scientific and Practical Conference of the ministry of foreign affairs, 25 July 1988, *Mezhdunarodnaia zhizn'*, 9/1988, p. 15.
22. V. Medvedev, 'Velikii oktiabr' i sovremennyi mir', *Kommunist*, 2/1988, p. 4. Medvedev is a member of the Politburo and CC Secretary.
23. E. Primakov, V. Martynov and G. Diligenskii, 'Nekotorye problemy novogo myshleniia', *Mirovaia ekonomika i mezhdunarodnye otnosheniia*, 6/1989, p. 16–17. Primakov worked with Gorbachev's confidant and Politburo member Iakovlev and succeeded him in his function as director of the Academy Institute for World Economy and International Relations. In 1989 he was elected chairman of the newly established Soviet of the Union (the first chamber of the Supreme Soviet) and after that became a member of the Politburo. Martynov was deputy chief of the Institute under Primakov and succeeded him in mid-1989; Diligenskii is chief editor of the Institute's periodical.
24. V. Vtorushin and Iu. Trusin, 'Soveshchanie v Prage' (citation of statements by A. Dobrynin), *Pravda*, 13 April 1988. Dobrynin was from February 1986 to September 1988 chief of the International Department of the CPSU Central Committee and then became one of the two advisers of the chairman of the Supreme Soviet (Gorbachev).
25. *Pravda*, 5 July 1989.
26. Cf. for example the report by E. A. Shevardnadze, 3 May 1987, op. cit., p. 18; 'Pervyi real'nyi rezul'tat perestroiki' (editorial), *Mezhdunarodnaia zhizn'*, 2/1988, p. 3.
27. *Pravda*, 16 January 1986.
28. For an instructive individual statement on this issue see Iu. Zhukov, 'Ot slov k deistviiam', *Pravda*, 13 February 1986.
29. The CPSU Programme (new version 1986) in Gert Meyer, *Sowjetunion zu neuen Ufern? Dokumente und Materialien mit Einleitung*, Düsseldorf, Bruecken Verlag, 1986, pp. 186–7.
30. *Inter alia*, Shevardnadze's remarks in his speech at the Twenty-seventh CPSU Party Congress, *Pravda*, 2 March 1986. For the Soviet assessment of the result of the anti-deployment campaign see Grigori Lokschin, 'Die gegenwaertige Friedensbewegung', *Wissenschaft und Frieden*, 1–2/1985, pp. 18–29.
31. A characteristic example of this is Gorbachev's Political Report to the Twenty-seventh CPSU Party Congress, *Pravda*, 26 February 1986.
32. Ibid.
33. I. Antonovich, 'Dialektika tselostnogo mira', *Mezhdunarodnaia zhizn'*, 4/1988, p. 47. Antonovich is vice-director of the Academy of Social Sciences of the CPSU Central Committee.
34. V. Vtorushin and Iu. Trusin (citation of statements by A. Dobrynin), op. cit.
35. Exposé by E. Primakov, op. cit., p. 7.
36. E. Primakov *et alia* op. cit., p. 6.
37. I. Antonovich, op. cit., pp. 52–3. This note refers to the citations in the

four preceding paragraphs.
38. In Soviet opinion the general reputation of the Soviet Union — in contrast to Gorbachev's personal reputation — leaves much to be desired.
39. V. Vtorushin and Iu. Trusin (citation of statements by A. Dobrynin), op. cit. In the same, the contribution by R. G. Ianovskii (rector of the Academy of Social Sciences of the CPSU Central Committee) at an official discussion of the international problems to be placed on the agenda of the nineteenth CPSU Party Conference (*Mezhdunarodnaia zhizn'*, 6/1988, p. 4).
40. Unpublished parts of the manuscript of Dobrynin's Prague speech of 12 April 1988.
41. E. Primakov *et alia*, op. cit., p. 8.
42. Ibid., p. 14.
43. *Pravda*, 28 June 1988.
44. *Pravda*, 6 February 1990.

4 Old and new thinking about international security

THE OLD IDEA OF SECURITY *VIS-A-VIS* THE OUTSIDE WORLD

During the Brezhnev period, the professed goal of the Soviet effort to provide for security *vis-à-vis* the outside world was the 'reining-in of imperialism' (*obuzdanie imperializma*). This implied that the Soviet Union needed 'reliable security' (*nadëzhnaia bezopasnost*) through 'reliable defence' (*nadëzhnaia oborona*). The adjective did not simply mean that the Kremlin felt security and defence had to be as reliable as possible — a desire which is certain to be shared by any politician or military leader who seeks to protect his country. In traditional Soviet terminology, 'reliable' meant that such protection must be guaranteed under any conceivable condition, particularly under the condition of war with NATO. That is, war prevention was seen not to be assured. Therefore, preparations had to provide security in the event of East–West war as well and hence to allow for the contingency of military defence (ie warfare). The requirement to 'rein in imperialism' expresses this view: the Western countries characterized as 'imperialist' powers were to be prevented from making war by the Soviet Union being fully prepared for it.

The Brezhnev security concept had far-reaching practical consequences at the military level. The perceived need to be prepared for East–West war entailed that:

— the West's anticipated aggression must not be allowed to advance, but had to be instantly stopped and indeed pushed back to the furthest limit of NATO territory (requirement of offensive defence);
— Western aggression was to be terminated with its originator being 'smashed' on his own territory (which presupposed that the Warsaw Pact countries had military superiority); and
— the risk of East–West war in Europe becoming nuclear and involving Soviet territory in large-scale military destruction, must be safely avoided (requiring the detachment of the European theatre from nuclear parity at the strategic level).[1]

The Brezhnev leadership displayed confidence that the first two requirements could be met. Given NATO's policy of nuclear deterrence (or, to put it more precisely, NATO's effort to link the European theatre to the American-Soviet mutual deterrence relationship thereby extending it to security relations in European so as to protect both sides allies from the prospect of devastating war), however, avoidance of nuclear escalation in the event of East–West war appeared far from certain. It was seen to be necessary to do away with NATO's extended nuclear deterrence. In Soviet rhetoric, this was expressed in violent denunciation of such deterrence as an allegedly aggressive strategy which sought to threaten and even to initiate war. To bring this point home, the term 'intimidation' (*ustrashenie*) was generally used to translate 'deterrence' into Russian. It was this point which Soviet spokesmen and experts had in mind when they polemicized against the West's nuclear 'deterrence'. The bilateral deterrence relationship between the United States and the Soviet Union was accepted as a fact of life which, additionally, aroused little fear, since it was taken for granted that Washington would be as reluctant as Moscow to enter a global, mutually suicidal duel. The nuclear danger which seriously concerned the Soviet leaders was that a European war might generate nuclear escalation which would draw their homeland into the war disaster.[2] At the level of practical action, the Kremlin sought to solve its problem by denying NATO an escalatory capability. The Soviet 1979–83 campaign against American missile deployment in Western Europe had this idea as the underlying motive.[3]

The Soviet Union's concept of security during the Brezhnev period was consistent with the general idea that the Western countries were the enemy and had to be suspected of an innate drive to unleash war should they be given the opportunity to do so. Consequently, the Soviet Union and its allies (who as socialist countries were peaceful and could not but seek to preserve peace) were confronted with the task of 'defending peace' against an 'imperialist aggressor'. So the prime objective was to prevent war by preventing potential warmakers from doing what they would like. From this premise, two postulates followed. The possibility of war threatened mankind only from one side: the Western one. Therefore, peace had to be defended exclusively against the countries of NATO. The best conceivable guarantee that war would not be unleashed was to confront the potential warmakers with a maximum of adverse conditions. Therefore, the task of war prevention would be served best if the socialist countries possessed overwhelming military strength, making clear to the Western aggressor that, in the event of war, he would have to face annihilation on West European territory.

This security concept was clearly antagonistic. The underlying idea that East–West relations were essentially prone to war and consequently war had to be seen as a permanent possibility did not allow for security to be created by a common effort of war prevention. To be sure, the Kremlin had adopted the social democratic term 'common security' (*vseobshchaia bezopasnost*) in the early 1980s, but this was merely a verbal claim for many years to come.

It is very difficult to judge whether the Soviet leaders of the Brezhnev period and the subsequent Andropov–Chernenko interlude really felt they were militarily threatened. They did behave, it is true, according to this assumption. None the less, many Western analysts are inclined to feel that the Kremlin was primarily motivated by political considerations. Since the Soviet Union was only a second- or even third-rate power by any standard other than the military one, it was natural for its rulers to rely on military power to influence world affairs. After all, power politics had been the very essence of Soviet policymaking ever since Lenin had taken power in 1917, and use of armed force, both direct and indirect, had played a prominent role. To be sure, the key concept of the 'correlation of forces' (*sootnoshenie sil*) is not only military in nature, but takes political, economic, social and a number of other power factors into account as well. However, the Soviets have always displayed a keen awareness of the political impact that may be made by possession of military strength. Their traditional rejection of a 'policy of strength' (*politika sily*) always pertained only to Western instrumentalization of military power.

In Europe, political utilization of Soviet armed force outside war was seen as an obvious possibility by many Western analysts — provided, of course, that the Soviet Union was successful in eliminating NATO's extended nuclear deterrence. As long as the Western alliance was capable of threatening selective nuclear escalation in the event of war, the Soviets would know they could not afford war and hence would be prevented from either threatening it or demonstrating their capacity to wage and to win it. If, however, this deterrent were removed, West European governments might see themselves exposed to such a challenge and feel constrained to agree to Soviet demands to avoid the risk of being involved in a war which the Soviet Union might feel it could afford.

THE GORBACHEV LEADERSHIP'S DE-NUCLEARIZATION CAMPAIGN

Within a few weeks after having taken over in March 1985, Gorbachev began to suggest that he wanted to press the United States on nuclear issues. A comprehensive nuclear test ban became the first focus of a heated campaign directed against the alleged American drive for overarmament and superiority. When, in the autumn of 1985, Washington responded by positing the ideal of nuclear weaponry being neutralized or even eliminated, the Soviet leader took the opportunity to demand that NATO's nuclear strategy be abandoned. On 15 January 1986, he proposed a programme of step-by-step elimination of all nuclear weapons.[4] The Soviet Committee for the Defence of Peace rushed to mobilize all kinds of organizations and groups in Western countries in support of the move.[5] At the Twenty-seventh CPSU Congress, Gorbachev revealed the rationale underlying his bid for de-nuclearization. He portrayed NATO's nuclear deterrence as a threat to the world which was both dangerous and immoral and hence not to be tolerated any longer.[6] Foreign Minister Shevardnadze intensified the anti-nuclear polemics and called for a brave new world 'without nuclear weapons and armed violence'. In this context, he blamed the West for seeking 'to eternalize its rule and to oppose the progressing course of history' (which, as every Marxist–Leninist had been taught to believe, aimed at eliminating capitalism).[8] This remark implied that it was the West's nuclear arsenal which allowed the Western order to prolong its existence against the laws of history.

For more than two years, the demand for de-nuclearization was a cornerstone of the Soviet policy line and a very highly publicized one at that. Moscow's spokesmen created the impression that they rejected any kind of nuclear weapon. A closer look, however, reveals that 'strategic parity' was commented upon more favourably. This indicated that it was nuclear deterrence extended to the European theatre which the Kremlin really opposed. And it was NATO's nuclear weapons in Europe on which diplomatic negotiations and public controversy were concentrated. Western audiences for the Soviet message were bound to relate their feelings primarily to the West's nuclear arsenal in Europe. Little appeared to have changed in comparison to the pre-Gorbachev period. Soviet rejection of the European theatre's linkage to the nuclear dimension had even been stepped up: not only were persons of lower rank involved in the campaign but also the highest leaders, including Gorbachev himself.

The anti-nuclear polemics became less noisy only in 1988 and 1989. Optimistic observers in Western countries saw some basis for the hope that the Kremlin would eventually move away from what they saw as propaganda and an unrealistic attitude. When addressing the Council of Europe on 6 July 1989, Gorbachev appeared to justify that expectation by expressing acceptance of minimum deterrence. A closer scrutiny of the Soviet leader's words, however, put such an interpretation in jeopardy. Gorbachev had in fact said that for the sake of allowing further progress in nuclear arms' reduction — which

was to approximate eventual elimination of all nuclear weapons —
he was willing to tolerate the minimum deterrence philosophy as the
West's underlying rationale. The Soviet Union would, of course,
stick to its de-nuclearization stand.[8]

The position taken by the Soviet president reflected only the
official attitude. In the intra-Soviet discussion which developed
under *glasnost*, quite a few voices advocated nuclear deterrence as an
appropriate means for war prevention. Even within official circles,
opinions were far from uniform. Among political experts and
spokesmen, there was an increasing tendency to soften previous
opposition to nuclear deterrence. The military, however, resented
such leniency and adamantly stuck to total nuclearization of Europe.
In their view, the crucial point was invariably that the Soviet
homeland had to be protected against any contingency. Nuclear
weapons which threatened to make war intolerable for the Soviet
Union, too, had to be eliminated from the theatre of potential war.
To the extent that the civilians began to feel that the contingency of
war would be avoided by a change in political relations, they were
less concerned over what might conceivably result in the event of
war. Some of them appear even to have internalized the Western
argument regarding the war-preventing effect of nuclear deterrence.

The Soviet leaders evidently do not reject nuclear deterrence
because they question its effectiveness in preventing war. Foreign
Minister Shevardnadze has made that clear. He believes, just as
NATO security experts do, that neither side can seriously consider
starting a nuclear war. There is 'no protection' against nuclear
weapons, whereas a 'war following a "non-nuclear scenario" ' seems
to him to be 'conceivable without mutual annihilation'. That has
prompted him to ask, as the West does, whether nuclear weapons
might therefore serve as 'a means to deter [conventional] war'. He
rejected this conclusion, however, citing the arms race, which he feels
developed under nuclear deterrence. He equally rejected the claim
that nuclear weapons have given us more than forty years of peace,
saying the nuclear powers have shown no signs of exercising military
restraint toward the world's nuclear have-nots.[9]

The first argument has nothing to do with the point it is meant to
prove: it is fully possible for countries to engage in arms competition
without ever waging war against one another. The second argument
actually supports what it supposedly disproves: despite political
tensions that were sometimes extreme, military restraint has
prevailed exclusively in East–West relations for the past decades —
due to mutual nuclear deterrence. The foreign minister is too shrewd
not to know that the reasons he cites in his attempt to prejudice the
public against nuclear deterrence actually argue for it. If he opposes
it none the less, then he has other motives. He said 'reliable security'

must be guaranteed and argued that nuclear use would render 'national security a fiction'.[10]

DE-NUCLEARIZATION IN THE KREMLIN'S POLICY TOWARD NATO

During the summit meeting in Reykjavik in October 1986 — which was decisive for the further development of American-Soviet relations — Gorbachev's operating motto was 'de-nuclearization', for which he sought and found a positive response from President Reagan. It was on this basis that the two reached a fundamental consensus which initially led to no solid agreement owing to Gorbachev's subsequent insistence that the Americans abandon their Strategic Defense Initiative (SDI). But when the Soviet leader dropped this demand in late February 1988, the way was finally clear. The result was the American-Soviet agreement on eliminating land-based missiles with a range of from 500 to 5,500 km (INF Treaty) which was signed on 8 December 1987. In subsequent statements, Gorbachev celebrated the agreement as a major success on the road to a world without nuclear arms. It was striking, however, that he refused to give the Americans any credit for the accord, claiming they did not act voluntarily but had been forced into reaching an agreement by the joint efforts — directed against the 'military activity in the European part of NATO' — of the Soviet Union, its allies and popular mass movements in the West. According to Gorbachev, the West was trying to 'circumvent' the accord by 'compensating' for the missiles to be withdrawn. Thus, the political struggle must be intensified.[11] Two things stand out in these remarks: first, Gorbachev's attempt to stir up antagonism in his Soviet audience and second, his tacit assessment that the INF Treaty was a severe blow to NATO's policy of deterrence.

The official appraisal of the INF Treaty was given in more detail in an authoritative statement to elite Soviet home audiences. On the surface, it was argued, the West had made a good deal: the Soviet Union had to scrap substantially more missiles than the United States. But numbers were said not to be decisive. The situation must be seen 'from the standpoint of our fundamental military and political interests', 'relative advantages must be weighed against each other' using the criterion not of the number of weapons systems, but of the ability to attain military objective. Seen in this light, the INF Treaty eliminated American ability 'to present an extremely unpleasant military threat to us at any given moment'. On the other hand, the Soviet Union had to sacrifice none of its military options vis-à-vis North America or Western Europe. Thus, it was explained, a factor was eliminated that had created complications in Europe and with the other superpower. At the same time, the INF Treaty was seen to serve the Soviet interest by weakening the 'military presence of the US at its forward-based positions in Europe and Asia'. In view of these benefits, the treaty appeared as a triumph of Gorbachev's 'new thinking', which essentially was not 'naked pragmatism', but a combination of realism and idealism.[12]

In Moscow, the INF Treaty was officially assigned the function of spearheading a development that would lead step by step to a Europe free of nuclear weapons.[13] This plan was put to the test in late 1988 when NATO began discussions on whether to modernize its arsenal of obsolescent land-based, short-range Lance missiles. According to West German calculations, the West's eighty-eight Lance launchers are pitted agianst substantially more numerous Soviet short-range systems whose ranges in some cases are significantly greater: more than 580 Scud Bs (300 km), 140 SS-21s (120 km) and 635 Frog-7s (70 km). The Warsaw Pact puts the total number of systems at 1,608.

According to NATO, the enormous numerical disparity was supplemented by a qualitative one: the East had already made great progress in replacing its old generation of missiles. Not modernizing the Lance systems (no longer usable at some time after 1995) would be tantamount to a unilateral cut by the West. Hence NATO planned to deploy eighty-eight Lance 2s with a range of between 400 and 450 km in order to maintain sufficiency. A reduction of that number was considered possible if the Soviets were to eliminate some of their systems. A 'zero option' was rejected, however, on grounds that NATO required an arsenal of land-based missiles in order to maintain a credible nuclear deterrent in Europe. If nuclear artillery were also dropped (as would be likely), American and other NATO forces in Europe would be stripped of their nuclear capability altogether (whereas the Soviet army would continue to rely on a nuclear potential behind it) — an essentially asymmetrical situation — Washington could be expected to respond by pulling out its troops from Europe. Western suspicion was further enhanced by a growing awareness among experts that the INF Treaty had done little to diminish the nuclear threat to which Western Europe was exposed given that the function of the intermediate-range systems due for liquidation was replaced by long-range systems with variable ranges (which were not liable to elimination under the Treaty).

The Kremlin seized the welcome opportunity to press for missile cuts as a further step toward the de-nuclearization of Europe. The NATO plans were publicly decried as being incompatible with obligations under the INF Treaty. The West was accused of trying to compensate for what it lost in December 1987, violating not only the spirit, but the letter of the treaty as well. All land-based short-range missiles must be eliminated Moscow declared. Largely overlooked by the public was the Kremlin's veiled but clear demand that its large missile cuts be balanced by large reductions in NATO's allegedly greater numbers of combat aircraft.[14]

The conflict heated up in early 1989. The chief concern of Western governments was that further de-nuclearization would intensify existing nuclear asymmetries between the Atlantic and the Urals, to the possible detriment of nuclear deterrence. The Soviet leadership saw no reason to allay Western fears. On the contrary, it carried on an intense campaign against the NATO measure with the declared aim of dealing nuclear deterrence another major blow, demanding that NATO begin speedy negotiations on a 'third zero option' encompassing short-range missiles.

During his visit to Bonn in mid-May 1989, Foreign Minister Shevardnadze struck threatening chords. Claiming — wrongly — that the Lance 2s planned by NATO had characteristics similar to the Soviet SS-23s to be scrapped under the INF Treaty, he said this 'most important of all international agreements' was in jeopardy and asked:

Why should we destroy SS-23 missiles if the other side plans to build and deploy analogous Lance 2 missiles? The problem cannot be solved by scholastic exercises. The fact is, there will be two equivalent missile types. The Soviet missiles are to be destroyed while the American missiles are to be built. That is unacceptable to common sense, not to speak of political sense.

In response to a journalist asking whether his remark meant that the Soviet Union planned to halt destruction of the SS-23s as agreed should NATO opt for modernization of its short-range missiles, Shevardnadze said it would have to be 'thought over'. He added, 'Does it make any sense to destroy these missiles? Or perhaps in this case we will have to create new systems and respond to NATO's decision in that way.' A follow-up question on whether he really meant 'new systems' drew a clear assertion. 'We will either have to halt destruction of SS-23 missiles or create new systems. But that,' he added, 'will not be our choice.'[15]

In a press controversy which ensued over whether the remarks implied Soviet willingness to neglect obligations under the INF Treaty, Shevardnadze went as far as to say that the Soviet Union would 'not stand idly by' if Lance modernization would 'undermine' this treaty.[16] A most serious conflict over nuclear security appeared to be in the making. Shortly afterwards, however, President Bush came up with a formula that allowed NATO to defer the modernization issue. This seemed useful since the West German government found itself in a dilemma which could not be overcome for the time being. In the second half of 1989, political change in Eastern Europe became so dramatic and so far-reaching in its security implications that the leaders of the West increasingly felt other priorities were being introduced. Thus the Kremlin was successful in preventing Lance modernization for a long time to come, while the issue remained unresolved in terms of philosophical principle.

NEW IMPERATIVES IN THE EUROPEAN THEATRE

In February 1987, Gorbachev announced 'reasonable, sufficient defence' as the new guideline for the Soviet military.[17] Underlying were two ideas. Armed forces would be needed only to the extent of 'reasonable sufficiency'. Their task would be limited to defence only. Seemingly, restraint regarding size and the task of the military instrument was put on the Soviet agenda, but the official statements were ambiguous. While the principle of 'reasonable sufficiency' (*razumnaia dostatochnost'*) reminded Western audiences of Nixonian sufficiency, which had been a rationale for putting a limit on nuclear force requirements, underlying Soviet intent remained clouded. The question was: sufficient for what? Nixon's idea that a situation of mutual superpower deterrence allowed for less than numerical nuclear parity was clearly not in the Soviet mind.

It was explained in Moscow that 'sufficiency for defence' (*dostatochnost' dlia oborony*) was the imperative. At that point, however, the ambiguity of the Soviet idea of defence was revealed. Official military doctrine had always stated that the Soviet military stance was bound to be defensive in character. After all, the Soviet Union was a socialist country which, in contrast to the countries that adhered to 'imperialism' (ie to the Western system), could only act in a peaceful and hence defensive fashion. This was a political, ideological argument which did not say anything about what kind of military action the Soviet Union would take in the event of war.

In fact, it was unequivocally postulated that the Soviet forces had to be on the offensive and to exploit the advantage of surprise if possible. What appears as an obvious contradiction to Westerners, was simply the two sides of the same coin in Soviet parlance. Military doctrine had two different components: a political one and a military–technical one. Soviet defensiveness expressed itself in the political statement that the Soviet Union did not threaten any country in the world and would, therefore, never commit aggression. It was another matter whether the Soviet Union, being confronted with an enemy's aggression, would regard a 'counter-offensive' (which might be a pre-emptive one) as an appropriate response at the military–technical level.

During the first years after the formula of 'reasonable, sufficient defence' and a number of similar terms had been introduced, official argument largely tended to lead back into the old mould creating the impression that little had changed except some of the terms. It was not simply the military establishment, including the defense minister, that was clearly reluctant to adopt new guidelines. High-ranking politicians and civil experts also joined the chorus of traditional voices. There were various arguments to adapt the new terms to the old concept. The sufficiency principle was used as a cover for the traditional claim to military superiority by saying that the 'existing parity' had to be maintained. Ever since Brezhnev's Tula speech of 19 January 1977, the Kremlin had taken the view that East–West military parity was already there and that, for this reason, any force reductions had to be symmetrical. Thus the existing parity argument amounted to insistence on Soviet superiority. Moscow officials also sought to prove their country's righteousness by pointing out that, in accordance with the imperatives of the military doctrine, their country's stance was exclusively defensive. The East Berlin Declaration which the Warsaw Pact issued on 29 May 1987 was cited to this end.[18]

The East Berlin Declaration, however, clearly reflected a situation in which new ideas had not prevailed over old concepts. It stated that the Eastern alliance kept its military strength strictly within the limits of what was needed to repel an aggressor. This implied that the level of minimum capability for defence had been reached already. Therefore, Eastern forces must not be reduced nor otherwise changed. At the same time, the prospect of a 'devastating rebuff' was held out to the enemy who, in the same manner as before, was mandatorily defined as the aggressor.

Under this formula, the traditional concept of pushing NATO deeply back into West Europe and of smashing Western forces had been advocated in the Brezhnev period. That such language might indicate a fundamental change of mind and concept was a very unlikely proposition. A number of military men in official positions were even blunter, using the harshest terms to describe their idea that, in the event of war, action had to be both offensive and overpowering. Certainly, the East Berlin Declaration emphasized the 'inadmissibility of war' (*nedopushchenie voiny*) as the crucial point. But, contrary to official assertion, this did not necessarily mean a defensive stance in military terms. The Soviet Union had always taken the view that war must be prevented which included the postulate that the enemy was to be dissuaded from war by the prospect of being smashed in the course of an offensive.

There is still another point which created some confusion among Western observers at the time. In 1986–7, Soviet spokesmen ceased talking about the need for 'reining-in imperialism'. Instead, they began to adhere to the principle that 'the aggressor must be deterred' (*nado obuzdat' aggressora*). Western audiences tended to feel that the Kremlin was moving towards NATO's idea of deterrence after all. In fact, however, Soviet understanding was completely different. It was posited that the Western side (which continued to be defined as the only possible aggressor in the event of war, given the Soviet Union's invariable peacefulness) had to be prevented from following its aggressive designs by a maximization of Soviet military power. It is on this basis that, as late as mid-1988, spokesmen expressed their belief that peace was secure to the extent that the socialist states acquired armed strength.[19] In this perspective, it was only the forces of the Soviet Union and its allies that provided for international peace and security to be maintained against the West.[20]

Such interpretation of the new terms notwithstanding, a concept change was gradually emerging. A crucial element of this process was *glasnost* which, to the military's dismay, was extended to military affairs and security policy. Regarding the structure of the military establishment, revisionist concepts such as abandonment of conscription and a transition to a professional army were increasingly discussed by a broad public. At the same time, civil experts began to question the old concept of external security and to replace it by a number of diverging proposals. Gorbachev clearly encouraged such re-thinking. This did not imply that he was necessarily in sympathy with the ideas and concepts which were submitted, but it did mean that he wanted alternatives to be generated which would fit in with conventional wisdom. In particular, Gorbachev appeared interested in breaking the military's previous monopoly of judgement on military and security matters. This was indeed decisive. From then on, the political leadership could, and did, choose among the solutions proposed by the military on the one hand and by civilian experts on the other. As it turned out, Gorbachev more often than not would prefer civilian advice.

Under these conditions, it was natural that Soviet statements on issues of security were divergent for a long time. When, in 1989, new tendencies had won the upperhand at last, another problem became apparent. Implementation of official guidelines such as, in particular, 'non-offensive defence' (*nenastupatel'naia oborona*) lagged far behind official rhetoric. Critical observers in the West asked whether the gulf which separated words from deeds indicated a lack of intent to put into practice what had been announced. There were, however, other valid explanations. Change of military structure was bound to take time. What is more, reorganization of forces and modification of armament mixes as undertaken from January 1989 onward in forward-deployed Soviet troops was ambiguous as to its true meaning. Tanks, which were being reduced in a declared effort to curtail offensive capability, were not needed to the same extent as before for the fulfilment of an offensive mission. Other systems which were kept such as helicopters were seen as more relevant for offensive action in the future. Confronted with the ambiguity problem of Soviet measures, both military and civilian experts in Moscow would reply that restructuring had to take a long time and could be expected to become unequivocally clear only in five or ten years. This is indeed an objective problem of evaluation, but there may also be a problem of transmitting political intent to professionals who are opposed to it. The Soviet military might seek to obviate some of the harsher implications which are inherent in the guidelines they received from the Kremlin.

The Soviet military do have grievances. They — including the defence minister — advocated that 'existing parity' be fully preserved only to learn shortly afterwards that Gorbachev, on 7 December 1988, announced unilateral cuts of half a million men and a sizeable number of weapons.[21] Spokesmen for the general staff, it is true, subsequently stated that they had been drawn into the decision-making process concerning the military details, but such participation certainly did not apply to the fundamentals of the scheme, and it can only have been shortly before Gorbachev went public. There is still another point of interest. The military stuck to the old argument of 'existing parity', saying that there was parity before the announced measure and that this parity had to be defended against any demand for unilateral reductions — a position which was officially adopted. The argument's inherent contradiction was explained away by the thesis that military options, not military numbers were relevant and that elimination of 500,000 soldiers did not make a difference in this respect.[22]

Western military observers tended to feel that this evaluation was indeed basically correct. The half million men — who would predominantly, but not exclusively be taken out of the European theatre and were only partially scheduled for dissolution (the others would simply withdraw into the Soviet Union) — did not make a difference so decisive as to eliminate military superiority and offensive capability.[23] Some Western military men even suggested that the Soviet Union had not abandoned any fighting power and might indeed have increased its potential for military action. On the one hand, the principle of replacing military quantity by military quality (as announced at the Nineteenth CPSU Conference in summer 1988) was seen to bear fruit. On the other hand, the Soviet general staff was perceived to have promoted military effectiveness by adopting a more balanced posture which relied less exclusively on offensive action and thus allowed for all kinds of unforeseen contingencies. As early as in 1981, the Soviet military had realized that their concentration on attack was becoming counterproductive under emerging new conditions. It was reasonable, therefore, for professional analysts in the West to suspect that Soviet force restructuring which strengthened the defensive component without renouncing offensive capability would result in gains rather than losses for the other side.[24]

WHAT KIND OF MILITARY SECURITY FOR EUROPE?

After World War II, two principal elements of military security emerged in Europe under the overarching umbrella of the American–Soviet strategic deterrence relationship. At the lower level of the potential war theatre, there is a balance of forces and armaments. A state of equilibrium would exist if neither side would possess military superiority and dispose of offensive options *vis-à-vis* the other one. In this event, war prevention would rest on either side's recognition that war can be waged but not won. This is, to be sure, a highly theoretical postulate, since such an equilibrium can hardly be defined decisively in the real world. It can suggest the direction into which arms control efforts should be oriented. Also, the prospect of not succeeding in war might not be a sufficiently powerful deterrent from waging it, particularly given the fact that the calculus is much less than certain. This security deficit is overcome if equilibrium is achieved at the level of linkage to the nuclear dimension. To the extent that theatre war entails the risk of escalation toward unforeseeable nuclear destruction, it becomes an unacceptable contingency (as the Kremlin realized just as much as Western governments[25]). If that risk relates equally to both sides, the strongest possible incentive to avoid war has been created.

For decades, the military situation in the European theatre has been characterized by imbalances which favour the Soviet Union against NATO, but the West's conventional wisdom has been that this is tolerable as long as equilibrium is maintained at the level of linkage. In this case, disequilibrium at the theatre level is prevented from resulting in an incentive to go to war, since potential gains are made meaningless given the risk of being exposed to unacceptable destruction if nuclear escalation were to ensue. During the Brezhnev period, the Soviet leaders had sought to eliminate this risk by depriving NATO of its capacity to initiate selective nuclear use. To the extent that Gorbachev and his aides pursue the objective of creating a 'nuclear-free world' in Europe, all military advantage that the Soviet Union can muster in the theatre would become exploitable again. The present leaders in Moscow assure the Western countries of their willingness not to have such a situation emerge. Equilibrium at the theatre level is to obtain as a guarantee for war prevention. Despite the ambiguities about sufficiency and defensive restructuring, it is plausible that they really mean it. At the same time, antinuclear sentiment in a number of West European countries is making it ever more difficult for NATO to maintain its posture of nuclear linkage. So a theatre equilibrium with no concomitant equilibrium at the level of linkage might eventually emerge.

Seen from a military angle, war prevention would be less safely guaranteed than under NATO's traditional concept. However, both political aspects and unforeseen changes to the situation have to be taken into account as well. If the territory controlled by Moscow were to shrink and the Soviet military would present a much smaller glacis against Western Europe, this would certainly reduce previous requirements of military security. Also, a conceivable Soviet decision to restrict military preparations to contingencies of 'small wars' (*malye voiny*) would fundamentally change the whole situation of Europe and allow for revision of quite a few security postulates.

After all, the Gorbachev leadership is under heavy pressure on many fronts. At the domestic level, the difficulties which have to be faced are reflected in a number of unprecedented arguments on security. After 1987–8, Soviet spokesmen began to emphasize that there is an important 'economic dimension' to external security. That is to say, economic development is understood to be extremely relevant to both the status and the protection of the Soviet Union *vis-à-vis* the outside world. After the Nineteenth CPSU Conference in the summer of 1988, the idea was added that there is a crucial 'social dimension' to external security as well. By that time, Gorbachev and his aides came to realise that Soviet security was in jeopardy to the extent that basic needs of the consumer at home were not being satisfied.

Such insights notwithstanding, the Kremlin was remarkably slow in transferring resources from the military sector to the civilian one. One can see this as an expression of official reluctance to diminish military strength, the only instrument of power upon which the Soviet Union can base its claim to world prominence. But there are also other possible explanations such as passive resistance of the military and length of implementation time in a centralized economy. Pressures are also mounting from abroad. The political change which has seized Eastern Europe has confronted the Soviet leaders with the need to respond to rising demands for troop withdrawal. In principle, Gorbachev and his aides appear to be willing to give in. This, however, might imply more than simply a geographical deployment change. Since it was already been shown to be extremely difficult to house soldiers coming home, the only way to evacuate foreign countries might be to disband the returning units.

WHAT POLITICAL ROLE FOR THE MILITARY INSTRUMENT?

Traditionally, military power has been accorded a crucial role in Soviet foreign policy, since the Soviet Union possesses little else but troops and weapons on which to base its claim to world prominence. Exploitation of military power in foreign policy corresponded to tenets of the official doctrine as well — Clausewitz's philosophy of war and peace which Lenin had taken over and adapted to his purpose of class struggle in which views vie in both peaceful and armed forms as the very essence of politics. So war and peace are the two sides of the same coin. War, or the threat of it, is simply another variant of politics in peacetime. In Marxist–Leninist terms, the struggle for socialism must be waged using peaceful and military means according to circumstances. To be sure, war must not be allowed for when nuclear weapons might possibly be employed, as has been made clear ever since the Twentieth CPSU Congress of 1956. None the less, the Soviet leaders from Khrushchev to Chernenko have sought and found ways of permitting military means to be utilized. On the one hand, use of armed force and the threat of it were ruled out only to the extent that direct East–West relations — and hence NATO's option of nuclear use — was involved. On the other, a sustained effort was made to deprive the West of a credible nuclear option in the event of war in Europe.

Doctrinal innovation as introduced by Gorbachev under the heading of 'new thinking' poses the question: to what extent has the traditional attitude undergone change? The principle of war prevention while not new has increasingly been voiced without reservation to such domains as the struggles for 'national' and 'social liberation'. De-ideologization of interstate or even international relations has been proclaimed. Security vis-à-vis the outside world, it is officially held, must be sought by political rather than military means. Interaction between countries and peoples is seen to require 'demilitarization' (demilitarizatsiia). All these new principles appear to imply that the Soviet Union is willing to stop relying on military power in promotion of its foreign policy. If the Kremlin were genuinely prepared to reduce its armed forces to levels much lower, this would be a practical indication that it is serious about abandoning the use, the threat of use and the demonstration of military strength for political purposes.

In an age when utilization of military power for satisfaction of political ambition is no longer accepted, there is a strong incentive to avoid being explicit on that. This consideration applies particularly to a leadership that is as propagandistically minded as the Soviet one. Therefore, blunt attempts to exert pressure and extortion such as

Khrushchev made, when he sought to impress the United States and its allies with his alleged missile superiority in 1958-9 to bring about the surrender of West Berlin,[26] are unlikely to be repeated. But veiled threats can still be made — and have in fact been made as late as under Andropov. When the East–West controversy over American missiles in Europe was at its peak, the Kremlin sought to persuade its crucial audience in the West, the West German public, to oppose NATO's projected measure and employed as a negative incentive the 'warning' that, if the missiles were put into place, the 'missile fence' would bar inter-German contact and communication. An 'ice age' would ensue and put an end to the 'benefits of *détente*'. But it was one thing to foster West German fears when missile deployment was imminent and quite another to carry out the threat after it had missed its object. Soviet propaganda had always portrayed the Western side in order to fuel tension. If Moscow were to have implemented what it had threatened, it would have adopted precisely the role which it had ascribed to the opponent. To avoid such an impression, jeopardizing the moral gains the Soviet Union had reaped among large parts of the Western public, the Kremlin chose not to resort to reprisals when the American missiles were stationed in Western Europe. The Gorbachev team declared a few years later that military threats had to be generally renounced in international relations. It should be noted, however, that the new leaders themselves do not always stick to this imperative. On 19 May 1989, Shevardnadze warned Bonn not to acquiesce in Lance modernization, saying that the Soviet Union might resort to some kind of response in armament.[27]

The limits which exist to instrumentalization of military powers are one potential motive for de-emphasizing reliance on force. Another is an awareness that superpowers cannot wage war against each other and their respective allies any longer. So they are seen to be unable to threaten it actively. Nor are they viewed to have to expect another side to be a threat against which they have to guard themselves. In this respect, however, the Soviet leaders were, and sometimes still are, ambivalent. Shevardnadze, it is true, explained 'that, on objective grounds, war and armed conflicts lose the function of being instruments of rational policy in the nuclear–cosmic epoch'.[28] Gorbachev made clear that it is the threat of nuclear warfare which makes war unacceptable to him and his peers. 'Nuclear war is senseless and irrational. In a global nuclear conflict there would be neither victors nor vanquished, but the world civilization would inevitably perish.' This, he went on, had created 'a completely new situation'. The 'classical formula of Clausewitz that war is the continuation of politics only with other means' has become 'hopelessly outdated'.[29] In Shevardnadze's words, nuclear weapons are 'unacceptable' as 'means of politics and, even more so, means of war'. 'From the standpoint of our national security, the existence and maintenance of such means of total annihilation against which there is no protection, is unacceptable.'[30]

This assessment does, however, not necessarily translate into confidence that war can be expected not to break out. 'The threat of war', Shevardnadze stated in July 1988, 'is not eliminated yet. There are no illusions in this respect.' For this reason, he felt that defence was 'the principal priority of the country'.[31] Nuclear warfare is believed to be disastrous but none the less a real possibility.[32] While the perceived threat of nuclear war is countered by policies of disarmament which posit total de-nuclearization, the need to prepare for the contingency of war is seen to remain. The priority given to disarmament 'does not eliminate under any circumstance whatsoever the requirement to strengthen defence by all means'.[32]

As a result, it is still conventional official wisdom in Moscow that what is now increasingly called 'national defence' must be secured. It is officially posited, though, that such defence can be organized such that it does not threaten other countries. This opinion essentially repeats the previous position that there is a peaceful Soviet Union which does not challenge anyone's security. In contrast to the earlier standpoint, however, it is not the Soviet Union's alleged peacefulness which is seen as a sufficient assurance for the outside world. Instead, Soviet military restraint, particularly the renunciation of offensive capabilities, is cited as a security guarantee for foreign countries.

PROMOTION OF SECURITY BY POLITICAL MEANS

In official portrayal, military power can be dispersed with not only in the perspective of foreign-policymaking. It is also of decreasing value when it comes to international security. Military power does not necessarily translate into political influence, as had been previously assumed. This means that the traditional interpretation of the correlation of forces theory must be revised. Strictly speaking, this theory was never meant to say that military potential was tantamount to political power which could be used against the outside world. It has always been maintained that quite a variety of factors such as political, societal, economic and moral ones determine the power equation among states and groups of states. In practice, however, the Brezhnev leadership was seen to have relied essentially on its military forces for projecting influence on other countries. This is now viewed as a great error. Military power was also seen to be potentially detrimental to the pursuit of the national interest if it created the impression of threat and resulted in defensive action. On the other hand, skilful diplomacy might succeed in achieving more, including improved force ratios, than a mere armament effort could have done.

In current Soviet assessment outside military circles, the military buildup of the Brezhnev period is largely equated with a self-defeating bid for absolute security. The damage that is seen to have resulted lies not only in the realm of having put a ruinous strain on Soviet resources — a strain which, as has been emphasized on occasion, greatly helped to make President Reagan's effort at 'killing the USSR through arms competition' work. Similarly, the Soviet Union impressed all the world, including communist nations such as China, with a military might which made the other countries unite against it. Thus the threat to which the Soviet leaders responded, was continually being created by Moscow itself. Excessive armament as practised by Brezhnev and his like was both a wasteful and counterproductive method for seeking security. The final result was that the Soviet Union's position in the world was weakened rather than strengthened and that the country's security needs became as insatiable as the postulate of 'reliable security' was permanently jeopardized. It was much wiser to seek security through predominantly political means, for example through a process of negotiated scaling down or through depriving the West of its traditional threat and enemy image. If the Soviet Union were no longer perceived by the Western countries as a hostile power, the most hard-headed governments would eventually be forced to reduce its military efforts as a result of pressure from their respective publics.

Differing views have been advanced on how the Soviet Union's security must be promoted politically. As a high-ranking Soviet academic close to the Gorbachev leadership explained in the summer of 1987, 'political measures in the field of security' designed to replace the old habits of armament imply maintaining 'the importance which is attached to an increase of the Soviet Union's defence capability' and require employment of 'political–legal means, among them international ones', in the first place. It was necessary 'to raise the combat capability as practically the only means to maintain the country's security at the appropriate level'. What emerges is an imperative to keep the Soviet Union as strong in military terms as ever. The only difference to previous behaviour is that the favourable correlation of military force which is deemed essential is sought more intelligently by negotiation and other political action rather than by costly and often counterproductive armament. The underlying rationale is, *inter alia*, that given the need for a 'sharp acceleration of the Soviet Union's economic and social development', the policy-makers must seek to provide for 'optimization of the relationship between productive and military expenditure' and hence cannot afford to maximize the armament effort any longer.[33]

The ground for this kind of argument had been laid at the Twenty-seventh CPSU when Gorbachev deplored the burden of armament imposed by 'imperialism' on the Soviet Union[34] and Shevardnadze concluded that this burden was a major obstacle on the road to economic development.[35] More than two years later, the foreign minister came back to the point saying that Soviet authority depended primarily on the country's 'general development and a high level of the scientific–technological infrastructure, not on a "land-roller" of arms and troops'. Since resources were scarce, they must not be overly consumed by military production but used for developing the country comprehensively. Therefore, he felt that the old effort to amass as many units and weapons as possible reflected 'the most primitive and distorted idea of what strengthens and what weakens the country'.[36] It is typical of this more enlightened traditional thinking that the crucial importance of force correlation was emphasized[37] and that, on occasion, the need to use military strength as compensation for economic weakness was stressed.[38]

In the course of time, however, other ideas about how political means must be used to provide for the Soviet Union's security began to be officially advocated as well. The role to be played by international organizations and institutions was increasingly stressed. It was also argued that use of force had to be absent from settling interstate conflicts. Political negotiations were the correct means for arriving at solutions to problems which gave rise to international controversy. In this sense, 'demilitarization of relations between states' was portrayed as indispensable for providing for both peace and security in the world. As another underlying object, the need to allow countries and peoples a 'free choice' (svobodnyi vybor) of their destinies was mentioned. Such key ideas seem to indicate a Soviet adherence to the imperatives of the non-use of force and to self-determination. 'Our ideal,' Gorbachev announced, 'is a world without weapons and forces, a world in which every people freely chooses its path of development, its way of life.'[39]

For quite a while, however, the Kremlin's intent remained in a twilight. The official formulas were ambiguous. 'Free choice' was defined as a given country's or people's freedom of choice only in social, economic and political respects.[40] National self-determination, particularly if it would imply changes of existing borders and state entities, would not be covered. On the platform of the Twenty-sixth CPSU Conference in 1988, Gorbachev even appeared to imply that 'free choice' had to be exercised according to the prescriptions of Marxism–Leninism when he equated it with the 'objective course of history'.[41]

Similarly, the idea of demilitarizing international relations could be, and was in fact, also interpreted along ideological lines. The point of departure for this is the Marxist–Leninist idea that history is bound to progress from capitalism, respectively 'imperialism', to socialism. This idea is then linked to the practical evidence that overthrow of old regimes rarely ever occurs without any armed clashes, particularly when a new regime comes to power seeking, as a Marxist–Leninist one is invariably inclined, forcibly to remodel the whole society of the given country. The use of such force is ascribed to imperialism's presumed unwillingness to surrender power and its concomitant presumed resolve to resort to employment of force in a desperate attempt to resist the onslaught of history. It is this putative Western response which is habitually termed 'militarism' seen as a trait closely linked to the capitalist system.

As the principal Western power, the United States has traditionally been accused of such hindrance of history's natural course more often than any other Western country. Gorbachev made this point at the Twenty-seventh CPSU Congress. 'Military power on which the US pins its hopes in order to preserve the status quo, to defend the interests of the monopolies and the military–industrial complex and to prevent further progressive change in the liberating countries, can only complicate the situation and give rise to new conflicts.' In this portrayal, capitalism 'does not dispose of positive goals and orientations' and has, for this reason, to rely on force. On the basis of its economic and technological resources, it can provide for the 'maintenance of concrete economic, military, political and other positions'. 'In particular sectors', there is 'even the possibility of social revenge, of gaining back what had been lost before'.[42] Shevardnadze completed the horrifying picture by denouncing Western policies as generally incompatible with the interests of mankind.

Imperialism renounces by no means the obtrusive idea that the most progressive ideas of the human mind embodied in the means of destruction are apt to perpetuate its rule forever and to stop the offensive course of history. But the possibilities and the character of present weapons are such that they make the policies of confrontation and rivalry senseless.[43]

The 'social developments which objectively occur in the world', ie the 'social innovation of the world' along Soviet lines, were portrayed as 'an objective requirement of mankind'. For this reason, 'stabilization of the international situation' as sought by the Kremlin could not be allowed to result in 'artificial maintenance of the social status quo' [through the use of military power]. It could not be bought 'at the expense of export of the counter-revolution'.[44] The gist of such demilitarization was that the Western system had to be stripped of all military means which could support its existence against socialism. In the Soviet portrayal, military force served exclusively Western ends; the Soviet Union and its allies did not really need soldiers and weapons, for their cause was promoted by history. 'The future', Gorbachev postulated in 1987, 'belongs to a society without exploitation of man by man', ie to the Soviet system when cleansed from Stalinist impurities. 'But it is every people's affair to decide whether it will accept them [the principles of socialism] as an orientation and follow them in restructuring its life, and, if it wants to follow them, in which forms and at which speed.[45] The Western side, however, could not dispense with military means to protect itself from socialist progress. According to this philosophy, demilitarization of international relations could only result in the world going socialist. In particular, elimination of nuclear weaponry would destroy NATO's political basis and open the road to socialism in Europe.

During 1989, all these and similar ideas ceased to be advocated by the Soviet Union. Eastern Europe was involved in dynamic political change which clearly demonstrated that the natural course of development did not proceed from capitalism to socialism but vice versa. Remarkably enough, the Gorbachev leadership was willing to accept the East Europeans' 'free choice' and to allow relations to be demilitarized, even though this unequivocally implied that the countries of the region were opting out of the socialist system, turning to Western partners for close cooperation and sometimes were even inclining to sever traditional security ties with the Soviet Union. To be sure, the Kremlin did voice reservations with regard to security implications from time to time, but it was less than categorical even in this respect, demonstrating an early willingness to acquiesce in any solution which would somehow take Soviet needs into account. That the East Europeans, including the East Germans, had a right to decide their affairs themselves, was never questioned. In the context of the German problem, the principle of 'free choice' was eventually so re-interpreted as to allow national self-determination to go under this heading as well.

The Soviet attitude toward political change in Eastern Europe was more credible in supporting the Kremlin's claim to promote the peoples' 'free choice' and to keep military force out of international relations than any rhetoric might have been. It is all the more astonishing that the Soviet leaders have been thus far comparatively reluctant to abandon military advantage and offensive capabilities in Europe. Is it the military's continuing influence, the sheer inertia of traditional behavioural patterns, or an inflated view of what the Soviet Union may need to sustain its security which hampers the revision of the earlier stance? A Western sceptic might argue that the Kremlin is following a long-term design which is directed at eliminating the American–Atlantic counterweight from Europe by persuading the West Europeans that they are absolutely safe. If the Soviet Union were then to gain economic and political strength, with the

West's active assistance naturally, it might dispense with its East European shield and become the dominant power on the continent none the less. Such suspicion, however, may seem not only far-fetched but also doubtful in the light of the incalculable risk to be run by Moscow. It is significant in this context that, since the Central Committee Plenum of February 1990, Gorbachev's foreign policy has come under strong attack from domestic critics who feel that the president's 'success' is likely to result in the break-up of the Soviet empire which was erected at the end of World War II.

NOTES

1. See, *inter alia*, 'Doktrina voennaia', *Sovetskaia voennaia entsiklopediia* (henceforth: *SVE*), edited by a commission chaired by Marshall N. V. Ogarkov, vol. 3, Moscow, Voenizdat, 1977, p. 228; N. V. Ogarkov, 'Strategiia voennaia', *SVE*, vol. 7, 1979, pp. 563–4; S. S. Tiushkevich, 'Zakony i obychai voiny', *SVE*, vol. 2, 1977, p. 337; V. Ia. Petrenko, 'Prevoskhodstvo nad protivnikom', *SVE*, vol. 6, 1978, p. 500; D. F. Ustinov, 'Sluzhim rodine, delu sotsializma', Ministry of Defence of the USSR (eds.), Moscow, Voenizdat, 1982, p. 59; D. F. Ustinov, 'Bessmertnyi podvig', *Pravda*, 9 May 1983; N. V. Ogarkov, 'Pobeda i sovremennost', *Izvestiia*, 9 May 1983.
2. For related evidence see Gerhard Wettig, *Die sowjetischen Sicherheitsvorstellungen und die Moeglichkeiten eines Ost-West-Einvernehmens,* Baden-Baden, Nomos Verlag, 198, pp. 49–56, 65–88.
3. For detailed presentation of the problem see Gerhard Wettig, *High Road, Low Road: Diplomacy and Public Action in Soviet Foreign Policy,* Washington D.C., Pergamon-Brassey's, 1989, pp. 81–6.
4. *Pravda*, 16 January 1986.
5. Iu. Zhukov, 'Ot slov k delu', *Pravda*, 13 February 1986.
6. *Pravda*, 26 February 1986.
7. *Pravda*, 2 March 1986.
8. *Pravda*, 7 July 1989.
9. E. A. Shevardnadze, 'Na puti k bezopasnomu miru', *Mezhdunarodnaia zhizn', 7/1988, pp. 6–9.
10. Ibid., p. 5.
11. Gorbachev's speech of 18 February 1988, *Pravda*, 19 February 1988.
12. 'Pervyi real'nyi rezul'tat perestroiki', [unsigned authoritative editorial], *Mezhdunarodnaia zhizn,* 2/1988, pp. 4–5, 3. The English version of the article ('A Real Step Toward a Safe World', *International Relations,* Moscow, 2/1988, pp. 3–12) does not contain the pertinent statements.
13. Cf. the official explanations to the Foreign Policy Committee and to the Presidium of the Supreme Soviet, *Pravda*, 6 February and 29 May 1988.
14. The Soviet Union excluded, *inter alia*, various categories of aircraft for which irrelevant roles were claimed. According to NATO's comparison, some of the subcategories were numerically balanced, whereas in others the Warsaw Pact was greatly superior. For a detailed discussion see Anton Krakau and Ole Diehl, 'Das Militaerpotential des Warschauer Paktes in Europa', *Die sowjetische Militaermacht und die Stabilitaet in*

Europa, Gerhard Wettig (ed.), Baden-Baden, Nomos Verlag, 1990, pp. 91–168. The aircraft component is particularly important to Moscow because in the assessment of the Soviet military Western airpower accounts for more than half of NATO's defence capability in the European theatre.

15. *Pravda*, 14 May 1989.
16. *Pravda*, 20 May 1989.
17. *Pravda*, 26 February 1987.
18. *Pravda*, 30 May 1987.
19. For an official expression of this view see P. Luzhev, 'Na strazhe zavoevanii revoliutsii', *Mezhdunarodnaia zhizn'*, 8/1987, p. 68.
20. Cf. S. F. Akhromeiev, 'Velikaia pobeda', *Krasnaia zvezda*, 9 May 1987; P. Skorodenko, 'Voennyi paritet i printsip razumnoi dostatochnosti', *Kommunist vooruzhennykh sil*, 10/1987, p. 15.
21. *Pravda*, 8 December 1988. Soviet discussions have been analysed by Ole Diehl and Anton Krakau, 'Die Militaerexperten der sowjetischen Westforschungsinstitute und die innersowjetische Strategiediskussion', *Die sowjetische Militaermacht*, op. cit.; Franz Walter, 'Die sowjetische Doktrin fuer den Einsatz der Streitkraefte, in *Europa*', ibid., pp. 19–69.
22. For detailed discussion of the announced reduction's explanation by official spokesmen see Gerhard Wettig, 'Gorbatschows Ankuendigung einer Streitkraefteverringerung im Lichte begleitender sowjetischer Aussagen', parts I and II, *Aktuelle Analysen*, Bundesinstitut fuer ostwissenschaftlich und internationale Studien, nos. 5 and 6, 1989, 13 and 14 January 1989.
23. Cf. Anton Krakau and Ole Diehl, op. cit.
24. During the Vienna CSCE Strategy Seminar, 16 January–8 February 1990, the Soviet military sought in vain to persuade their Western and N + N (i.e. neutral and non-aligned) counterparts that the Soviet Union's forces had adopted a defensive structure. Their argument that the unilateral cuts made according to Gorbachev's 7 December 1988 announcement convincingly testified to a defensive orientation was found wanting.
25. E. A. Shevardnadze, op. cit., p. 6.
26. Arnold L. Horelick and Myron Rush, *Strategic Power and Soviet Foreign Policy*, Chicago and London, University of Chicago Press, 1966.
27. *Pravda*, 20 May 1989.
28. Shevardnadze on 25 July 1988 at a foreign ministry conference, *Vestnik MID SSSR*, 15/1988, p. 35 (similarly p. 36).
29. M. S. Gorbachev, *Perestroika dlia nashei strany i dlia vsego mira*, Moscow: Izdatel'stvo politicheskoi literatury 1987, pp. 143–4.
30. E. A. Shevardnadze, 'Na puti k bezopasnomu miru', *Mezhdunarodnaia zhizn'*, 7/1988, pp. 7, 6.
31. Shevardnadze on 25 July 1988, op. cit., p. 35.
32. N. Chervov, 'Moguchii faktor mira', *Mezhdunarodnaia zhizn'*, 2/1988, p. 11.
33. E. Primakov, 'Novaia filosofiia vneshnei politiki', *Pravda*, 10 July 1987.
34. *Pravda*, 26 February 1986.
35. Shevardnadze's address to members of the Soviet foreign policy establishment on 27 June 1987, *Vestnik MID SSSR*, no. 2, 26 August 1987, p. 33; official documents in preparation for the Nineteenth CPSU Party Conference, *Pravda*, 27 May 1988.
36. Shevardnadze on 25 July 1988, ibid., pp. 36–7.

37. Gorbachev at the Twenty-seventh CPSU Congress, *Pravda*, 26 February 1986; A. Iakovlev, 'Mezhimperialisticheskie protivorechiia — sovremennyi kontekst', *Mezhdunarodnaia zhizn'*, 17/1986, p. 6.
38. A. Iziumov and A. Kortunov, op. cit., pp. 54–5, 56–7.
39. Gorbachev at the Twenty-seventh CPSU Congress, *Pravda*, 26 February 1986.
40. Vadim Zagladin, 'Prioritet doveriia', *Sovetskaia Rossiia*, 23 June 1988. The article interprets the foreign policy concepts of the official documents of the Nineteenth Party Conference. Shevardnadze on 25 July 1988, op. cit., p. 39.
41. Gorbachev at the Nineteenth Party Conference, *Pravda*, 29 June 1988.
42. Gorbachev at the Twenty-seventh CPSU Congress, *Pravda*, 26 February 1986.
43. Shevardnadze at the Twenty-seventh CPSU Congress, *Pravda*, 2 March 1986.
44. E. Primakov, op. cit.
45. M. S. Gorbachev, *Perestroika*, op. cit., pp. 154–5.
46. M. Amirdzhanov and M. Cherkasov, op. cit., pp. 31–2.

5 A new policy towards Western Europe

A FUNDAMENTAL CHANGE OF POLICY

Until 1985, the Soviet attitude toward West European integration was essentially negative. The European Community (EC) was portrayed as little other than an instrument to bolster NATO by strengthening its European pillar. NATO, in turn, was evaluated as an offensive 'imperialist' bloc with aggressive designs against the socialist countries. To be sure, the Kremlin professed adherence to the idea of Europe and displayed a keen interest in promoting West European 'independence' from the United States. But this attitude did not translate into Soviet acceptance of West European integration. The West Europeans could only conclude that the Soviet leaders wanted them to be both deprived of American backing and disunited among themselves. Such a perspective, of course, was bound to be appalling.

Shortly after Gorbachev's takeover, the Soviet leadership began to display signs of re-evaluation which became more outspoken when the Kremlin was successively confronted with political challenges that made departure from a previous standpoint appear imperative. On the one hand, the West European integration process gained momentum. In particular, establishment of a common market without barriers at the end of 1992 became a concrete prospect. The Soviet Union, which had decided to abandon previous policies of socialist autarky and to seek cooperative economic relations with Western countries, could not afford to ignore the EC any longer. On the other hand, the situation within the Soviet Union and the Council for Mutual Economic Assistance (CMEA) increasingly produced incentives for policy change. Both the failure of socialist integration and the need to redress an ailing economy created the necessity to seek a positive relationship with the successful and prosperous EC. Therefore, Moscow dropped its ban on 'unequal' relations with the EC and permitted relations between the Community and individual CMEA countries.

Gorbachev argued in May 1987 that the revised stand was indispensable so as not to view Europe 'through the prism of relations with the United States'. By getting away from previous 'dogmatic positions concerning the European Economic Community [sic]', he sought a 'principally new approach to this organization in practical matters'.[1] A leading Soviet official explained that the processes of integration in Western Europe had intensified. Their 'contradictory' nature notwithstanding, the realities had to be taken into account. Another 'channel of dialogue with Western Europe' was needed. The official made clear that the new policy line was not simply shaped by pragmatism. A new concept, the idea of a 'common European home' (*obshcheevropeiskii dom*), was to open the perspective of a 'pan-European process' (*obshcheevropeiskii protsess*). The envisaged purpose was to eliminate confrontation and to promote dialogue on the continent.[2]

SOVIET ASSESSMENT OF THE EUROPEAN COMMUNITY

It is felt in Moscow that the EC has entered a qualitatively new phase of development.[3] The supranational elements of decisionmaking in the EC are duly acknowledged.[4] On this basis, the twelve West European countries are seen to be more closely interconnected than any other group of states in the world.[5] In the Soviet view, the EC is approaching the status of a confederation.[6] The juridical and political foundations for further progress in integration appear to be laid.[7] The success of West European integration is ascribed to the fact that the member countries have managed to work out 'realistic procedures' of cooperation and have developed sufficiently flexible instruments to coordinate their views and to strike compromises.[8] This is viewed as the very basis of their capacity for common action, frequent conflicts and rivalries notwithstanding.[9] As a result, a high level of integration particularly at the economic–technological level is seen to exist among the EC countries.[10] It is also felt in Moscow that the EC has strengthened the military–political and military–economic ties both within and outside NATO.[11] As a result, what otherwise would be a cluster of secondary states has emerged as one of the leading centres in the contemporary world.[12]

The Kremlin's high rating of the EC does not mean that deficiencies and imperfections are overlooked. It is clearly noted that the attempt to create a political federation and thus to attain the rank of a superpower has failed. Even the effort of forming an economic union is viewed to have been successful only after long delays.[13] The member states are still seen not to have a genuinely common foreign policy.[14] Soviet analysts expect common decisions to become more difficult as will more advanced integration.[15] Further development of the EC is also expected to be retarded by differing domestic political tendencies. Neoconservative, social-democratic, and communist groups, it is held, equally favour integration but their ideas about the practical details differ widely.[16] All these problems, however, are not considered to be a barrier to further integration progress. In the Soviet perception, the West European countries can only seek to pool their highly developed national economies and thus create a geographically wider framework.[17] The formation of a common market, in turn, is seen inevitably to create the conditions for common policies.[18] While Soviet observers note with interest that difficulties have arisen in promoting West European integration,[19] they none the less see a secular trend toward uniting the efforts and the resources of the region in meeting the economic and technological challenges posed by the United States and Japan.[20]

The perceived need that the Soviet Union adapt to West European integration as an irreversible reality is not necessarily tantamount to positive evaluation. How do, then, influential Soviet personalities view the advantages and disadvantages for their country? The traditional negative attitude continues to be reflected in some of the arguments. West European integration, it is held, is to consolidate capitalism in Europe against socialism. It also reflects the effort to put up a common West European stand against the Soviet Union's disarmament offensive.[21] But other, more positive considerations move into the foreground. In general, West European integration is seen as expressing an objective historical tendency toward internationalization of economic life. Accordingly, it is acknowledged as a development which is both inevitable and progressive in character.[22]

It is also noted positively that, since the 1950s, integration has served to overcome military conflict within Western Europe.[23] On occasion, this way of handling traditional discord is hailed as a model for coping with ethnic conflict in Eastern Europe and in the Soviet Union.[24] Evaluation of the West European integration's intra-Western aspect is ambivalent. On the one hand, West European willingness to reduce dependence on the United States is well received in Moscow.[25] On the other hand, concomitant intensification of military cooperation both within and outside NATO is regarded as a challenge to the Soviet Union and its allies. It is argued that such a development threatens to result in 'serious consequences' for the correlation of forces between East and West.[26]

PERCEIVED BENEFITS AND LIABILITIES

Prior to 1986–7, the Soviet side tended to emphasize the negative economic implications which West European integration would be likely to have for the socialist countries. To be sure, arguments to this effect continue to be made, but their relevance is more narrowly circumscribed and simultaneously counterbalanced by other considerations. For example, it is expected that exports from the Soviet Union to Western Europe will generally become more difficult but that the principal Soviet trading commodity, raw material and energy, will be sold as easily as before.[27] Also, coordination of West European credit policies appears to restrict Soviet latitude. Similarly, socialist countries are seen to meet with greater difficulties in founding banks in Western Europe. However, compensation seems possible by having recourse to indirect methods of financial penetration of Western Europe. At the same time, it is felt in Moscow that the increased financial potential of an integrated Western Europe will be better equipped to extend credits to the Soviet Union and Eastern Europe.[28] In general, the EC is expected to be increasingly interested in the socialist countries as a market. This fact, it is argued, will make the West Europeans more forthcoming to Eastern needs and wishes. In particular, a shortening of the COCOM list is anticipated.[29]

Soviet observers and analysts have also modified their political evaluation. They no longer view the EC as necessarily being supportive to NATO. Rather they feel that it can possibly also serve as a divisive element in the West. In particular, the strengthening of Western Europe which results from integration is seen to imply a lessening of Western Europe's dependence on the United States.[30] It appears equally certain that the growing economic and technological potential of Western Europe serves Soviet interests. The Soviet Union can expect to have a resourceful partner; the economic aspects of European security will be stabilized. These favourable consequences, however, are not perceived to obtain automatically. It would necessitate the EC being willing to develop its relations with CMEA in parallel with its internal integration. There is confidence in Moscow that mandatory mutual coordination of policies in the Community will not allow 'extremist' positions to prosper. The Soviets also cherish the hope that the EC and CMEA are united by a sufficiently broad commonality of interest.[31] It has also been argued, however, that such commonality goes together with a competitive relationship.[32] Therefore, the EC might actively promote restructuring of relations in Europe, but will not necessarily do so.[33]

On the other hand, there are also serious political liabilities which have to be faced. The Soviet Union will find it harder to develop relations with West European nations on a bilateral basis:[34] ie the traditional policy of appealing to one West European country and to play it off against another will be less likely to work in the future. There is also a clear concern that Western tendencies to intensify rather than reduce confrontation in Europe might gain the upper hand. To forestall such a development, Soviet experts recommend their country's positive involvement in the shaping of a future Europe.[35] As a worst-case scenario, the possibility of the EC being transformed into a military–political alliance is envisaged.[36] This would be viewed as a most serious challenge. NATO would be fortified as an anti-socialist bloc; the correlation of forces in the world would be gravely altered.[37]

It is not only the confrontationalist and military potential of the EC which arouses concern among Soviet policymakers. The imbalance of the integration process in both parts of Europe is another disquieting factor. While the EC has developed common procedures, institutions and policies, the CMEA has failed in its integration effort and has a real prospect of falling apart. Inability to coordinate economies, the socialist system's inefficiency and an increasingly felt need to do business with the EC have contributed to the plight of the CMEA.

This situation is reflected in Moscow's assessment that the EC intensifies the divisive trend in the Eastern economic organization and adds to its difficulties in reaching consensus among its member countries. As the only method for coping with these problems, encouragement of close East European contacts with the EC is recommended. If the Kremlin were to seek to prevent the East Europeans from developing ties with the Community, severe tension in the COMECON would result.[38] It must, however, be assured that the member countries' development of close relations with the EC is complemented by parallel integration in the CMEA. Otherwise, Soviet experts expressed their concern as early as in winter 1988/89, Eastern Europe would gravitate toward Western Europe and, as is made implicitly clear, gradually opt out of the Soviet sphere of influence.[39] Underlying is a distinct feeling of political inferiority vis-à-vis Western Europe. The EC and, to a lesser degree, the EFTA group are seen as overwhelmingly attractive compared to what the Soviet side can offer.

This is indeed the most serious concern of the Soviet policymakers: Eastern economic and political integration being non-existent, West European integration is bound to be overwhelmingly attractive for the East European countries unless CMEA and other Eastern organizations can finally overcome their weakness and provide a counterweight. If the Soviet Union does not manage to create a sufficiently viable alternative, the present lagging behind of socialist integration will produce a political disaster. The EC will then irresistibly attract the East Europeans and destroy what euphemistically has been called the 'socialist community'. The Soviet idea that, for some time to come, economic relations in Europe must be based on equal cooperation between essentially two sides, would have to be abandoned in favour of a Europe which would be grouped around the European Community as the centre. This was a frightening prospect for the Kremlin at the time.[40] To avoid such an outcome, socialist integration in Eastern Europe is viewed as imperative.[41]

The need to make the East Europeans draw together is seen not only in the economic realm. The Warsaw Pact is also ascribed great importance in this respect. While the Pact's military role is expected to be on the decline, increasing emphasis is put on its politically coordinating function. There is, however, a difficulty. The Warsaw Pact, while an unquestionably efficient military organization, lacks most of the political qualities which would be needed in this mission. For this reason, a restructuring of the Pact has been called for with a view to revamping it for the envisaged political role.[42]

The Soviet leaders are aware that, ultimately, the problem is linked with socialism's lack of attractiveness. To compensate, they demand that the Western governments exercise political restraint. If Europe is to have a common future, they argue, 'one cannot allow for a return to the ideologized stereotypes of the past' which would imply the danger of getting 'close to another "cold war" '. With a view to the breathtaking changes in Hungary, Poland, East Germany and Czechoslovakia, the Kremlin warns against Western attempts at turning them against socialism. 'In the West, voices are heard which tell us that current changes [in Eastern Europe] result from [the West's] policy of strength, that the development goes into the direction of Western values and that the guarantor of its irreversability is a strong West.' Such reasoning is portrayed as utterly misleading. Instead an Eastern

feeling of increased security has allowed for a trend toward reform in the socialist countries. Considering democracy and freedom as only Western values is tantamount to demonstrating maximum arrogance and to suffering from a mania of 'Western greatness'. The 'all-human' values cannot be curtailed to 'Western values'. What else would be the focus of rallying mankind![43]

Despite their awareness of existing risks, the Soviet leaders profess confidence that their idea of shaping the relationship with the EC will prevail in the end.[44] Underlying this publicly declared evaluation is the perception that there is no economic and political option but to cooperate with the EC. For better or for worse, the Soviet Union must take into account the realities which have emerged in Western Europe. Also, the requirements of restructuring in the Soviet Union make establishment of ties with the EC imperative. Last but not least, there is no hope of keeping the East Europeans with Moscow except to authorize their dealings with the Community. In sum, the Kremlin feels it is wise to be with the prevailing trend rather than to stand up against it.[45]

THE SOVIET VISION OF A FUTURE EUROPE

The inference that the realities created by the EC are accepted in Moscow by necessity rather than free choice follows from various evidence. One indication is provided by terminology. Soviet authors invariably refer to the EC as a mere 'society' or 'association' by using the word 'soobshchestvo'. The term which would transmit the idea of 'community' more closely — 'sodruzhestvo' (with the implied sense of friendship or at least friendliness) — is reserved for the commonality between the socialist countries aligned to the Soviet Union. Thus the word which suggests a closer relationship is employed when such a relationship appears ideologically and politically mandatory but is in fact lacking. Soviet unwillingness to use a similar term to characterize the EC indicates an attitude of reservation. This impression is reinforced by the fact that, more often than not, the EC is generally termed only an 'economic' one. Obviously, there is still some unwillingness in the Kremlin to note that the original European Economic Community dropped this epithet long ago and thereby established its claim to be a community which transcends the economic sphere.

Seen from Moscow, the EC is deficient in that it is West European, not pan-European, in nature. As the official Soviet argument has it, all the countries of Europe must draw together if the continent is to re-assert itself. One part of Europe should not be kept separate from another one. The 'holistic nature' (tselostnost) of Europe is stressed. It is posited that Europe must establish a political, economic, cultural and other identity of its own. The existence of countries with differing socio-political orders must not be seen as an impediment. The states of either system, it is held, should not only coexist but also cooperate. As a result of such 'analysis of the situation on the continent' the idea of a 'common European home' must emerge as a guideline for future relations.[46]

The new Europe envisaged for the future will be 'more open and orientated to a greater extent toward mutually beneficial cooperation, toward development of free exchange of people, ideas and cultural values'. The Europeans' common effort must be directed at 'scientific–technological progress, exchange of advanced technology and the creation of a European juridical, economic and informational realm'. In the domain of security, mutual adherence to the concept of 'sufficiency for the needs of defence' is advocated. As a result, the military potentials of the countries involved are expected to conform to a minimum standard and to be defensively structured.

At the same time, military activity is to become mutually transparent so as to enhance confidence in Europe.[47]

The original idea of the 'common European home' implied that reunification rather than partition of Europe be sought.[48] This implies, inter alia, the vision of a common market including all of Europe as an ultimate goal.[49] For the sake of rapprochement which is to further the end of pan-European unity, the principle has been postulated in Moscow that the adherents of the two systems must not view each other as ideological or class enemies but enter a dialogue leaving aside ideological conflict. Co-development is the professed goal.[50]

As Gorbachev has justified the idea, 'the prevailing historical tendency lies rather in an approximation than in a divergence of differing economic structures'. The Soviet president equally stated that the Soviet Union had 'embarked on a course of developing market relations' and would fit, therefore, into the global pattern of economic exchange and cooperation. Building a 'pan-European economic area' could be effected by bringing together countries and groupings of integration 'on an equal footing'. The relations which would ensue had to 'be flexible and capable of changing forms and methods quickly, of also changing priorities depending on the partners' needs'. It was on this foundation that Gorbachev felt the 'pan-European integration process' had to develop. The first organizational step toward creating a 'European economic area', he added, might be a 'mechanism of consultation between the EC, the EFTA and the CMEA'.[51]

The Soviet concept which implies that all divisions in Europe be overcome has been incoherent from the start. In economic respects, for example, Gorbachev professed in the spring of 1988 the goal of creating a 'common pan-European market'.[52] In autumn 1989, the Kremlin began to advocate that a 'common economic area' be established in Europe.[53] Given the fact that the Soviet Union and the East European countries are in full economic disarray and in desperate need of Western help (with some East Europeans questioning the very existence of the CMEA, and, respectively, their membership in it), this was a bold statement indeed since the Soviet Union had practically no incentive for luring the West Europeans out of the European Community and for convincing its own economic partners that they must not allow themselves to be attracted by the EC.

To be sure, the Soviet leaders accepted that, for the time being, there was no alternative to doing business with the economic 'bloc' which had emerged in Western Europe. A 'most active cooperation with the European integrationist institutions' was declared to be crucial. But the goal to be pursued ultimately had to conform to a pan-European guideline. 'Only a deepening of the pan-European process and a resolute dismantling of the structures of military confrontation with parallel planning and construction of the common European home and of integrating structures [for all of Europe] in the various spheres can promote the formation of a truly united Europe.' As the spheres in which Europe must assert its unity, economy, ecology, law and humanitarian affairs, ie human rights, are mentioned.[54]

Moscow's professed long-term concern is to foster the 'pan-European process' and to provide for 'overcoming the schism of Europe'.[55] Since the Soviet Union's current state of weakness in political, economic, technological and other respects makes it appear most unlikely that its appeals to replace the present European institutions by pan-European structures might succeed, the Kremlin has chosen another road to promote its goal. Both military alliances and the economic groupings are to continue as they are for the time being, but they must transform themselves and cooperate with each other in such a way that they gradually fuse together. Strengthening rather than weakening East European integration is seen as imperative for the sake of this end. On this basis, Gorbachev emphasized that, in the economic realm, 'we also have to seek ways of integration between such economic formations as the CMEA and the pan-European market'. The perspective of a 'European economic area' with 'pan-European mechanisms' operating would result from cooperation and opening up as envisaged by the Eastern side.[56]

Soviet statements on Europe are thus characterized by a dual message. When policy goals are discussed, it is the creation of European unity from the Atlantic to the Urals which is vehemently advocated, but when practical business is focused upon, it is equally clear that the transnational institutions and groupings which exist in the two parts of Europe are the points of reference. In particular, the European Community is understood to be a fact which can hardly be expected to give way to another 'reality' in too soon a future. 'Dissolution of the military blocs' figures prominently in many official statements, but Soviet policymakers knew already prior to the summer and autumn of 1989 that relations in Europe would need the stabilizing power of the two alliances for quite a while. Therefore, the maximum of change which was seen from the very beginning was modification of the existing dualism of alliances.[57]

Moscow's double-talk can be interpreted by the analyst in two ways. Logical consistency would be provided by the assumption that the professions of pan-Europeanism indicate the ultimate goal, whereas acceptance of dualistically structured relations is tantamount to handling current affairs. Plausibly, this is part of the truth. To some extent, however, there also appears to be a difference of emphasis among different policymakers. In particular, the diplomatic cadres appear to be more inclined to accept existing realities as durable norms than party workers or, to a lesser degree, high-ranking leaders such as Gorbachev.

It must be emphasized that the Soviet president rarely omits an opportunity to criticize the dualist structure which prevails in Europe. As has already been mentioned, the Kremlin accepts the two blocs for the time being. None the less, Gorbachev makes invariably clear that, in the long run, West and East must allow themselves to get involved in political developments which will provide for an increasing measure of commonality, thus gradually initiating a process for overcoming the differences. Demilitarization of East–West relations is one of the things to be set into motion for the attainment of this goal. Withdrawal of foreign troops from European countries and dissolution of the military blocs are seen as the final results of the process. The idea of West European defence which underlies NATO, is accorded no recognition.[58]

The Soviet leaders seek to promote the pan-European idea in a number of ways. They advertise their own willingness to renounce their country's military presence abroad,[59] while they clearly feel that such a step cannot possibly be taken while America and other Western troops continue to be deployed in West Germany. Although they advocate that integration processes in both parts of Europe be interconnected,[60] they can hardly expect the West Europeans to halt their integration effort when the Eastern side is unable to make progress. What remains uppermost is the Kremlin's appeal to the Europeans to forget about their quarrels and act on the assumption of a common interest with the Soviet Union. The idea of an all-encompassing dialogue pervades Soviet statements on the 'common European home'. Fear and distrust, it is added, must be eliminated. All kinds of institutions which transcend bloc barriers such as, most notably, the Conference on Security and Cooperation in Europe, are hailed as agents of the desired development in a pan-European direction and hence deserving of active promotion.

CONCLUSIONS

Under Gorbachev, Soviet policy toward Europe has simultaneously become more pragmatic and more principled. Previous unwillingness to accept the EC as a fact of international life has been overcome. The Kremlin understands that the process of West European integration is irreversible and too important to be ignored. Even more, the Soviet Union can hope that the EC, while entailing risk, offers economic and political opportunities as well. It is at this point that the Gorbachev leadership's principles for restructuring inter-European relations become relevant. For some time to come, the EC will be perceived as an association of West European states which both excludes Eastern Europe and the Soviet Union and thus provides for a dualistic structure.

Moscow policymakers feel that this reality must be gradually transformed into a monistic structure which would include the socialist countries as well. It is, however, not extension of the EC which is sought. Instead, the very character of the Community must change in order to allow for both a common market and a political association of all of Europe. For the Soviet leaders, the impossibility of simply extending the European Community follows from their insistence that their country's socialist character must be preserved and that two different socio-political systems must coexist and cooperate. Thus a new, all-European Community would have to be free of capitalist premises and suitable for both capitalist and socialist members.

Thus far, the Soviet policymakers have not developed any concept of how to effect the transformation to a wider European community. The few ideas which are there are both vague and divergent. Traditionally, Soviet authors and spokesmen have cherished the hope that mutual interest in economic and technological cooperation is the cement which can be used to build the 'common European home'. This view continues to be expressed by influential person-alities including Gorbachev himself,[61] but this idea is increasingly open to doubt in a period when the Soviet Union's economic potential and capacity for production are declining. Inclusion of an ailing economy is certainly not an attractive option for a successfully developing West European community.

For this reason, the Soviet leaders increasingly emphasize other domains for all-European cooperation. In the light of the growing West European awareness of ecological problems that require a common effort, they stress their willingness for far-reaching co-operation in this sphere. The most important topic, however, is international security. Cooperation in an all-European framework is offered as the crucial guarantee that the threat of war will be eliminated from the continent. The ways and means of how to do this are not spelt out in very concrete terms. It is simply held that 'overcoming confrontation' (ie creation of a monistic European framework) and 'eliminating military violence from interstate rela-tions' (with little explanation as to how this will be achieved) will produce the desired result.[62] A number of principles are expounded to demonstrate that international security in Europe will be safely guaranteed, but it remains vague how this will be effected in concrete terms. The only rationale which is cited says that involvement in cooperation provides the best conceivable safeguard for the maintenance of either side's security.[63]

The crucial problem for the Kremlin is that its far-reaching aspirations contrast starkly with a situation which does not allow for much ambition. *Perestroika* in the Soviet Union is a political venture which increasingly absorbs its leaders' energies and resources instead of yielding assets for active involvement in foreign policy. The winds of political change blowing into the face of Gorbachev and his aids discourage rather than encourage their inclination to accept uncertainties and risks. The best hope they have is that their political weakness might paradoxically help them to achieve what they seek in Europe — by making Western audiences feel secure and careless to an extent that attainment of the West's objectives appears generally dispensable.

NOTES

1. Gorbachev's address to leading cadres of the ministry of Foreign Affairs on 23 May 1987, *Vestnik ministerstva inostrannykh del SSSR*, no. 1, 5 August 1987, p. 6.
2. Address by deputy foreign minister A. G. Kovalev to the party secretaries of Soviet institutions abroad on 28 July 1987, *Vestnik ministerstva inostrannykh del SSSR*, no. 3, 10 September 1987, pp. 10–11.
3. 'Posledstviia formirovaniia edinogo rynka Evropeiskogo soobshchestva, Material podgotovlen Otdelom zapadnoevropeiskikh issledovanii IMEMO AN SSSR' (henceforth Material IMEMO), *Mirovaia ekonomika i mezhdunarodyne otnosheniia*, 4/1989, p. 40.
4. 'Evropeiskoe soobshchestvo segodnia. Tezisy Instituty mirovoi ekonomiki i mezhdunarodnykh otnoshenii AN SSSR' (henceforth, Tezisy IMEMO), *Mirovaia ekonomika i mezhdunarodnye otnosheniia*, 12/1988, pp. 10–11. The Moscow Institute of World Economy and International Relation (the IMEMO in Russian) can be regarded as being both influential and close to official circles. Its director in winter 1988–9, Evgenii Primakov, had political ties to Gorbachev's aide and Politburo member Aleksandr Iakovlev (his predecessor) and was both president of the Union Soviet and a Politburo candidate in 1989.
5. Ibid., p. 9.
6. Ibid., p. 11.
7. Ibid., p. 10.
8. Ibid., pp. 9, 10.
9. Ibid., p. 8.
10. M. Amirdzhanov and M. Cherkasov (staff members of the European security and cooperation department of the Soviet Foreign Ministry), 'Etazhi obshcheevropeiskogo doma', *Mezhdunarodnaia zhizn*, 11/1988, p. 37.
11. Tezisy IMEMO, op. cit. p. 17.
12. Ibid., p. 6.
13. Ibid., pp. 8–9.
14. Ibid., p. 17.

15. Ibid., p. 13–14.
16. Ibid., p. 12.
17. Ibid., p. 7.
18. Material IMEMO, op. cit., p. 41.
19. Ibid., p. 40.
20. Ibid., p. 39; Tezisy IMEMO, op. cit., pp. 15–16.
21. Ibid., p. 7.
22. Ibid., p. 5.
23. Ibid., p. 7.
24. A. Iazykova, 'Problemy mezhnatsional'nykh otnoshenii i obshcheev-ropeiskii protsess', *Mirovaia ekonomika i mezhdunarodnye otno-sheniia*, 9/1989, p. 6.
25. Tezisy IMEMO, op. cit., p. 7.
26. Ibid., p. 17.
27. Material IMEMO, op. cit., pp. 42–3.
28. Ibid., p. 43.
29. Ibid.
30. Ibid., p. 44.
31. Ibid.
32. Tezisy IMEMO, op. cit., p. 5.
33. Ibid., p. 18.
34. Material IMEMO, op. cit., p. 44.
35. Ibid.
36. Tezisy IMEMO, op. cit., pp. 17–18.
37. Address by Ambassador Kvitsinsky to the Nineteenth CPSU Party Conference, 2 July 1988, *Pravda*, 3 July 1988.
38. Material IMEMO, op. cit., pp. 43–4.
39. M. Amirdzhanov and M. Cherkasov, op. cit., pp. 35–6.
40. Ibid., pp. 36–37; Material IMEMO, op. cit., p. 43; address by Ambassador Kvitsinsky on 2 July 1988, op. cit.
41. Cf. Gorbachev in his Warsaw speech on 11 July 1988, *Pravda*, 12 July 1988.
42. See, *inter alia*, the Falin interview in *Sovetskaia Rossiia*, 12 July 1989, and the analysis by Vladimir V. Kusin, 'A Soviet Proposal to Make the Warsaw Pact into a New Cominform', Radio Free Europe Research, RAD Background Report/196, 20 October 1989.
43. Address by Foreign Minister Shevardnadze to the Supreme Soviet, *Pravda*, 18 November 1989.
44. See, *inter alia*, Gorbachev's political report to the Supreme Soviet on 1 August 1989, *Pravda*, 2 August 1989.
45. Cf. Tezisy IMEMO, op. cit., p. 5; Material IMEMO, op. cit., p. 44.
46. Gorbachev in his Prague speech of 10 April 1987, *Pravda*, 11 April 1987; Gorbachev's dinner speech on 14 October 1988, *Pravda*, 15 October 1988; Gorbachev's address to the Council of Europe on 6 July 1989, *Pravda*, 7 July 1989; Tezisy IMEMO, op. cit., p. 18.
47. Shevardnadze in an interview with the Polish news agency PAP, *Pravda*, 26 October 1989.
48. Ibid., p. 18; Gorbachev in his Belgrade speech of 15 March 1988, *Pravda*, 16 March 1988.
49. Ibid.; remarks by E. A. Shevardnadze in Brussels on 18 December 1989.
50. For detailed elaboration of the point see A. Kozyrev, 'Vostok i zapad. Ot konfrontatsii k sotvorchestvu i sorazvitiiu', *Mezhdunarodnaia zhizn*, 9/1989, pp. 3–14, especially pp. 3, 8–10.
51. Gorbachev's speech on 1 December 1989, *Pravda*, 2 December 1989.

52. Gorbachev in his Belgrade speech of 15 March 1988, *Pravda*, 16 March 1988. Gorbachev expressed himself in a largely similar fashion in his address to the Council of Europe on 6 July 1989, *Pravda*, 7 July 1989.
53. 'Vneshnepoliticheskaia i diplomaticheskaia deiatel'nost' SSSR (aprel' 1985g. – oktiabr' 1989g.)', report given by the Ministry of Foreign Affairs of the USSR to the Supreme Soviet on 23 October 1989, *Mezhdunarodnaia zhizn'*, 12/1989, p. 50; Gorbachev during a press conference held in conjunction with Andreotti in Milan on 2 December 1989, *Pravda*, 3 December 1989; address by Shevardnadze to the European Parliament in Brussels on 19 December 1989, *Pravda*, 20 December 1989.
54. Ibid. See also the Soviet Foreign Ministry's report of 23 October 1989, op. cit., pp. 48–52.
55. Address by Shevardnadze to the European Parliament, op. cit.
56. So, inter alia, Gorbachev during the press conference with Andreotti in Milan, op. cit.
57. M. Amirdzhanov and M. Cherkasov, op. cit., p. 30.
58. For an exemplary statement of this idea see Gorbachev's address to the Council of Europe on 6 July 1989, *Pravda*, 7 July 1989.
59. Shevardnadze in his speech before the UN General Assembly on 26 September 1989, *Pravda*, 27 September 1989.
60. Gorbachev's dinner speech on 14 October 1988, *Pravda*, 15 October 1988.
61. Gorbachev in his Belgrade speech of 15 March 1988, *Pravda*, 16 March 1988.
62. For a comparatively detailed portrayal of this philosophy (which, in this case, was not specifically applied to Europe) see Shevardnadze's UN speech of 26 September 1989, *Pravda*, 27 September 1989.

6 The two alliances and the vision of a pan-European security system

THE TRADITIONAL PROBLEM OF EUROPEAN SECURITY

Europe appears to have entered a period of fundamental change. It is not only the political development in Eastern Europe which departs from previous patterns. European East–West relations seem to have reached a point of at least some restructuring as well. Essentially, there are two possibilities. The dualistic system of the two alliances in West and East will either be complemented by elements of mutual cooperation or eventually be replaced by another, monistic system of European security. In the first case, NATO and the Warsaw Pact would continue to coexist, but would also transform their relationship. Alternatively, the two alliances would increasingly lose their importance, ultimately terminating their existence so as to merge into a system of collective security as has been proposed by the Soviet Union ever since 1954.

Either of the two options can be sought in both a global and a European framework. The current dualistic security system which extends beyond Europe might be so modified as to reduce the American role and to provide for a West European military nucleus. Conversely, transition to a system of collective security might be seen to be viable in an American–Soviet context. It would be more likely, though, that a collective security arrangement would, intentionally or inadvertently, result in American withdrawal from Europe. Thus it appears plausible that the choice made between a dualistic and a monistic direction of development might determine whether American and Soviet troops will remain in Europe. It appears sufficiently safe to assume that once American forces would have fully withdrawn from Europe the Atlantic alliance is very unlikely to continue. However, West Europeans feel the American military presence is a structural counterweight to the potential which a retrogressive Soviet Union would possess on the continent based on its military establishment (which continues to be impressive) and its geostrategic weight (which might be politically exploited once the Soviet Union and its sphere of influence were reconsolidated).

Getting rid of both NATO and the American presence is the very goal toward which Moscow's efforts have been traditionally directed. If the Western alliance were eliminated as a military and political factor, the Kremlin had expected its country to become the dominant European power. By virtue of its geostrategic position and its military might, the Soviet Union then would be stronger in Europe than all other countries combined. The underlying premise was, of course, that the Soviet Union's political stability and territorial integrity were assured. While the prospect of inspiring awe to the Europeans by military means has been traditionally tempting for the Kremlin leaders, it is less than certain that they will actually direct their efforts to this end again. In the Gorbachev era, weighty reasons of practical expediency have been voiced against the renewal of such ambitions.

First of all, the attempt to pursue maximum goals is seen to be counterproductive. If the West Europeans perceive a Soviet effort directed at destroying the military and political foundation of Western self-preservation and at seeking expansion of Moscow's influence to the Atlantic, they may be expected to feel inescapably threatened and to take strong countermeasures. As a result, the Soviet political advance would be halted rather than promoted. Also, Soviet awareness that a period of dynamic change is developing counsels against a policy which would antagonize NATO and the United States. Caution of this kind is greatly enhanced by the current state of potential political disintegration. In particular, the Soviet Union's diminishing capacity to control developments such as the East European dynamism and hence to cope with the spectre of potential chaos has given rise to the idea that the United States and NATO might offer themselves as sources of support against unpredictable spontaneity. Of course, Soviet inclination to think along these lines depends, *inter alia*, on the Kremlin's perception of the American attitude *vis-à-vis* the Soviet Union.

THE FIRST PHASE OF DEFINING THE SOVIET ATTITUDE

Gorbachev and his aides have gone a long way in reassessing American intent. When the new leader took power, his first foreign policy statement reflected grave concern over what he portrayed as dangerous American 'imperialism'. He assured the world that the Soviet Union steered a 'Leninist course of peace and peaceful coexistence' and wanted 'equal, correct, and, if you want, civilized interstate relations', but warned that 'only if imperialism renounces its attempts to decide the historical conflict between the two societal systems, will it be possible to get international relations into the channels of normal cooperation'. Additionally, he denounced NATO as an 'aggressive bloc' and blamed the United States, for claiming a ' "right" of intervention anywhere and at any time' and also for both intensifying 'subversive action' and coordinating 'activities against the socialist countries'.[1]

When, more than four years later, Gorbachev gave an account of his visits to London, Paris and Bonn to the Supreme Soviet, the picture he drew was quite different. To be sure, it was primarily Western Europe which he had in mind when he argued that a 'possibly decisive breakthrough of the ideological barriers on the way to a new, peaceful Europe' had been achieved and that he felt the time was ripe for a 'common working out of important initiatives'. But it was equally clear that the United States and NATO were similarly credited with a large measure of commonsense and with a willingness for compromise, even though not all objections to their policies were abandoned.[2] Obviously, the fundamental change of tone presupposed a fundamental change of attitude as well. It would be surprising if this shift would have left the Kremlin's previously hostile assessment of both the Atlantic alliance and the American presence in Europe unaffected.

It is characteristic of the early Gorbachev period that attitudes toward the United States and NATO were expressed in ideological terms. 'Capitalism' was accused of having taken 'the birth of socialism as a "mistake" of history which had to be "corrected" ' by all means. 'US imperialism' was portrayed as seeking to intensify all kinds of conflict and to instigate a dangerous nuclear arms race. 'Washington's diktat' was also directed at pushing the Western allies into submission, while a 'policy of total confrontation' was pursued against the Soviet Union. 'Anti-communism' and 'anti-Sovietism' were declared as characteristic of both American foreign activities and domestic politics in the West where 'pressure on all progressive forces is exercised'. A general crisis of capitalism notwithstanding, the West continued to be capable of holding its positions and even embarking upon 'social revenge and recuperation of what had been lost before'. These statements made by Gorbachev in his report to the Twenty-seventh CPSU Congress[3] implied that the United States and the Atlantic alliance under its alleged control had to be vehemently fought. In private, he was even more blunt. He spoke of 'our enemy' who had 'started a campaign against our leadership with all kinds of means including terror'.[4]

The ideas expounded by the Soviet leader at the time were elaborated further by minor figures. In an official commentary to the party programme submitted to the Twenty-seventh CPSU Congress, it was held that the 'capitalist system' was approaching the 'limits of the possibilities for growth' and 'had become a barrier for the further development of mankind'. It was on this basis that the concept of according priority to 'all-human values' was put forward as an instrument of political struggle against the West, particularly against NATO's strategy of nuclear deterrence.[5] Other statements contained the accusation that the Western system, especially the United States and NATO, sought to preserve the 'social status quo' against socialism.[6]

Against this background, the Soviet effort to emphasize East–West commonality in Europe has a distinct anti-American and anti-NATO flavour. When, in the context of the Twenty-seventh CPSU Congress, the Soviet leaders took over the slogan of 'common security' (*vseobshchaia bezopasnost*) from West European social democrats, there was a clear implication that nuclear deterrence as practised by the United States and NATO was incompatible with the new postulate. For this reason, the transatlantic alliance had to be combatted. Also, the idea of creating a 'system of all-encompassing security' (*sistema vseob "emliushchei bezopasnosti*), respectively an 'all-encompassing system of security' (*vseob "emliushchaia sistema bezopasnosti*) which continues to be voiced to this day, implies that there must be a replacement for the current 'military confrontation' (*voennaia konfrontatsiia, voennoe protivoborstvo*) resulting from the simultaneous existence of NATO and the Warsaw Pact. The idea of a European security system which would eliminate military confrontation has taken concrete shape in the proposal to seek a 'pan-European system of collective security' in the future.[7] This means that the idea of European security on the basis of two alliances is rejected. An anti-NATO attitude is also evident from the continuing demand to create regional nuclear-free zones in Europe.[8]

This Soviet policy is equally expressed in the demand for a 'common European home' (*obshcheevropeiskii dom*). From the start, the Kremlin felt that the Soviet Union had to be accepted as an integral part of Europe. At the same time, however, there were increasing indications that the Soviet Union's previous anti-American, anti-NATO position might be a kind of principle which would allow for deviation in political practice. The question arises as to what status is envisaged for the other world power, the United States. Is Moscow willing to allow the United States to remain as a Western counterweight? A number of Soviet statements seem to suggest that the United States is a non-European country which must be left outside. When, during the early Gorbachev period, Soviet spokesmen were asked by Westerners whether their country would acquiesce in American participation, the reaction was typically evasive.[9] Obviously, the Soviet side wanted to avoid a frank answer which would have been negative, to avoid alienating its Western audience.

DIFFERENTIATION OF THE SOVIET ATTITUDE

The Kremlin's unwillingness to clarify its attitude with regard to the American role in Europe increasingly proved to be a handicap to the on-going Soviet campaign for a 'common European home'. More and more people in the West began to suspect that Gorbachev, who had adopted this formula from Brezhnev,[10] identified with his predecessor's anti-American policies. Additionally, the Soviet leader had himself publicly declared that the Americans should be kept out of the 'common home Europe' as late as November 1984.[11] Two and a half years after having taken office, he appears to have realized that Western suspicion had to be allayed. His book on *perestroika* which was addressed primarily to audiences in the West carried a denial at last.

When we stress the importance of an independent (*samostoiatel'naia*) position of Europe [*vis-à-vis* the outside world], we are frequently confronted with the accusation that we seek to provoke a quarrel between Western Europe and the United States. We did not have such an intention and we do not have it. We are far from ignoring or minimizing the historical bonds which exist between Western Europe and the United States. It is absurd to treat the European policies of the Soviet Union as an expression of some 'anti-Americanism'.

Gorbachev also asserted that his 'idea of a "common European home" ' indicated 'in no way an intention to close its doors to anyone'.[12]

It should be noted that Gorbachev chose to be very imprecise when he defined what kind of role the United States was to be accorded in Europe. What did it mean to acknowledge some historical ties and to keep doors open for others who, by implication, were seen as non-Europeans? The rest of what Gorbachev had to say about his policies *vis-à-vis* Europe followed an anti-American and anti-NATO line. The Anglo-Saxon powers of the postwar period were blamed for indulging in 'old thinking', which had resulted in 'splitting Europe in two opposed military blocs' and in creating 'the bloc of NATO as a weapon of military–political confrontation in Europe'. The Kremlin leader presented himself as the protagonist who would overcome previous 'bloc confrontation' and who, for this reason, had developed the idea of a 'common European home'.[13] Also, the governments of the NATO countries were negatively portrayed for allegedly following the American lead in fostering the arms race and international tension.[14] Gorbachev's assessment implied that both American policies and the existence of NATO ran counter to the requirements posed by the 'common European home'.

The Soviet leader's line of argument as expounded in his *peres-troika* book did not differ much from the statements which had been made before. Gorbachev had always denied that he wanted to drive a wedge between the United States and its allies. He had equally assured the public that, in principle, the socialist countries were positively inclined toward 'American participation in the pan-European process'. But Eastern willingness to tolerate the United States in Europe, the argument had continued, was nullified by Washington's policies, which were directed at 'diametrically opposed goals' since they were directed against security and cooperation in Europe. This denunciatory portrayal was accompanied by blaming the United States for allegedly exerting pressure on the West Europeans to follow suit.[15] Consequently, the Soviet leader's apparent change of mind in the autumn of 1987 inspired little confidence.

In the subsequent two years, however, there were increasing signs that the Kremlin's attitude toward the role of both the United States and NATO in Europe began to alter. Addressing the Council of Europe on 6 July 1989, Gorbachev expressed himself more positively than ever on the role to be played by the Americans. In the same fashion as the Soviet Union, the United States was a 'natural part of the European international-political structure'; its participation in European affairs was 'not only justified but also historically qualified'. He added that 'no other approach' to the European problem was acceptable and could be expected to yield positive results. To be sure, these remarks were made in the context of defending the thesis that the Soviet Union (not the United States) had to be included in Europe and that the continent could not have an identity of its own without the Soviet Union and for the sake of superpower equality, also North America. None the less, the message was clear that the United States must not be left out.[16]

The Soviet leader's advocacy of American participation in Europe was not tantamount to acceptance of an American military presence. Among the goals which Gorbachev defined for the Europe of his vision, the demands for both a 'complete evacuation of foreign troops from the territories of other countries' and 'liquidation of military blocs plus instant development of a political dialogue between them to this end' were prominent. Taken at face value, these proposals implied that the Kremlin was willing to give up its military presence and its claims to military control of Eastern Europe if the United States would withdraw its forces from the continent.[17] Such a bargain, it is true, would require serious sacrifice on the part of the Soviet Union which, to be sure, might be seen as inevitable in the longer term. Such an arrangement would put the West at a decisive geostrategic–military disadvantage. Without the military counterweight thus far provided by the United States, the Soviet Union was bound to be the only military superpower in Europe and, by virtue of this fact, would be able to extend its influence all over the continent. On occasion, this point has been explicitly mentioned by Soviet negotiators when they insisted that Europe must not consider its situation in the light of geopolitics.[18]

For the time being, Soviet spokesmen are generally willing to say that the venture of constructing a 'common European home' presupposes American participation. They equally emphasize that 'military confrontation' in Europe must be eliminated. This statement traditionally implies that the system of the two alliances must be abandoned. If this goal were accepted, there would be no political or juridical basis for keeping American troops in Europe any longer. The same consequence results when one identifies with the Soviet protest against 'splitting Europe'[19] and with the postulate that policies have to be orientated 'not at eternalization of the split but at its gradually being overcome'.[20] When it comes to discussion on operational matters, rejection of an American military presence in Europe tends to be stated in some form or other. As the principal political merit of the American–Soviet INF Treaty, its capacity to weaken the 'military presence of the United States on the forward-based sectors [of combat] in Europe and Asia' was emphasized.[21] Public advocacy of foreign troop withdrawal from the territories of other countries implies that NATO's concept of an integrated defence being prepared on West German territory must be abandoned.

To the extent that Soviet control over Eastern Europe was shattered in the second half of 1989 by a dynamic process of democratic emancipation, the Kremlin began to emphasize the need to preserve crucial elements of the territorial and political status quo. Previous appeals for the dissolution of the two military blocs were relativized, saying that this was no matter of immediate concern. For the time being, the 'realities of today' such as the two alliances had to be respected, even though they were not 'durable factors of the future'. What was presently needed was that the alliances gradually transformed from military institutions into 'political–military organizations predominantly by developing the civil directions of their activities and reducing all the military elements'. This concept was expressly designed to enable the Warsaw Pact 'to play the role of a stabilizer and guarantor of the territorial–political realities' and simultaneously 'to make a more fundamental contribution to the construction of a new Europe'.[22]

The Kremlin clearly felt that both the Warsaw Pact and NATO were needed in a period of rapid change to channel Eastern Europe's ongoing development in a benign direction. Washington was willing to be helpful to the other side in this respect, feeling that such an attitude would both allow Gorbachev to relax about what was going on in Eastern Europe and equally protect all of Europe from the risks of destabilization. The Gorbachev leadership did not seek to bring military pressure to bear on the East Europeans. On the contrary. When a number of countries in the region began to assert their respective armies' commitment to national security thus distancing themselves from the previous Soviet-imposed 'internationalist' orientation, it agreed to Hungary's and Czechoslovakia's demand for negotiations on the removal of Soviet troops in early 1990. There was a clearly expressed willingness to accede to the demand. In addition, prominent military leaders began to indicate that other withdrawals such as the evacuation of Soviet troops from Poland and even from their key deployment area of East Germany might follow in due course.[23] To be sure, the latter statements were accompanied by the express expectation that the United States and other Western powers would reciprocate. The new line was presented as an outcome of the 'principle of free choice' (*printsip svobodnogo vybora*) adopted by the Soviet Union. This position was supplemented by Moscow's call for the 'demilitarization' of relations between states in order to make such a principle prevail in Europe.[24] The political quality of the Warsaw Pact, which was to undergo restructuring along political lines, was seen to be more essential than the military one.

Underlying the idea that the Warsaw Pact must change its role was the Soviet leaders' increasing realization that it was unprepared to discuss and resolve acute political issues. As long as the Soviet Union had imposed its will on the other countries by diktat, a clearing-house function had appeared dispensable, but when the East European allies had begun to assert their independence, adoption of a political coordinating function became imperative. A permanent dialogue among the Eastern countries was required if common policies were to result. Also, increasing divergence of domestic structures and politics would be conducive to conflict and rupture unless some mechanism of joint policymaking were to be established. The Warsaw Pact's transformation into a political body would provide a framework for the establishment of an agreed commonality. Preservation of the member countries' allegiance to the Pact became the prime Soviet concern with regard to Eastern Europe in late 1989.[25] At the same time, however, the Kremlin continued to call for the two Pacts' dissolution, if less vocally. By February 1990, Moscow began to recognize that one or two members, presumably East Germany and Hungary, might opt out of the Eastern alliance.[26]

Soviet adoption of the pragmatic stance that the Warsaw Pact must be used as an instrument to reconsolidate waning political influence in Eastern Europe was hailed in Moscow as a major step toward East–West cooperation and peacemaking. 'Transformation of the Warsaw Treaty from a military–political organization into a political–military one', it was held, would be the single 'most important step on the way towards creating a Europe free of violence'.[27] Such demilitarization of the Eastern alliance was seen to imply a strengthening rather than a weakening. The Warsaw Pact was to provide a new foundation which would allow the Soviet Union to combat disruptive trends in Eastern Europe and to create a framework for Eastern integration so as to be competitive with the efforts of NATO and the EC. The Kremlin had no substitute for the Warsaw Pact as a centre for coordinating policies and managing crises in Eastern Europe and for allowing the Eastern countries to take joint economic and political action to ensure the kind of stability it felt to be imperative.[28] Invigoration of the process would eventually allow the Soviet side to channel European security into an increasingly pan-European direction.

In principle, the East Europeans' willingness to maintain 'their alliance obligations to the Warsaw Treaty', which would be transformed into a political body, was viewed in Moscow as a crucial 'prerequisite for preserving stability under current conditions'. This urgent requirement notwithstanding, the Soviet leaders continued to envisage a European world without 'blocs' in the long run. This perspective was linked to the idea that the Soviet Union must not give up its political identity, which is different from that of the West. 'We remain ourselves.' The experience of past East–West conflict was portrayed as a crucial incentive for seeking a monistic rather than a dualistic international order. With regard to relations in Europe, the 'level of the concrete and practical question' was defined as follows: 'Will Europe remain a zone of [two] poles of [military] strength, or will it turn into a polycentric community [*sodruzhestvo*] of peoples and states?' The latter choice implied, in particular, that 'the necessity of these alliances [NATO and the Warsaw Pact] will cease to exist in the future' despite the expectation that 'the road toward this goal will not be easy'. Restructuring of the two alliances along political rather than military lines was seen as the crucial point of departure for the 'pan-European process'. The two Pacts' character had to be so changed as to make 'the political traits prevail over military contents'.[29]

DETAILED DISCUSSION OF AMERICAN MILITARY PRESENCE IN EUROPE

The Soviet policymakers increasingly realized that some vague acceptance of America participation in European affairs would not allay Western suspicion. There was also a growing awareness that, at least for the time being, the Soviet Union had little to gain from jeopardizing the American presence even if this related simply to the military aspect. In particular, the diplomats in the Ministry of

Foreign Affairs were inclined to feel that it was unwise in the short term to seek such goals as the dissolution of military blocs and concomitant American military withdrawal from Europe. This 'would inevitably lead to vehement quarrel and intensive resistance'. There was no use in taking 'beautiful initiatives which do not have the chance of being put into practice in the foreseeable future'. Instead, it appeared necessary 'to take into account the fact that not a single country will presently renounce the established structures of its integration ties and relationship with other countries for the sake of introducing "from scratch" the frame of a fundamentally new relationship'. This was seen to relate in particular to the problem of 'the American role in the pan-European home'.[30]

Two reasons were given to support the point. On the one hand, the Americans were thus far perceived to have shown little interest in the concept of a 'common European home' since they realized that they would not be accorded a room in the new building and that Soviet-inspired Europeanization would mean that Moscow supplanted American influence. On the other hand, it was recognized by Moscow that many Europeans would be unwilling to abandon their ties with the United States. 'In the European NATO countries, one does not think of security in [terms of] separation from America and in any considerations which omits the role of the United States in the affairs of the old world what one principally sees is an attempt by Moscow to drive a wedge into Atlantic unity.' In view of this situation, the Soviet diplomats tended to feel that excluding the United States 'from the list of the participants in the construction of the [pan-European] home being planned' ran the risk of making the whole idea a 'still-born' venture.[31]

Two practical imperatives resulted from this analysis. Construction of a 'common European home' must not be made dependent on a preceding change in the system of security on the continent. Instead, the measures designed to effect transformation of the security relationship in Europe had to 'run parallel to the creation of new cooperation structures' in general. Without succumbing to the 'tyranny of reality over ideas', acknowledgement was accorded to the fact that the 'system of security in Europe' must be 'based on the existence of two military blocs for a long time'. Therefore, progress in matters of security had to be sought through 'correction' of the blocs' mutual relationship rather than through their 'dissolution'. The second conclusion of the Soviet professional foreign policymakers was that American participation in European affairs must not be 'equated' exclusively with American military presence on the continent. Other dimensions of the American involvement in Europe, especially transatlantic ties in the political, economic or cultural spheres required attention.[32]

This policy clearly deviated from the course pursued under Brezhnev when all aspects of American involvement in Europe were indiscriminately attacked. The Gorbachev leadership's changed attitude was not entirely clear. There was an inherent contradiction between acceptance of an American presence in Europe (either inclusive or exclusive of troop stationing) on the one hand and the imperative of a pan-European community on the other. There is strong evidence that such a contradiction was resolved by the concomitant via that American forces and NATO served a positive function in a short- and medium-term time perspective, but did not correspond to Europe's needs in the long run. It is also possible that the status quo was not criticized for reasons of tactical expediency or, conversely, that the more distant pan-European goal was felt to be no more than a pious hope to which lip service must be paid.

The most likely assumption is that the position which prevailed in the Kremlin accorded temporary recognition to an American military presence. This hypothesis begs more questions. How long was the stationing of American troops in Western Europe to be tolerated? What means would be used in the future to prepare for their withdrawal? Since the answers to these questions remained open, the Soviet attitude continued to be ambivalent. Acceptance of an American presence for an interim period might result in either ultimate acceptance or in a particularly subtle manner of non-acceptance. This was one of the problems being discussed when, from 25 to 27 July 1988, Shevardnadze held a foreign policy conference. One of the discussants advocated American military withdrawal from Europe within a short period of time. Another one argued against him saying that this would never happen and hence was not worth trying. The prevailing opinion was that it was 'not productive' to pin one's hopes on disuniting the United States and Western Europe.[33] On the basis of this diagnosis, the foreign policymakers in Moscow appear to have concluded that they must continue their ambivalent public stance. They appealed, therefore, to the West that the 'bloc logic mentality' might be overcome and both *rapprochement* and dialogue sought.[34]

Those favouring an American military presence in Europe emphasized that a close relationship between North America and Western Europe was not so much problematical as it was beneficial on its own merit. A Soviet expert who held this view argued

that the American presence in the European security system has not only instigated the arms race and enmity [between East and West] but has also exerted a certain stabilizing influence. It has neutralized former mistrust and controversy among some West European states. In addition to that, the possibility of relying on the power of the United States has diminished the

West Europeans' fear of the 'Soviet threat' and has consequently allowed them to militarize their societies and policies to a lesser degree.

At the same time, he already foresaw in the spring of 1989 that

the European continent in both West and East is entering a period of rapid change which goes along with a certain potential for destabilization. Therefore, the stabilizing role of an American presence in the European security system is increasing. Without it, the gradual transition of Europe to a new security system which is based on the concept of the common European home, ie not on military confrontation but on political guarantees and on all-European institutions, might be more difficult.[35]

To the extent that there was Soviet willingness to accord a 'worthy place' to the United States in Europe, this did not imply unreserved acknowledgement of the Americans' status as Europeans. The United States was viewed as a 'part of Europe', it is true, but it was equally portrayed as having traits of its own which put it, in contrast to the Soviet Union, at some distance from Europe.[36] At a non-philosophical, political level, the United States appeared increasingly unable to make its weight felt in Europe. According to the Soviet analysis, the prevailing trend increasingly moved the United States away from military involvement in Europe. This was seen as providing an 'unprecedented combination of objective and subjective possibilities to go forward on the way to gradually overcoming military confrontation and creating a new, more stable and humane security system in Europe'.[37]

In other words: Washington was felt to be more and more unlikely to maintain its military presence in Europe, at least on the present scale. This would be even less likely if there was a political development which aimed at creating a 'common European home'. The Soviet side equally expected that American leaders would themselves feel the necessity to go along with the pan-European process, all their misgivings about it notwithstanding. In the seventies, it was argued, the correlation of military forces in Europe changed crucially to the detriment of the United States. As a result, Washington was understood to be no longer able to prevent a pan-European *rapprochement* from making progress.[38]

IMPLICATIONS OF POLITICAL CHANGE IN EASTERN EUROPE

When, in the autumn of 1989, the extent of both change and destabilization in Eastern Europe became clear, the Soviet attitude toward European security acquired some additional nuances. Significantly, the position's inherently contradictory nature intensified. On the one hand, the Kremlin sought to strengthen the two alliances as a political counterweight to domestic change in Eastern Europe. The Warsaw Pact was to be transformed into some kind of interstate community to keep the member countries together and to provide them with a body for conflict resolution and common action. The United States and NATO were exhorted to assist the USSR effort by supporting the preservation of an Eastern status quo. On the other hand, the Soviet leadership was confronted with developments which threatened to weaken both the posture and the cohesion of the Warsaw Pact. Czechoslovakia and Hungary announced unilateral reductions of forces and a deviation from the Pact's military structure. Demands for Soviet troop withdrawal were raised and negotiated. To compensate for impending losses, the Kremlin began to step up its appeals that all troops on foreign soil be evacuated. The target date for completion of the process was changed from 2000 to 1995.

It appears plausible that the Soviet leaders perceived the dramatic development in Eastern Europe as greatly reducing their military prowess *vis-à-vis* the Western countries. It would be logical, therefore, if for this reason they began to emphasize the political components of European security even more than previously. Capitalizing on the general idea of a 'common European home', they proposed that 'interstate relations of a new type' be established in Europe. The basis of the arrangement was to be 'cooperation in every respect'. As the guiding principles, 'respect for the [peoples'] choice' to take their individual roads of development and equally 'unconditional taking into account of the territorial–political realities' were mentioned.[39] The European countries had to be accorded the right to determine their own affairs, but their freedom of choice had to be limited by the imperative that the international status quo, particularly existing frontiers and blocs, must not be jeopardized.

In this context, the idea of a 'system of all-encompassing security' for Europe was advocated with renewed emphasis. In fact, it was a system of collective security which was suggested to the Europeans. If the scheme were to be put into practice, a fundamental change in the rationale for safeguarding security would result. The postwar security system in Europe has been based on the principle that there are two alliances which opposed each other. Member states in each alliance were united by a feeling of common interest. Each gave themselves the task of preventing the other side from either going to war or obtaining a military superiority which would allow it to threaten war without inviting serious risk to itself. That is, each group of allies responded to a common challenge by a common effort.

If a system of collective security were to be adopted instead, the principle of all-inclusiveness would be the basis for membership. That is, countries with greatly differing and even opposing orientation would have to join together. Commonality of interest and purpose would inevitably be lacking. Diverging perceptions of security would not allow for agreement on decisions and for joint actions. Since security needs would differ widely, there would be no common feelings about what must be done in case of emergency. Lacking consensus about the values and interests to be protected and the kind of challenge to be met, security would be common but limited to words. In every practical respect, common decisions would be most unlikely. Such a security system would inspire little confidence among its members that protective action would be forthcoming in the event of crisis. Similarly, a potential challenger would feel that he would not run a great risk if he chose to threaten members of the system. In the European context, collective security appears fraught with the additional danger that the United States, relieved of its clear-cut commitment to Western Europe's defence, would feel encouraged to withdraw from the continent altogether.[40]

The difference between alliance and collective security explains why the postwar situation in Europe has not generated war, periods of high East–West tension notwithstanding, whereas the two decades before 1939 which were under the aegis of the League of Nation's collective security arrangement resulted in disaster. A system of collective security is inherently incapable of structuring the member states' security perceptions and deriving a mechanism of practical, predictable action from them. When an emergency arises, every measure has to be determined *ad hoc*. More often than not, the decisionmaking process will be paralysed by conflicting aspirations and effort. What then emerges is that the strongest country, or group of countries within the larger system will take action on its own and push the other countries' interests aside.

Viewed in the light of such analysis, Soviet advocacy of collective security gave rise to Western suspicion, but more likely than not, the Kremlin's scheme was more a matter of momentary expediency than a long-term intent. In a period of change when Soviet troops appeared to be less usable *vis-à-vis* the outside world than usual, it was natural for Moscow to seek for ways of safeguarding security by some political arrangement. The process which centres around the Conference for Security and Cooperation in Europe (in which all European countries plus the United States and Canada participate) appeals to the Soviet leaders as a framework in which some kind of common security on the continent may be promoted.

Western statesmen were understandably reluctant to undertake steps toward anything resembling collective security. They rather tended to feel that NATO, and implicitly the Warsaw Pact as well, should not be replaced but complemented by a wider European system. It is in this sense that President Mitterrand talked with Gorbachev in Kiev at the end of 1989. He suggested to his interlocutor an overarching European confederation with both the United States and the Soviet Union as associates. Apparently, the Soviet leader was willing to consider the French idea alongside his own proposal. Conceivably, a line of thought may emerge which will allow both West and East to approximate their respective ideas about European security.

ASSESSMENT OF OPTIONS FOR EUROPEAN SECURITY

As the only foreign policy speaker at the Nineteenth CPSU Party Conference in the summer of 1988, Ambassador Kvitsinsky gave his assessment of the state of relations with the West. He felt that there was a chance to consolidate the 'positions of socialism' and to open up 'new possibilities'. Particularly important in this respect, he argued, is, *inter alia*, a 'resolute activization of our policy in Europe'. As the principal task, he advocated promotion of 'new thinking'. It is under this slogan that Soviet appeals to join the effort of building a 'common European home' are subsumed. As the ambassador declared, to provide for 'new thinking' to prevail is a 'problem of intensive struggle which requires a comparatively long time and a great effort'. There are 'politicians abroad who have hoped they can put into practice all kinds of plans' to dislodge socialism and to 'realize territorial–political and other ambitions with regard to us and to our allies'.[41]

When, later in his speech, Kvitsinsky addressed himself to West European integration, he made it clear that he also saw a military dimension in it. He predicted that a 'serious change in the correlation of forces' would result. While his evaluation tended to the negative side, he suspended judgement until the direction which would be taken by the EC would have become clear. 'Much will depend on what this organization will want to be: an additional [source of] support to the NATO bloc in Europe or a factor in new European thinking and of the construction of a common European home.' The ambassador felt that the possibility of West European military integration supporting NATO rather than weakening was particularly grave given the fact that East European integration was lagging behind. Therefore, promotion of 'socialist integration' was seen as imperative. 'If we don't have genuine integration [in Eastern Europe], a "sucking in" of an increasing number of European states into the EEC [ie the European Economic Community as he miscalled the EC], and through the EEC into NATO may set in: in other words, the founding of a pan-European branch of the North Atlantic bloc.' This danger, the Soviet diplomat emphasized, was 'real'.[42]

Seen in this light, the Kremlin was defensive when it sought to promote a pan-European process. It was a crucial Soviet objective to preserve the East European grouping, even if under arrangements different from those advocated previously. Like the traditional goal of eliminating NATO, this goal would make it necessary for the proposed pan-European process to be developed beyond a mere political and military *détente*. A fundamental *rapprochement* of the two parts of Europe appeared indispensable.[43] Therefore, the idea of a 'common European home' was understood as an alternative, rather than a complement, to the current division of Europe into two blocs and camps.[44] This was officially sanctioned by Gorbachev himself when he explained that commonality, not weaponry directed against each other, was needed in Europe.[45]

In conformity with the Kremlin's assessment that it was counter-productive to attack NATO and the American presence directly, the Kremlin sought to change the security system in Europe by departing from what existed. Gorbachev proposed that NATO and the Warsaw Pact serve as the very bases to initiate transformation of current security relations. A 'European centre for reducing the military danger' was to serve as a 'place of cooperation between NATO and the Warsaw Pact'. The centre's work was envisaged 'on a permanent basis' and intended as a 'useful structure which increases the reliability of European peace'. To this end, the Soviet leader referred to his breakthrough nuclear arms control meeting with President Reagan in October 1986 in order to suggest that a 'second, this time in pan-European Reykjavik' be held on 'how to break the present vicious circle and to safeguard a transition from words to deeds in the field of reducing conventional armaments'.

The question arose how performance of this arms control task related to the idea of a 'common European home'. Emphasis was put on 'dialogue rather than mutual accusations, the effort to understand the interests and arguments of the other side and the failure to ascribe bad intentions [to it]' constituted important elements of building the 'common European home'.[46] At the same time, negotiating conventional forces reduction on the basis of military 'sufficiency' and 'non-offensive defence' was portrayed as being directed at creating a new basis for European security. Contrary to the stand taken by previous Soviet leaders, Gorbachev was willing to consider all kinds of suggestions from Western governments if only they opened some prospect of fusing security in Europe. For example, he was willing also to accord to NATO a positive role provided that the process of military 'deconfrontation' would be promoted.

CONCLUSIONS

In recent years, Soviet policies concerning European security and European restructuring have become more sophisticated. Direct political attacks on NATO and the American presence have been replaced by a new line which takes the Western interest into account. This does not mean, however, that the Kremlin is willing to acquiesce permanently in the present dualism of alliances. In principle and in the long run, the tendency still appears to prevail in Moscow that the security relationship in Europe must be transformed along monistic patterns. It seems likely to a number of analysts and politicians in Moscow that the United States will be increasingly inclined to disengage itself from Europe. If, as a consequence, a monistic structure were to result in Europe, a Soviet Union which would have regained its political strength would reap substantial political benefits. It would rid itself of being juxtaposed with both NATO and the EC. The Kremlin would thus be freed from the risk of being confronted with the prospect of West European integration becoming so attractive that East European allies were tempted to join in. Last but not least, many Soviet leaders appear to hope that, after a period of political reconsolidation and economic–technological revitalization, the Soviet Union might be able to exploit a position of geostrategic advantage and military superiority, allowing it to make a political impact on Europe beyond the traditional East–West divide.

The policymakers in Moscow have become sufficiently sophisticated to understand that such considerations, while important, are not the whole story. In the current period of destabilization, particularly in Eastern Europe, American involvement on the continent, military and/or other, might prove useful. On the basis of this assessment, the Soviet leaders tend to feel that the best choice they can make is to accept the Americans, including their military presence, in Europe for some time to come. They appear inclined, however, to reserve the option of getting the United States out later when, hopefully, the Soviet Union will have regained strength. For this reason, NATO's existence and an American presence in Europe must not be recognized definitively. Many diplomats seem to disagree with this view feeling that American-Soviet cooperation in Europe provides a permanent basis for political relations with the West.

Most Soviet policymakers, however, give the impression that, at least in principle, they regard American military withdrawal from the European theatre as highly desirable. In this view, getting the

Americans out remains an important goal which must be pursued again once the present domestic and intrabloc difficulties have been overcome. Presumably, the underlying perception is that the military factor, rhetoric about demilitarizing relations notwithstanding, continues to be a beneficial factor in international politics in Europe. If the United States were eliminated from the continent as a military power, this would result in giving the Soviet Union a strong, presumably dominating military and political position in Europe. Non-military forms of American involvement in European affairs tend to be seen as less important. In this perspective, it is the United States' capacity to offer armed protection to the West Europeans which ultimately counts. If Washington would lose this capacity or become unavailable to provide a counterweight to the military world power Soviet Union in Europe, the correlation of forces would change fundamentally and allow a Soviet Union which would re-adopt previous ideologic and power politics to prevail on the whole continent.

For the time being, the adherents of the anti-NATO view in Moscow do not recommend policies which would greatly differ from those advocated by the pro-Americans. They equally feel that NATO and the American presence must not be openly put into jeopardy. For the pro-Americans, this postulate follows from a fundamental belief in the long-term benefits of comprehensive cooperation with the United States. In the anti-Nato perspective, acceptance of the current security structures in Europe is imperative for reasons of tactical expediency, if only for the time being. Otherwise, the Soviet Union will not have a chance to cope with political change in Eastern Europe and simultaneously to exploit the West's diminishing threat perception as a result of the East European events. Both factors, it is concluded, should be instrumentalized for fostering the 'pan-European process'. Differing in their outlook on the future, the two schools of thought have reached a temporary consensus on short- and medium-term policies: NATO's existence and the American presence must be accepted for some time to come, if for differing long-term objectives.

NOTES

1. *Pravda*, 24 April 1985.
2. *Pravda*, 2 August 1989.
3. *Pravda*, 26 February 1986.
4. Remarks made by Gorbachev in a talk with Soviet writers on 19 June 1986. For translated versions of the Russian text which has become available from two independent sources, see *La Repubblica* and *L'Unità*, 7 October 1986.

5. V. V. Zagladin, 'Programmnye tseli KPSS i global'nye problemy', *Voprosy filosofii*, 2/1986, pp. 3–15.
6. Sh. Sanakoev, 'XXVII s''ezd KPSS ob osnovykh napravleniiakh sovetskoi vneshnei politiki', *Mezhdunarodnaia zhizn'*, 9/1986, p. 10; E. Primakov, 'Novaia filosofiia vneshnei politiki', *Pravda*, 10 July 1987. Primakov has been a close associate of Gorbachev's aide A. Iakovlev (who was to take a leading political role afterwards) for a long time and was later (in 1989) elevated to the position of the Supreme Soviet's chairman.
7. Communiqué of the foreign ministers of the Warsaw Pact countries, *Izvestiia*, 27 October 1989.
8. See for example Gorbachev's speech in Helsinki, *Pravda*, 26 October 1989.
9. This pattern could be observed as late as on 8 November 1987 when, after a presentation at the Friedrich Ebert Foundation in Bonn, the head of the International Department of the CPSU Central Committee, A. Dobrynin, avoided replying to this question which had been asked several times by West German social democrats.
10. *Pravda*, 23 November 1981.
11. Gorbachev before the British House of Commons, *Pravda*, 13 November 1984.
12. M. S. Gorbachev, *Perestroika i novoe myshlenie dlia nashei strany i dlia vsego mira*, Moscow – Izdatel'stvo politicheskoi literatury 1987, pp. 218–19. The book was written in the summer of 1987 and published in the following autumn.
13. Ibid., pp. 201–4.
14. Ibid., p. 217.
15. *Pravda*, 1 July 1986.
16. *Pravda*, 7 July 1989.
17. Ibid. For another plea that 'no Soviet or any other soldier be stationed outside his own country', see Gorbachev's address to the UN General Assembly on 26 September 1989, *Pravda*, 27 September 1989.
18. A. Kozyrev (head of the international organizations department in the Ministry of Foreign Affairs), 'Vostok i zapad: Ot konfrontatsii k sotvorchestvu i sorazvitiiu, *Mezhdunarodnaia zhizn'*, 9/1989, p. 3.
19. Gorbachev's speech in Belgrade on 15 March 1988, *Pravda*, 16 March 1988.
20. Documents of the very influential Institute of World Economy and International Relations on the trends prevailing in the EC, *Mirovaia ekonomika i mezhdunarodnye otnosheniia*, 12/1988, p. 18.
21. Pervyi real'nyi rezul'tat perestroiki', *Mezhdunarodnaia zhizn'*, 2/1988, p. 5. An editorial in the Foreign Minister's journal clearly expresses official opinion. It is significant that the English version of the article (*International Affairs*, Moscow, 2/1988, pp. 3–12) does not contain the assessment.
22. See, *inter alia*, the interview by Foreign Minister Shevardnadze given to the Polish news agency PAP, *Pravda*, 26 October 1989; 'Vneshnepoliticheskaia i diplomaticheskaia deiatel'nost' SSSR (aprel' 1985g. – oktiabr' 1989g.)', report given by the Ministry of Foreign Affairs to the Supreme Soviet on 23 October 1989, *Mezhdunarodnaia zhizn'*, 12/1989, pp. 11, 49, 67–68.
23. Cf. for example Chief of General Staff Moiseiev's interview in *Krasnaia zvezda*, 10 February 1990.
24. Report by the Foreign Ministry to the Supreme Soviet of 23 October

1989, *Mezhdunarodnaia zhizn'*, 12/1989, p. 10.
25. This pattern of behaviour which can be generally observed has been analysed in more detail for the Polish case by Michael Shafir: 'Soviet Reaction to Polish Developments: Widened Limits of Tolerated Change', *Radio Free Europe Research*, RAD Background Report/179, 20 September 1989.
26. See the Moiseiev interview mentioned in note 23.
27. V. Falin (head of the International Department) in reference to relevant remarks by Gorbachev in an interview in *Sovetskaia Rossia*, 12 July 1989.
28. For a more detailed analysis see Vladimir V. Kusin, 'A Soviet Proposal to Make the Warsaw Pact into a New Cominform', *Radio Free Europe Research*, RAD Background Report, no. 196/1989 (20 October 1989), pp. 1–6.
29. Address by E. A. Shevardnadze to the European Parliament in Brussels on 19 December 1989, *Pravda*, 20 December 1989.
30. M. Amirdzhanov and M. Cherkasov (two staff members of the European security and cooperation department in the Soviet Ministry of Foreign Affairs), 'Etazhi obshcheevropoiskogo doma', *Mezhdunarodnaia zhizn'*, 11/1988, p. 30.
31. Ibid., pp. 30–1.
32. Ibid.
33. Report given by First Deputy Foreign Minister A. G. Kovalev, *Mezhdunarodnaia zhizn'*, 9/1988, p. 38.
34. Shevardnadze's address to the ambassadors of the EC countries in Moscow on 7 February 1989, *Vestnik ministerstva inostrannykh del SSSR*, 3/1989 (1 March 1989), pp. 24–5.
35. S. Karaganov (staff member of the influential Institute for World Economy and International Relations), 'SShA i obshcheevropeiskii dom', *Mezhdunarodnaia zhizn'*, 7/1989, pp. 28–9.
36. Ibid., p. 28.
37. Ibid., pp. 21–4.
38. Ibid., pp. 26–7.
39. Report given by the Soviet Foreign Ministry to the Supreme Soviet on 23 October 1989, *Mezhdunarodnaia zhizn'*, 12/1989, p. 49.
40. For a more detailed discussion of the problem see Gerhard Wettig, 'Kriterien der Friedenssicherung in Europa', *Beitraege zur Konfliktforschung*, 3/1974, pp. 13–40.
41. *Pravda*, 3 July 1988.
42. Ibid.
43. See discussion between Iu. Borko and B. Orlov in *Mirovaia ekonomika i mezhdunarodnye otnosheniia*, 9/1988, pp. 47–54.
44. G. Vorontsov, 'Ot Khel'sinki k "obshcheevropeiskomu domu', *Mirovaia ekonomika i mezhdunarodnye otnosheniia*, 9/1988, pp. 43–4.
45. *Pravda*, 11 July 1988.
46. Ibid.

7 The Soviet Union and the political transformation in Eastern Europe

FUNDAMENTAL ELEMENTS OF CHANGING SOVIET POLICY TOWARD EASTERN EUROPE

In the course of 1989, all the Soviet Union's European allies underwent a profound political transformation. In all these countries, the communist party's monopoly on power was broken. A trend towards democracy and a Western-style market economy set in everywhere, even if the pace differed from country to country. In the German Democratic Republic (GDR), the overthrow of administrative socialism marked the end of seclusion from the West, opening up the prospect of unification with the Federal Republic of Germany. By traditional Soviet standards, these developments were changes that threatened the very core of the socialist system and thus could not be tolerated. Nevertheless, the Kremlin decided to accept the new situation. Without doubt, a major factor in that decision was the fact that in the previous years the Gorbachev leadership had been none too happy with the orthodox ideological policies pursued by its allies, with the exception of Hungary and, in some respects, Poland. So in Moscow's view a change of course was, in principle, not a bad thing. But it soon became clear that the change was going far beyond Soviet intentions. This makes the Soviet decision not to apply pressure or force even more worthy of note.

The official line followed by the Soviet Union, as formulated earlier and put into practice in 1989, was based on the principle of 'free choice' (*svobodnyi vybor*) and an associated 'demilitarization of relations'. Each country and people had the right to determine its fortunes on the basis of its own decisions. It was stressed that no foreign power must be allowed to intervene with the use or threat of military force, or in any other way, to impede those fortunes. Initially, however, this position was ambiguously presented. On the one hand, the pertinent Soviet comments were made with reference to the choice of a 'way of life' (*obraz zhizni*) and of a 'path of development' (*put' razvitiia*) and thus gave the impression that the option concerned solely the choice of politico-social system, with no provision being made for a right of national self-determination. On the other hand, the Soviet spokesmen frequently expressed themselves so as to make it evident that the choice was to be made in a predetermined direction — namely in favour of socialism.[1] These ambiguities in wording were not eliminated until after the political transformation of Eastern Europe had already outflanked such reservations.

The events of 1989 had been preceded by a fundamental revision of the Soviet Union's priorities towards its allies. When the Kremlin found itself forced to concentrate its efforts on economic and technological development and on implementing *perestroika* within its own borders, it started to view its relations with its client states abroad more and more as costly commitments. Not only their proliferating demands for financial support but also the pattern of economic cooperation as a whole were now seen as liabilities on a balance sheet for which there was no recompense in the form of political assets. The Soviet Union, it was apparent, was losing countless billions every year just from the fact that its energy and raw materials exports to the socialist countries were not bringing in any hard currency. Besides, the Soviet Union would have to be integrated into the competitive rivalry on the world market if it was to attain the higher level of economic performance on which it had set its sights. In this new scenario, the barter trade practised to date between the state-controlled-economy countries was an obstacle to the development of the Soviet economy's productive forces. Then came Shevardnadze's promulgation of the imperative of the 'economization of foreign policy' (*ekonomizatsiia vneshnei politiki*), which establishes the principle of material gain as the guideline for the handling of foreign relations.[2] This new precept rules out the continued use of scarce Soviet resources to bolster power elites in allied countries.

Since 1987, Moscow had been attempting to make the leaderships in Eastern Europe aware that they were in future going to have to stand on their own feet economically and that it would be up to them to adapt to the harsh conditions prevailing on the world markets. A schedule was drawn up for the gradual reduction of Soviet energy and raw material supplies in the barter trade between the socialist countries. The countries of Eastern Europe have since then been faced with the need to follow the Soviet Union in its efforts to become competitive on the world markets. It was the Kremlin's intention that they should awake from their decades of torpidity and mobilize their forces — and one of the main instruments in doing so was to be, specifically, systemic reforms to cure their chronic economic and technological debility.

Moscow's refusal to continue accepting the responsibility for its allies and to burden itself with economic imbalance just for the sake of preserving the political status quo in Eastern Europe had far-reaching political consequences. Wherever the countries of Eastern Europe found it impossible to cope with their problems on their own, they had no choice but to look to the West for help. But by taking on the burdens that had been cast off by the Soviet Union, the Western countries inevitably also gained influence in the region previously dominated by the Soviet Union. The Soviet pretension to absolute control as embodied in the 'Brezhnev Doctrine' became untenable.

The Kremlin's decision to press on with *perestroika* at home also helped to change conditions abroad. Whereas reformist forces in Eastern Europe, if they had been tolerated at all, had hitherto remained outsiders in the international communist movement, they now became Moscow's favourites. The Hungarian party was the first to benefit from this change of heart. Though even Brezhnev had accepted Hungary's experimenting with unconventional economic reforms, in the hope that these experiments might generate experience that would be of benefit to the Soviet Union, too, the leeway allowed for such reforms had been modest by comparison with the need for radical innovation. Thus the new Soviet course opened up far greater opportunities for the Hungarian reformers. In particular, their freedom of action was extended to include political reforms. The next country to profit from the pro-reform attitude in the Soviet Union was Poland. Though the communist party there tried to preserve the status quo as far as possible, the ongoing, worsening crisis and a more and more vociferous opposition forced it to abandon its old, fruitless policies and to look around for new approaches. But Soviet sympathies were not restricted to reforms that were already on the drawing board. The advocates of socialist change in those countries that still adhered to traditional policies could also count on encouragement from Moscow.[3]

As far as can be judged from known statements by Soviet politicians, it would appear that the Kremlin leadership had also become aware of the lack of public acceptance of Soviet dominance in Eastern Europe and had come to the conclusion that it was time to draw the consequences from this politico-psychological circumstance. For instance, towards the end of the winter of 1989-90, Foreign Minister Shevardnadze recalled that even in the early to mid-eighties the Soviet embassies in the allied countries had pointed out that the further deployment of Soviet armed forces in those countries could cause problems. All in all, Moscow in 1989 had an aptly critical picture of the situation in Eastern Europe. A dispassionate assessment of the prevailing trends in the region had been imperative, even if only because following the eruptions of 1953, 1956 and 1968 and the Solidarity movement of 1980-1 nobody could be left in any doubt as to the workforce's sentiments regarding the 'barracks socialism' practised in the past. That so many GDR citizens had 'voted with their feet' was a clear indication of widespread dissatisfaction with the existing situation.[4]

The Soviet foreign minister summed up his portrayal of the official appraisal of the situation in Eastern Europe in 1989 to the effect that nobody had had any illusions as to the general nature and the basic direction of the incipient changes. What had come as a surprise, of course, had been the speed and intensity with which events had developed.[5]

THE EMERGENCE OF A NEW SOVIET ATTITUDE TOWARD EASTERN EUROPE

The Gorbachev leadership had not always been willing to tolerate, much less to encourage change in Eastern Europe. In his first statement of his programme, his speech to the Central Committee in April 1985, the newly elected general secretary had outlined his policy in entirely traditional terms. He had praised the 'closed community of the socialist states, their economic and defence power, and their unity of action in the international arena' as an 'invincible force in the struggle for a peaceful future for mankind'. The strength of socialism, he added, was urgently required in order to restrain the 'aggressive efforts of [Western] imperialism'.[6]

When Gorbachev came to address the Polish communists' party congress one year later, his speech was already a little less orthodox. He rehabilitated the Solidarity opposition by declaring that, during the crisis of 1980–1, it had only criticized 'deformations of socialism'. Contrary to the interpretation common up to that time, he appreciated that Solidarity's efforts had not been directed against socialism as such. At the same time, however, the general secretary followed familiar stereotypes by insisting that the 'life-nerve of a socialist society' was 'the place and the role of the working class and its party', that only the working class was 'capable of being the initiator, the stimulator and the prime force of socialist construction', and that only the communist party could 'organize and steer the energies of the masses of the people towards the creation of a new society'.[7]

The first signs of Gorbachev having largely cast off Marxist–Leninist orthodoxy came in April 1987, when he addressed the party congress of the Czechoslovak communists. On this occasion, the appraisal he delivered of the blessings of the traditional socialist system was no longer free from criticism. He went on to explain *perestroika* in his own country by saying that although the existing system was firmly established it was still unsatisfactory in many ways and was 'lagging behind existing necessities and requirements'. For that reason it was time for a 'major reconstruction'. The Soviet leader obviously had the orthodox Czechoslovak regime in mind when he castigated the ' "no-problem" portrayal of reality', adding that this was doing a disservice to socialism because it created a 'chasm between words and deeds' and led to 'social passivity and loss of credibility for the proclaimed slogans'. Gorbachev also pointed out that production methods must be constantly adapted to changing conditions if socialism was to remain efficient. This adaptation, he qualified however, must remain within certain bounds. The 'proletariat' and the 'poor farmers' must be the ones to exercise power. That was the immutable 'political basis of society' and the 'unshakeable foundation of socialism'. He also expressly stated that the 'party of the communists' should act as the initiator of change, while the people should merely participate in the process.[8]

In the same speech, Gorbachev addressed with unprecedented openness the problem of relations between the socialist states. While endorsing the view that socialism had developed into a 'powerful international formation' and stressing the 'complex network of mutual relations in the fields of party, state and society', he also pointed out that 'many forms and methods that have evolved in the past' were no longer in keeping with 'present-day possibilities and requirements'. But since socialism was in the process of establishing itself as a 'world system', it was necessary to 'raise the entire system of interaction between our countries onto a qualitatively new level'. He called for 'the entire system of political relations between the countries of socialism' to be founded 'strictly on the basis of equality and mutual responsibility'. Nobody had 'the right to lay claim to a special position in the socialist world'. 'The independence of each party, its responsibility towards its own people, and the right to decide on questions concerning the development of its own country in a sovereign fashion — these are unconditional matters of principle for us.' Thus he proclaimed the right of each communist party to look after its own affairs according to its own judgement. But Gorbachev went on to add a reservation: while each party and each country was entitled and obliged to act of its own accord, at the same time all bore responsibility for the 'common interests' of socialism.[9]

This was the same small print that the Brezhnev doctrine had used in 1968 to justify the military intervention by the Soviet Union and its vassal states in refractory Czechoslovakia in the name of the 'socialist community' (*sotsialisticheskoe sodruzhestvo*). It was not until his visit to Belgrade in March 1988 that the Soviet leader unambiguously disclaimed any right to decide what type of system was to be binding on other socialist countries.[10] But not all his audience were convinced that Gorbachev had really and unconditionally renounced any right of intervention. Some were of the opinion that his statement had referred not to all socialist countries but only to Yugoslavia, which had been outside the Soviet power sphere ever since 1948 and enjoyed a different status from the Warsaw Pact countries, anyway: Khrushchev had formally recognized Yugoslavia's independence as early as 1955.

In the following months, Gorbachev reiterated on several occasions his rejection of interference in Eastern Europe, incorporating this view into a pan-European context, for instance in a speech delivered before the Council of Europe on 6 July 1989. The countries of Europe, he stated, belonged to different social systems. This was a reality that had to be respected. Gorbachev spoke out in favour of the 'recognition of this historical circumstance' and of the 'observance of the sovereign right of each people to choose its social structure according to its own designs'. This was 'the most important precondition to a normal European process'. Decisions as to the social and political order in any country were 'the exclusive affair of the peoples themselves and their choice.' 'Any interference in the internal affairs [of others], any attempt to restrict the sovereignty of [other] states — of allies and friends just as of any others — is inadmissible.' The Soviet leader added that the renunciation of the use and threat of force both between and within the alliances was an essential element of the international order to be established in Europe.[11]

The Soviet leadership had obviously come a long way since those beginnings in April 1985 when it had still portrayed the global situation in general and relations with its allies in particular in the long-standing traditional fashion. However gradually this change of stance may have come about, the question is when precisely the decisive step towards respecting the independence of the other Warsaw Pact countries was taken. On the basis of various indications, Ronald Asmus concludes that the basic new conception had already been elaborated and adopted by the late autumn of 1986.[12] This fits in with the fact that it was at about this time that the first contacts intended to encourage reformist forces in allied countries were made.

THE SOVIET REACTION TO THE POLITICAL CHANGE IN POLAND

The transition toward democracy and market economy first got under way in Hungary and Poland. The course of events in the land of the Magyars gave the Soviet leadership little ground for interference. There were no incidents that could be seen to change the power constellations in the country dramatically and thus to constitute an evident caesura. In Poland, by contrast, the semi-free elections to the Sejm in June 1989 marked a distinct turning-point. Contrary to the expectations that arose out of the agreements reached beforehand, the discussion about the possibility of a non-communist government came to a head in August. The virtually incredible electoral defeat suffered by the Polish United Workers' Party had induced the two hitherto slavishly loyal minor parties in the National Unity Front to dissociate themselves from the communists. Thereupon, the moral leader of the victorious Solidarity movement, Lech Wałęsa, issued an appeal to these parties to form a coalition with the former opposition and help push the communists out of the government. The prospects opened up by this suggestion were breathtaking at that time. For the first time in more than four decades, there was the possibility of a non-communist government in Eastern Europe. This posed the question as to whether the Kremlin would be willing to permit its Polish comrades to be ousted from power and at the same time accept as partners forces that were openly opposed to the existing system. The first commentaries to appear in the Soviet press were negative. Fears appeared confirmed that the Kremlin would exert its influence to keep the Polish communists in power.[13]

Solidarity was aware of the risk. Its representative at the coalition talks, Jaroslaw Kaczyński, contacted the Soviet ambassador in Warsaw, whose reports to Moscow on the situation in Poland in the preceding weeks and months had been devoid of all illusions[14] and who, together with his superiors in the Foreign Ministry, was convinced of the need for a fundamental political change. Accordingly, he raised no objections. The Kremlin had apparently come to terms with the prospect of a Polish government which, as Wałęsa had urged, intended to put an end to the power of the communist party as the culprit responsible for the economic, political and moral crisis engulfing the country. The public stance subsequently adopted by the Soviet Union, however, suggested that it still had reservations about such a settlement to the government deadlock. A spokesman of the Foreign Ministry in Moscow warned against any attempt to destabilize Poland and to infringe the country's obligations within the alliance or its cooperative relations with the Soviet Union. The Soviet government newspaper *Izvestiia* accused Wałęsa of having broken his promise. The official party organ *Pravda* even went so far as to claim that the initiators of the new coalition were acting contrary to valid political principles. When one spokesman for the Soviet Foreign Ministry was asked to explain this comment, he replied that it was only logical for the Soviet Union to express such an opinion. Moscow wanted to preserve a stable and friendly Poland, but Solidarity's 'manœuvres' had given rise to a difficult situation.[15]

The pressure from Moscow induced Solidarity to give a number of political guarantees. Wałęsa gave his assurance that the new government would respect the authority of the communist President Jaruzelski and would fulfil Poland's commitments within the Warsaw Pact. He also abandoned the idea of a completely non-communist cabinet and agreed that the Ministry of Defence and the Interior Ministry should remain in communist hands.[16] This concession settled the matter to Moscow's satisfaction. The communist party was to retain control not only of the domestic security forces but also of the military apparatus. This gave the Soviet leadership two decisive guarantees that Poland would continue to live up to its obligations within the alliance.

The Polish communists, however, were not so happy. Their leader Rakowski telephoned Gorbachev to gain his support for further demands.[17] To no avail. Two days later, the Sejm elected Tadeusz Mazowiecki prime minister without having given way to the communists' demands and without having come up against Soviet opposition. Another two days later, on 26 August, CPSU Politburo member and KGB Chairman Kriuchkov arrived in Warsaw from Moscow to talk to the head of the new government. This senior Soviet official gained a positive impression of Mazowiecki and subsequently stated that the Soviet Union was not worried about the changes that had taken place. The new prime minister was a 'sound man' who knew how things stood. 'We wish him success, and we are convinced it will be coming his way.'[18]

GORBACHEV'S WARNINGS TO THE HONECKER REGIME IN THE GDR

Even more so than Poland, the GDR was a key element in Soviet control over Eastern Europe. It had always been the political and military cornerstone of the forecourt hegemony which the Soviet Union built up beyond its Western borders after 1944–5. It was thus with good reason that Gorbachev spoke of the East German state as a 'strategic ally' which had exercised a 'profound influence on the entire post-war history of Europe' and which was also involved in determining the 'course of global affairs'.[19]

However, the policies pursued by Honecker and his advisers had little in common with Soviet conceptions. Soviet Foreign Minister Shevardnadze in February 1990 voiced the opinion in retrospect, that the leaders of the GDR had been left behind by the course of events. If they had carried out reforms, the situation would have been 'a different one', ie the collapse of the communists in the autumn of 1989 could have been avoided.

But they insisted stolidly on their opinion: We have built up socialism, we need no corrections, we are on the right path, all social problems have been solved . . . Honecker was out of touch with the sentiments of his people. And so the time for reforms was allowed to slip irretrievably away.

But because of the principle of free choice, the Soviet Union had been unable to do anything to change this course of events. 'For after all, we could not impose our position on Honecker.' The Soviet side had felt obliged to exercise this reserve 'although we by all means understood that the leaders of this country would sooner or later run into very serious difficulties'. The same applied to the dogmatic course followed by the Czechoslovak leaders at that time. 'One could not help but see it. One need only remember the reception given to Gorbachev by the people in Prague and Berlin. They welcomed him like a saviour, they asked him to help and to bring his influence to bear . . .'.[20]

This retrospective assessment of the situation on the part of the Soviet foreign minister is demonstrably in keeping with the critical appraisal formulated in Moscow in the spring and summer of 1989 regarding the state of affairs in and the prospects for the future of the GDR.[21] Furthermore, all the evidence supports Shevardnadze's claim that, despite its concern, the Kremlin had made no attempt to bring about a change of regime in the GDR. This claim must be seen as plausible, even if long-standing contacts between reformist forces in East Berlin and persons from Gorbachev's entourage have come to light since the change of leadership in October 1989.[22] Interestingly enough, important feelers were extended via the foreign divisions of the security services of the GDR and the Soviet Union. It would appear that these tentative contacts centred around Markus Wolf, head of the foreign division on the East German side until 1987, and his Soviet counterpart, Vladimir Kriuchkov, who was appointed Chairman of the KGB in 1988 and subsequently rose to membership of the Politburo.

In August and September 1989, the Kremlin's unease over the situation in the GDR intensified as, on the one hand, a mass exodus of East Germans to West Germany via third countries, mainly Hungary, set in and, on the other, those in positions of responsibility in East Berlin made it more and more apparent that they were resolved to use armed force, if necessary, to suppress expressions of discontent in their country. As if that were not enough, the East German leadership was propagating the view that *perestroika* might be good for peoples at the standard of development of the Soviet Union but was of no use whatever in such an advanced country as the GDR. The dissatisfaction felt by Gorbachev and his advisers escalated to annoyance when they found out that Honecker was maintaining close contacts with their opponents in the Kremlin, principally with Ligachev, and was banking on their emerging victorious from the altercations within the Kremlin walls.[23] It cannot yet be stated with certainty whether this induced Gorbachev to use his visit to the GDR (scheduled for early October to attend that state's fortieth anniversary celebrations) as an opportunity to trigger off a long overdue process of change in the country. But even if that was not originally his purpose, the Soviet leader's visit to East Berlin developed *de facto* along those lines.

At the GDR's commemorative event on 6 October 1989, Gorbachev gave the impression of a friendly and trusting relationship by paying homage to the purported perspicacity of his hosts.

We do not doubt that the Socialist Unity Party of Germany with its intellectual potential, its wealth of experience and its political authority will succeed in interaction with all social forces in finding answers to the questions that have been placed on the agenda by the course of development of the [German Democratic] Republic and which are causing concern to its citizens.

This formulation itself revealed that the Soviet leader rejected Honecker's course in opposition to his own people. This was further underlined by a reference to the fact that 'diversity of the forms of organization of production, of social structures and of political institutions' was necessary and that 'attempts at uniformization and standardization in questions of social development in conjunction with the imposition of some or other mandatory models' led not into the future but back into the past. Gorbachev also stressed the GDR's right to solve its own problems in its own way — thereby imputing that such problems existed, despite the SED's assurances to the contrary — and to follow its own decisions. At the same time, however, he confronted his hosts with the need to keep pace with the changes that were going on in the world beyond their own borders and presented as exemplary the *perestroika* under way in the Soviet Union.[24]

In his talks with Honecker the following day, the General Secretary of the CPSU expressed himself in even plainer terms. As he later reported in public, he had placed great emphasis on the 'topic of the development and changes currently going on under the influence of the impetuses proceeding from domestic political and international processes'. In this context he had admonished: 'Life is constantly posing new tasks, and the most important for communists is to keep in sensitive touch with the trends of the times and to react to contemporary social needs and the sentiments of the masses.' A 'new breath' was necessary. The 'vast opportunities' that socialism harboured were very promising, but they had to be put into practice by dedicated efforts towards specific objectives. A 'new revolution' was under way as a 'revolution within the Revolution' — a theory that essentially amounted to the warning that it was not sufficient to rest on past achievements but imperative to embark on something new.[25]

Gorbachev reiterated the Kremlin's message to the GDR leadership in an even more direct form at a press conference held in East Berlin on 6 October. Every country must be interested in *perestroika* in order to draw 'its own lessons' from the experience of these times. He voiced his confidence that this was adequately appreciated in the GDR, too. 'We know our German friends well, and their ability to reflect upon life and thereby to learn how to preplan politics and apply corrections if necessary.' In reply to a question posed by a journalist as to whether he thought the GDR was in a dangerous situation, he dismissed this suggestion with the remark that 'dangers lurk only for those who do not react to the burning questions of life. But anybody who responds to their stimuli and incorporates them into suitable policies has no difficulties to fear.'[26] This implied that the only ones who need fear danger were those who shunned tackling problems — as Honecker and his advisors had done in the past.

In the wake of Gorbachev's visit to East Berlin, more and more signs emerged to indicate that the Kremlin no longer wished to see Honecker at the head of the East German government. Members of the Soviet delegation leaked to a West German journalist with a reputation for scrupulously passing on the latest Soviet gossip to his audience a message to the effect that a 'very strong majority in the Politburo of the SED' was trying to get rid of Honecker and to enter into a dialogue with the East German public. If the present first secretary managed to retain his position, it must be feared that the GDR would no longer be able to play its prominent role in international politics.[27]

THE POLITICAL U-TURN IN THE GDR AND THE SOVIET RESPONSE

The Soviet leadership continued to make every effort to avoid interfering in the internal affairs of the GDR. But that did not prevent it from using the one lever it held in the GDR to bring to bear indirectly: via the Soviet armed forces stationed in that country. It was common knowledge that the regime ultimately owed its political existence to the military support it received from the Soviet Union. But the declared intention of Honecker and his henchmen to use force to suppress any display of unrest among the populace put cooperation between the East German security forces and the Soviet troops in the GDR in a new light. It is known that a general instruction was issued to all Soviet military personnel in Eastern Europe as early as in August 1989 to keep out of any domestic altercations that might arise in the countries in which they were stationed. This instruction was evidently reiterated specifically to the GDR when, at the end of Gorbachev's visit, the East German security forces were making preparations for the imminent use of force to suppress the spreading demonstrations.[28] There is every reason to suspect that the uncertainty and the hesitation that became apparent on 9 October 1989 among the East German troops deployed in and around Leipzig was at least to some extent attributable to the knowledge that they could expect no support from their Soviet comrades.

The tension between leadership and populace in the GDR was rapidly taking on crisis proportions. After 7 October, Honecker and his advisers felt relieved of the need to exercise the restraint that the anniversary celebrations and Gorbachev's visit had imposed upon them. They now sought to stop the rampant protest with all the means at their disposal. The brutality of the security forces escalated. A demonstration scheduled for 9 October in Leipzig and which was expected to break all attendance records was to be the showdown. Honecker signed an order which provided for the full use of firearms if necessary. The deterrent effect that this was no doubt intended to have did not occur. A bloodbath of Peking proportions appeared imminent. In the light of these prospects, spokesmen for the demonstrators and for the security forces' operations coordinators met in secret to discuss how the catastrophe could be averted. The assembled company addressed an urgent appeal to those responsible in East Berlin to repeal the order authorizing the use of firearms. At the very last moment — three-quarters of an hour before the demonstration was due to start — their plea was granted.[29]

Following the involuntary handover of power in the GDR, Honecker's successor, Egon Krenz, with the backing of his political friends, claimed credit for having prevented the massacre by having repealed the disputed order.[30] This version has been refuted by Honecker and also suspected by others of being no more than an attempt to polish up Krenz' blemished personal image among the East German public, a theory which is not devoid of logic. But being the Politburo member responsible for security matters, Krenz was more than any other in a position to retract an order by Honecker in this field. Besides, vehement personal animosities had long been brewing between the two men,[31] and Krenz may well rightly have viewed the revocation of Honecker's shoot-to-kill command as an opportunity to overthrow Honecker and to take his place instead of

Günter Mittag, whom Honecker favoured as his potential successor.[32] None the less, the matter must still be viewed as most uncertain.

From then on, Honecker's fall was only a matter of time. His removal from office was decided on 10 October 1989 in the Politburo and sealed one week later by the Central Committee. The Soviet reaction was a mixture of joy and relief. The Soviet Union media made a point of stressing that for all his promises of reform Krenz expressly emphasized his intention of adhering to the socialist system. Apparently Moscow expected that a new man at the top of the SED who committed himself to implementing the desired reforms and to dialogue with the people would be enough to dispel the discontent among the populace. It very soon became clear that this expectation was not going to be fulfilled. The protests continued to spread and became more and more radical. Krenz, who initially made no more drastic changes to the inner circle of power than to replace a number of Honecker's particularly close confidants, was unable to shake off his popular image as a man of the *ancien régime* who was not to be trusted. It would appear that the Kremlin was not particularly concerned about the people turning against Krenz. For Soviet confidence in Krenz was also limited. The Kremlin's favourite was a man who had up to then been kept out of the Politburo of the SED and had been tolerated as SED district secretary for Dresden only by virtue of his links with Moscow — Hans Modrow. By the beginning of November, Krenz ultimately found himself forced to appoint Modrow prime minister. Soon afterwards, he himself resigned his post as leader of the SED, making way for Gregor Gysi as his successor. In the meantime, however, the position of prime minister had become the more important.

THE CHALLENGE OF A RUNAWAY REVOLUTION

In the weeks that followed Honecker's removal from power, the prime demand of the people of the GDR was the right to travel to the Federal Republic of Germany as and when they liked. In response to this demand, Krenz and his aides quickly put forward the draft for a Travel Act which, however, still contained many restrictions and accordingly met with unanimous rejection, whereupon a more liberal bill had to be drawn up. Meanwhile, public pressure was still building up. At the same time, the government found itself on the defensive on other issues, too. The calls for its resignation became universal. It was a time of expanding mass demonstrations throughout the country. On 4 November, Czechoslovakia opened its borders to allow citizens of the GDR to leave for West Germany in order to relieve the by now intolerable conditions in the West German embassy in Prague, where in the end 6,000 East Germans had taken refuge while they waited for the opportunity to turn their backs on their country. This triggered a massive outflow of emigrants from all parts of the GDR. During the next five days, 40,000 citizens of the GDR set off for West Germany via Czechoslovakia. At the same time, the mass demonstrations continued unabated. The largest meeting of this kind took place in East Berlin on 4 November, with an estimated attendance of 600,000 – 800,000.

In this quandary, Krenz resolved on 8 November — on the spur of the moment, it would appear — to instruct the competent authorities as of the next day, and pending the passing of a new Travel Act, to issue instantly and on the spot to any GDR citizen who asked for one a permit to travel to the Federal Republic or to West Berlin. When Politburo member Schabowski announced this decision in the media the same evening, it sparked off an unexpected reaction. People flocked in droves from East Berlin and the border regions of the GDR to the crossing points to the West to pay an impromptu visit. Countless thousands gathered at the checkpoints demanding immediate passage. The GDR leadership, or at least those members of it who could be reached at that time in the early hours of the night, were eventually forced to instruct the border guards to give way to the insistent crowds, whereupon tens of thousands streamed into the West. Until the morning of 10 November, all checks ceased at the border crossings. The Berlin Wall, for more than twenty-eight years the symbol of the GDR's forced seclusion from the West, was traversed by crowds of climbers in both directions without the police intervening. As of that night, it would have been inconceivable for the GDR government even to attempt to restrict travel to the West. The people had by their own spontaneous action won their freedom to travel.

The repercussions of this incident were not just far-reaching but without doubt went beyond any liberalization which Krenz and his aides may have had in mind. Its most significant outcome was not that it relieved the pressure on the leadership and appeased the discontent in the country. Though it did — not immediately but in the course of a protracted process — have this effect to some extent, the decisive element for the further course of political development was something completely different: the opening of the borders changed the course of the revolutionary process in the GDR. The younger and working-age sections of the population who up to then had been denied any glimpse of West German life became fully aware of the relative poverty of conditions in their own country and reacted by demanding that the prosperity gap be closed rapidly. The best way of achieving this appeared to be unification with the Federal

Republic as soon as possible. If demonstrations up to then had been marked by the slogan 'We are the people', the emphasis now changed to 'We are one people!'.

The old opposition, the majority of which had been working for a better, democratically rejuvenated GDR, now found its conceptions of a future to be shaped within the framework of the existing East German state pushed aside and was compelled to fall into line with the new trend. At the same time, pressure was building up on the governments in both parts of Germany to put a rapid end to the parallel existence of two German states. The influx of immigrants from East Germany into the Federal Republic swelled again, forcing those in positions of responsibility to look for ways for the GDR to make up its economic and prosperity backlog as quickly as possible. Otherwise, it would be only a matter of time before the West German side became unable to cope with the burden of the resettlers from the East, while the GDR would dry out under the population drain and would forfeit every prospect of stable development.

THE GROWING PROSPECT OF A GERMANY UNIFIED IN ONE STATE

The published Soviet response to the opening of the Wall was positive. After all, it was an event which fitted in with Gorbachev's notions of ending decades of seclusion from the West. Besides, voices had already been heard in Moscow — even if only from unofficial quarters and intended for the ears of a West German audience — calling for the Berlin Wall to be demolished. But this did not mean that the political developments that had been under way since the opening of the borders were not being followed with concern in Moscow. Immediately after the borders were opened, the Soviet embassy in East Berlin had addressed a note of censure to the GDR leadership. Headquarters in Moscow was or now became aware that this step on the part of the GDR could have serious consequences. The Soviet criticism — voiced in private only — was not levelled at the lifting of seclusion as such: the opening up of the societies of Eastern Europe remained desirable in principle. But the precipitate manner in which this step had been taken gave rise to fears. Would the GDR be able to continue in existence as a second German state, and would it be able to continue playing the role of the Soviet Union's 'strategic ally' ?

The ensuing statements from the Kremlin made it clear that it attached decisive importance to this question. Internal changes in the countries of Eastern Europe could be accepted unconditionally. The

Soviet leadership insisted only that those countries must continue to honour their commitments within the Warsaw Pact. But in the case of the GDR, the pre-condition for the ability to fulfil those commitments — namely the country's membership of the Eastern alliance — was being called into question by growing doubts as to whether the GDR could continue to exist as a separate state at all. Accordingly, the position adopted by the Soviet leadership up to the end of January 1990 was to admit that there was a special relationship of cooperation between the two German states, but to insist that a process leading to full unification could not be countenanced.[33]

But even at this stage it was already apparent that any attempt to keep up this distinction was to walk a tightrope. Nobody could deny that the economy and society — and thus the body politic in the GDR — could not be consolidated without assistance from West Germany on a massive scale and that this must necessarily entail close links between East and West Germany that would without doubt go beyond the terms of conventional economic and technological cooperation. The question thus arose as to where the Kremlin wanted to draw the line between allowable involvement and inadmissible union. The term 'treaty community', which appears to have first been coined by the Soviet side, afforded no clarity in this respect. It served Federal Chancellor Kohl as the point of departure for his Ten-Point Plan of 28 November 1989, the basic idea of which was for the Federal Republic and the GDR to develop a close treaty relationship as a background for the stage-by-stage unification of Germany in a single state.

The official reaction from Moscow varied between discreetly raised objections and utterances of outright rejection. The more negative signals came from the foreign minister and his officials, while comments from the inner circle around Gorbachev himself were couched in more conciliatory formulations.[34]

The general Soviet attitude can be identified as intense unease at the thought that the West German government had made the 'treaty community' a part of a dynamic chain of events leading towards eventual state unity. It would have been more in line with Soviet intentions if the West German Chancellor had — like the East German Prime Minister Modrow, appointed on 8 November 1989 — viewed the envisaged 'treaty community' as a static relationship aimed at consolidating the dual-state status of Germany. The GDR was, according to the official theory in Moscow, completely free in its internal affairs. But the elimination of its borders, as would occur in the event of a merger with the Federal Republic, could not be accepted. The old formulations of 'neo-Nazism' and 'revanchism' were conjured up again to discredit all who called for the elimination of the German–German border.[35]

REPERCUSSIONS OF THE EAST GERMAN REVOLUTION ON CZECHOSLOVAKIA

The political victory over the old regime in the GDR encouraged the people of Czechoslovakia to stage mass demonstrations calling for the removal of the orthodox communist government there, too. The demonstrations did not take long to produce the desired results. One of the first responses to these expressions of public demand was the formation of a new government consisting mainly of non-communists. At this point, the course of development in Czechoslovakia went beyond the successes achieved in the GDR, where even after the elections of 18 March 1990 a communist-led government, the Modrow cabinet, remained in office and was able to influence events from above.

The Czechoslovak government of December 1989 also went further than the borderline that had been drawn in Poland with the appointment of Mazowiecki. Though there was a communist defense minister in Prague just as in Warsaw, the Ministry of the Interior, which was to be of extreme importance to the further course of political development, came into non-communist hands. The Kremlin accepted this configuration without objection and took no action even when shortly thereafter the newly elected president, the former dissident Vaclav Havel, introduced radical changes to the political structures in his country, including the army and the internal security organs, to bring them into line with Western democratic models. After the elections in the GDR, when a conservative/liberal coalition with or without social-democrat participation was on the cards, Foreign Minister Shevardnadze told his West German counterpart Genscher that the Soviet Union respected the 'choice of the people of the GDR' and was prepared 'to work with the government that is to be formed'.[36]

The compromise on which the Soviet leadership had insisted when the first non-communist-led government in Eastern Europe had been installed in Poland was no longer universally mandatory. This was an important step towards the lifting of all preconditions for the elections scheduled to be held in all the countries of Eastern Europe as of the turn of the year 1989–90.

THE PROBLEM OF THE SOVIET FORCES STATIONED IN EASTERN EUROPE

The standpoint taken by the Soviet leadership from November 1989 to January 1990 on the German question boiled down to the attempt to maintain a strict distinction between the emancipation of the

GDR's internal affairs on the one hand and the preservation of the foreign and security-policy status quo on the other. Inside the country itself, political change was to be allowed to evolve freely, while the GDR was still required to meet its commitments to the Soviet Union, to the Warsaw Pact and to the Council for Mutual Economic Assistance as in the past — which presupposed the continued existence of the GDR and of its borders with the Federal Republic of Germany. The security and stability of Europe, Moscow had insisted, did not permit any change to the international status quo. This same conception had apparently formed the basis for the demand made of the new non-communist government in Poland in August 1989 that the two ministries responsible for security affairs must remain in communist hands: irrespective of all domestic changes, Poland had to preserve a situation which assured the continuation of its traditional links with the Soviet Union.

Especially after December 1989, more and more signs emerged to indicate that the postulate of the separate co-existence of change at home and continuity abroad might be being relaxed. A link-up between domestic and foreign policy was established not just by the restructuring of the armed forces and the security apparatus introduced in various countries of Eastern Europe. At least as important a factor were ever louder calls in Hungary and Czechoslovakia for the withdrawal of the Soviet troops stationed in those countries.

The Kremlin was in principle prepared to accede to these demands. By the end of December, the Soviet government had indicated to Hungary that it would be prepared to enter into talks on the issue. Shortly thereafter, a similar declaration of intent was conveyed to Prague. Both were only logical, since the Soviet leadership had in the preceding months endorsed the theory that the military interventions of 1956 and 1968 had been unlawful and that there was thus no legitimate basis for the continued presence of Soviet troops in these two countries. Thus, in the talks that followed, the complete withdrawal of the Soviet armed forces was not in dispute; instead, the talks centred around the timetable, with the Soviet side favouring a longer time scale extending to the end of 1991. The official statements on the subject suggest that the main reason given for this preference were difficulties in finding enough accommodation and other requisites for the large numbers of soldiers to be repatriated to the Soviet Union.

An agreement was concluded with the Czechoslovak government as early as 26 February 1990.[37] On 10 March, a similar agreement with Hungary followed.[38] In both cases, the Soviet side demonstratively started the repatriation of the first of its military units immediately after the conclusion of the agreements. The United States' administration did what it could to facilitate the withdrawal of the Soviet troops from Eastern Europe. In order to give the Kremlin something in return, President Bush changed his proposal at the Vienna conventional forces reduction talks for the number of American and Soviet soldiers allowed to remain between the Eastern border of Poland and the Atlantic to be lowered from 275,000 to 195,000. Gorbachev was glad to accept this offer.

One surprising fact is that the Soviet leadership not only responded to requests by others for troop withdrawals but in the case of Poland took the initiative itself in proposing the withdrawal of its forces stationed there.[39] The Polish leadership's answer was hesitant, however. Though Lech Wałęsa of the Solidarity movement spoke out vigorously in favour of such a step, the reservations held both by the communist President Jaruzelski and by the non-communist Prime Minister Mazowiecki won the day. It was above all the feelings of uncertainty about the status of the Oder–Neisse border which, coupled with the prospect of a re-united Germany, made it appear advisable, at least for the time being, not to relinquish the political protection afforded by the presence of Soviet forces in the country.

The Soviet willingness to give up its military presence in Hungary, Poland and Czechoslovakia, which it had only shortly before still regarded as indispensable, should be seen in connection with the increasing emphasis the Kremlin had been placing on the call, first made in 1988, for the removal of all foreign troops from the territory of the countries of Europe. This envisaged the United States and other Western allies recalling their armed forces from the Federal Republic of Germany as the price to be paid for the Soviet military pullback to within its own borders. The Soviet leadership in principle included the GDR in its offer of withdrawal. In return, of course, it expected NATO to abandon the nucleus of its defence system, the Federal Republic of Germany. Such an arrangement would necessarily have amounted to banishing American military power from Europe, while Soviet forces would remain in the European theatre, albeit farther to the East.

Unlike in the case of the other countries of Eastern Europe, the Soviet leadership was not willing to withdraw its forces from the GDR without a prior binding assurance of Western reciprocation. The Kremlin considered its military position in Germany too important to give up without knowing for certain what it was going to get in return. The presence of Soviet forces in the GDR, it explained, was 'a special issue that is connected with the obligations of the Four Powers victorious in the Second World War'. It could be solved 'only in consideration of the security interests of all states involved'.[40]

Foreign Minister Shevardnadze insisted that the primary concern of his country was to achieve a new security status for Germany on the road to unity — which amounted to the elimination of the

Atlantic defence system on the European continent. He rejected the argument that it would be expedient to keep a united Germany in rein by integrating it into NATO. On the other hand, he did not want this rejection to be understood as a reversion to the old stereotype of the Atlantic enemy. He stressed that he and his colleagues in the Kremlin no longer regarded the United States as an adversary and that they had given up their earlier aim of driving the Americans out of Europe. But if anybody tried to tell him that it need not worry the Soviet Union if Germany were to be integrated into NATO, then he had to point out that there was no guarantee that the friendly attitude of the Atlantic alliance would continue indefinitely. 'Today, everything would be fine, we have normal, civilized relations with all NATO countries, but tomorrow the situation might be different . . . .'[41]

The Soviet willingness to forego military presence in Eastern Europe and not to insist on a tit-for-tat with the West except in the case of the GDR can be explained by a changing Soviet understanding of security. The Kremlin applied the principle of the 'demilitarization of interstate relations' not only to Eastern Europe. It was also intended to refer to relations with the countries of the West. The most candid expression of this viewpoint can be seen in the increasing Soviet emphasis placed on the need to transform the Warsaw Pact from a military/political into a political/military organization. The traditional nature of the Eastern alliance as a primarily military apparatus was no longer adequate if the military confrontation between East and West was to give way to a politically determined relationship between states. In the Kremlin, this consideration was linked with concern that, through being geared exclusively towards the military/technological sector, the Warsaw Pact would not be able to keep pace with the multi-faceted political West that had numerous instruments of political integration at its disposal. Even if Moscow painted a symmetrical picture of the need for a 'politization' (*politizatsiia*) not only of the Eastern but also of the Western alliance, it was perfectly well aware that it was only the Warsaw Pact that was in need of such a transformation because NATO had from the very beginning been an instrument of political coordination and of the harmonization of interests among its member countries.

As the Soviet leadership progressively detached itself from its earlier preoccupation with the military, it could not avoid becoming conscious of the weakness of its alliance as regards political integration, and it had no choice but to endeavour to build up an organization along the lines of NATO. In a period of rampant change in Eastern Europe, such an organization appeared all the more urgently necessary. At the same time, the Soviet leadership also sought to take advantage of NATO and of the United States as its leader to promote its own security interests. The cooperative relationship with the Western alliance on which Shevardnadze placed such emphasis would serve those interests. But at the same time his doubts as to whether the present good relations would continue revealed that Soviet confidence regarding the durability of amity with the West had yet to be consolidated and that Moscow was still interested in seeing NATO eliminated.

THE DEVELOPMENTS IN EASTERN EUROPE IN 1989 FROM MOSCOW'S RETROPERSPECTIVE

Looking back on the events of 1989, Shevardnadze re-affirmed the principle of 'free choice' with its logical conclusion that the Soviet Union must not interfere in the affairs of the countries of Eastern Europe. He made a point of emphasizing that 'neither Czechoslovakia [ie the 1969 invasion] nor Afghanistan [the 1979 intervention] [will be] repeated'. In express reference to the Brezhnev doctrine, he insisted that both these military actions had been motivated by 'solidarity and internationalism'. 'But one thing', he added, 'is clear: there is and there can be no justification for military intervention [in a foreign country], no matter in what lofty words it may be couched.'[42]

This commitment to respect the sovereignty of other countries and to renounce the use of armed force was linked with the conviction that the developments under way in the allied countries were historically necessary and were creating a better situation. Shevardnadze identified the 'striving for an acceleration of the renewal of socialism, of its political system, its economic foundations, and its intellectual sphere' as the main motive force behind those developments. This viewpoint included the admission that there were some things in the Western countries that were exemplary. 'Indeed, there is something to be learned from capitalism; it has proved to be more viable than the founders of scientific communism imagined.' In this connection the question was also being posed as to how this affected the Marxist–Leninist parties' claim to a leading role in Eastern Europe. The answer was: 'The right to be the vanguard in a country' had to be earned by merit, as envisaged in the new situation in the countries of Eastern Europe. The fact that the communists were now forced to prove themselves against the political competition would have a curative effect. Though the task at hand was 'not easy', 'the future not only of the Marxist–Leninist parties in that part of Europe but also of the entire communist world movement' would depend on its outcome.[43]

The conceptions and principles of the new Soviet policy toward Eastern Europe were presented in an article on the party programme in the CPSU's theory journal. Earlier attempts to mix ideology and interest in the Warsaw Pact had been misguided. An alliance must be based on concurrent state interests. Not all countries united by reciprocal alliance obligations need necessarily pursue the same ideology. And conversely, not all countries that were in one form or another adherents of Marxism–Leninism were eligible as allies. The notion that membership of an alliance must be identical with membership of a certain class was described as equally erroneous. This had in the past resulted in intervention in the affairs of weaker countries and in those countries having been made into satellites. According to this analysis, the traditional ideological view of relations with the countries of Eastern Europe had had still further adverse consequences: the confrontation between NATO and the Warsaw Pact had been intensified and the deceptive appearance of a 'class solidarity' between the Soviet Union and its allies had created blindness to the existing difficulties and conflicts. Instead of a confraternity in international and legal categories, an ideological chimera had been created that had glossed over the problems in mutual relations.[44]

The authors of the article termed it a fundamental desire of the Soviet Union to maintain friendly relations with the countries along its borders. But this did not imply that the respective neighbours must necessarily adopt the same social system. Good relations could also be struck with non-socialist countries, as the example of Finland showed. Conversely, the case of China proved how badly one could get along with some neighbours even though they were socialist. The improvement in Soviet relations with Afghanistan was cited as evidence of the benefits to be gained from relations with partners rather than with satellites. An alliance, the article went on, must be based on real interests from which concrete obligations could be derived. An imposed alliance remained a formality and thus, ultimately, worthless. To attempt to build on it would be to create a mere illusion.

In the past, this mistaken approach, in the opinion of the authors, was severely detrimental to Soviet interests. For the sake of preserving an ostensible community, the Soviet Union had made concessions to its allies — that is to say had given in real terms without receiving anything real in return. The Soviet Union had also suffered as a result of having felt obliged to render its allies unconditional support. In this belief, it had not infrequently passed over opportunities for *détente* in its relationship with the West. In contrast with past practice, it was in the Soviet interest to assume obligations even with respect to socialist countries only to the extent that such obligations coincided with the Soviet Union's own needs. The authors also considered it necessary to abandon the traditional idea that it was advantageous to have as many allies as possible. The loss of an ally did not automatically weaken the Soviet position in the world. If there was no coincidence of interests, it was better to give up the vain appearance of alliance and to place the relationship on a new basis of partnership, for example of agreement on a case-by-case basis.[45]

The conclusion to be drawn from these considerations was that alliance policy must be detached from all ideological criteria. But this was not possible as long as state policy copied party policy. For this reason, the authors deemed it expedient for control over Soviet foreign policy to rest no longer with the Central Committee but with the Supreme Soviet.[46]

Following this line of thought, it was only logical for Gorbachev to continue at the February 1990 plenum of the Central Committee the phase-out of party domination that he had initiated with the rejuvenation of the Supreme Soviet. By introducing a resolution on a multi-party structure,[47] he opened up the prospect of a pluralism of organizations being able to establish itself in the political decision-making sphere, thus contributing to the demise of those structures which were encouraging the claim to ideological exclusivity.

From this new perspective in which policy was to be based on state interests instead of on ideological postulates, the Soviet leadership could see some significant benefits to be drawn from the ongoing changes in Eastern Europe. It no longer needed to burden itself with allies that were constantly demanding political and economic assistance but were at best reluctant when it came to cooperating with the Soviet Union in support of Soviet interests. It could in future pursue its interests more freely and at its own discretion, choosing on the basis of pragmatic rather than ideological criteria the allies and partners that appeared most suitable for the purpose in hand. This calculation was evidently based on the assumption that there would remain enough common interests in relations between the Soviet Union and Eastern Europe, or perhaps that such common interests would really start to develop, when the ideological ties that were now felt to be more of a hindrance than a help had been severed. In particular, the Eastern Europeans would recognize that they could profit from Soviet backing in security matters when such long-standing points of irritation as, especially, ideological rape and the Soviet military presence had been eliminated. From now on, relations between the Soviet Union and Eastern Europe should be based essentially on a reform-policy consensus that was to take the place of the dissension over *perestroika* that had marked the preceding years. The new relationship problems resulting from the emancipation of

Eastern Europe from the Soviet Union were evidently considered to be manageable.[48] However, the makers of Soviet policy also perceived serious difficulties in mutual relations that were being aggravated by pressure of time.[49]

From the Soviet viewpoint, the relaxation in Eastern Europe was also an indispensable counterpart to the fundamental transformation of relations with the West which appeared to be essential both with a view to the creation of new security structures and for the sake of the envisaged economic and technological cooperation. Only if the Soviet Union relented from oppressing Eastern Europe, as one protagonist of the new Soviet policy put it, could it reduce confrontation with the countries of the West and in the long term eliminate the need for the existence of NATO. The threat to which the Western Europeans felt exposed emanated most essentially from the force-based hegemony that the Soviet Union had up to now been exercising over Eastern Europe.

Gorbachev himself went public with considerations along the same lines. He spoke of the 'global problems and dangers' that made 'a transition from confrontation to cooperation between peoples, irrespective of their social order' mandatory in the interests of humankind, and he stressed that the Soviet Union saw itself as 'part of human civilization'. While the Soviet leader still insisted on the special nature of the socialist system, he defined this nature as being in accordance with the 'needs of mankind'. It was to the Soviet Union's benefit to embark upon a course of international integration with the developed Western industrialized nations. Though the Soviet Union should not 'copy the West', it should 'make greater use of the advantage of the integration process than is currently being done within the framework of the global socialist system'.[50]

As Foreign Minister Shevardnadze reviewed, the new Soviet approach toward Western Europe in 1989 was also based on the desire for a radical transformation of relations with the West. The Soviet Union had stopped thinking in traditional friend and foe patterns. For a state that built its existence on fears of an imaginary foe had no *raison d'être*. History had shown that attempts to use bogeymen to stabilize their own order had led to the downfall of entire civilisations. And, Shevardnadze added in recollection of history in the Soviet Union, too, 'I hope to God that there will never again be talk of enemies of the people, of socialism or of anything else for that matter'.[51]

The objective of securing a leading role for the Soviet Union on the European continent remained as valid as ever, but the methods to be used in pursuit of that aim were changing. If previously the Soviet Union had attempted to achieve its desired role in Europe by means of confrontation within the framework of East/West antagonism, it was now endeavouring to construct its role on the basis of a broad consensus among the European countries concerned. This was not just a change of path towards its target. The manner in which the target was to be achieved, and consequently its configuration in real terms, was also changing.

NOTES

1. Cf. for example Shevardnadze's remarks at the scientific and practical conference of the Soviet Ministry of Foreign Affairs, 25 July 1988, *Mezhdunarodnaia zhizn'*, 9/1988, p. 15.
2. Particularly characteristic are the related remarks of Shevardnadze of 25 July 1988, ibid., pp. 19–21.
3. For evidence of corresponding contacts with East Berlin since 1986 see: 'Eine Strategie mit langem Atem', *Der Spiegel*, 15/1989, p. 61; 'Radikale Veraenderungen', speech by Manfred von Ardenne in the Volkskammer, 13 November 1989, *Sonntag* (East Berlin), No. 48, 26 November 1989.
4. Interview by L. Pleshakov with Shevardnadze, *Ogonek*, 11/1990, p. 4.
5. Ibid.
6. *Pravda*, 24 April 1985.
7. *Pravda*, 1 June 1986.
8. *Pravda*, 11 April, 1987.
9. Ibid.
10. *Pravda*, 17 March 1988.
11. *Pravda*, 7 July 1989.
12. Ronald Asmus, 'Evolution of Soviet–East European Relations Under Mikhail Gorbachev', Background Report/153, 22 August 1989, *Radio Free Europe Research*, pp. 2–3.
13. Cf. Michael Shafir, 'Soviet Reaction to Polish Developments: Widened Limits of Tolerated Change', *Radio Free Europe Research*, RAD Background Report/179, 20 September 1989, p. 3.
14. Interview of Pleshakov with Shevardnadze, op. cit. (note 4).
15. Ibid., pp. 2–3.
16. Ibid., pp. 2–4; Anna Swidlicka, 'Kiszczak Fails to Form a New Government', Polish Situation Report/13, *Radio Free Europe Research*, RAD Background Report, 23 August 1989, pp. 10–13.
17. Anna Swidlicka, 'The 14th PUWP Plenum and its Aftermath', Polish Situation Report/14, *Radio Free Europe Research*, RAD Background Report, 12 September 1989, p. 31.
18. Michael Shafir, op. cit. (note 13), p. 8; 'KGB-Chef nennt Polens neuen Premier zuverlaessig', *Koelner Stadt-Anzeiger*, 28 August 1989.
19. For example on the occasion of the fortieth anniversary of the GDR: 'Druzheskaia vstrecha', *Pravda*, 8 October 1989; speech in East Berlin, 6 October 1989, *Pravda*, 7 October 1989. In the following months the formula 'strategic ally' was used repeatedly.
20. Interview with M. Iusin and Shevardnadze, *Izvestiia*, 19 February 1990.
21. Cf. the related parts in a memorandum by V. I. Dashichev of 18 April 1989 (*Der Spiegel*, 6/1989, pp. 148–52) and the appraisal given by V. Falin to the Soviet leadership in summer 1989: 'Moskau befuerchtet Aufstand in der DDR', *Die Welt*, 15 September 1989, a report,

allegedly based on secondary information by the BND.
22. See citations in note 3.
23. Cf., *inter alia*, Wjatscheslaw Daschitschew 'Die deutsche Einheit kommt . . .', *Frankfurter Rundschau*, 8 February 1990; David B. Ottaway, 'Gorbachev Did it, a Bonn Official Says', *International Herald Tribune*, 13 November 1989.
24. *Pravda*, 7 October 1989.
25. *Pravda*, 8 October 1989.
26. *Pravda*, 7 October 1989.
27. Uwe Engelbrecht, 'Moskauer Delegation rechnet mit rascher Abloesung Honeckers', *Koelner Stadt-Anzeiger*, 12 October 1989.
28. See the interview with Willy Brandt, *Sueddeutsche Zeitung*, 14 December 1989. Brandt's information is based on high-ranking Soviet sources.
29. Reiner Dederichs, 'Praeses Beier betont den Wert der DDR-Kirche', *Koelner Stadt-Anzeiger*, 15 November 1989; 'Modrow verringert den Einfluss der SED', *Die Welt*, 17 November 1989; third programme of the *West German Broadcasting (WDR)* Television network, 19 November 1989, News Magazine at 10.05 p.m. (report of an evangelical superintendent from Leipzig); Otto Joerg Weis, 'Courage schon vor der Wende', *Koelner Stadt-Anzeiger*, 29 November 1989. Later on, Honecker declared that he had not intended to let the police shoot (*Der Spiegel*, 9/1990, p. 28). This statement is, however, hardly reliable since it can be seen as an exculpatory statement.
30. Cf. particularly the interview with Krenz, *Time*, 11 December 1989, pp. 20–1.
31. See for example the interview with Horst Sindermann, *Junge Welt*, 27 December 1989; statement by Manfred Gerlach on West German *Second Channel Television (ZDF)* 'Journalisten fragen — Politiker antworten', 16 November 1989, 10.10 p.m.
32. The disputes in the GDR leadership in the period from 10–18 October, after which Honecker was ousted, seem to support such an assumption.
33. Cf. for example Gorbachev's answers to the questions at an All-Union Students' Forum, 15 November 1989, reported by *TASS*, 17 November 1989; statements by Shevardnadze, 17 November 1989, to the Supreme Soviet's International Committee, *Pravda*, 18 November 1989; Gorbachev's answers to journalists during a joint press conference with Italian Prime Minister Andreotti, 2 December 1989 in Milan, *Pravda*, 3 December 1989; Gorbachev's answers to journalists during a joint press conference with the president of France, 3 December 1989 in Kiev, *Pravda*, 8 December 1989; speech by Shevardnadze to the European Parliament, Brussels, 19 December 1989, *Pravda*, 20 December 1989.
34. See especially the TASS report of 5 December 1989 on the talks between Shevardnadze and Genscher on that day.
35. See especially the declaration of the Warsaw Pact states of 27 October 1989, *Izvestiia*, 27 October 1989.
36. 'Prebyvanie v Namibii', *Pravda*, 23 March 1990.
37. Text: *Pravda*, 27 February 1990.
38. Text: *Pravda*, 11 March 1990.
39. Cf. for example the interview with the Chief of Staff of the Soviet Armed Forces, M. A. Moiseev, *Krasnaia zvezda*, 10 February 1990; declaration of the Soviet government, *Izvestiia*, 12 February 1990; interview with Shevardnadze, *Izvestiia*, 19 February 1990; 'Bez inostrannykh soldat i baz', *Pravda*, 26 February 1990.

40. Ibid.
41. Interview by M. Iusin with Shevardnadze, *Izvestiia*, 19 February 1990.
42. Interview with Shevardnadze, *Argumenty i fakty*, 2/1990, p. 2.
43. 'Vostochnaia Evropa na puti k obnovleniiu', *Mezhdunarodnaia zhizn'*, 1/1990, pp. 115–17.
44. A. Bogatyrev, M. Nosov and K. Pleshakov, 'Kto oni, nashi soiuzniki?', *Kommunist*, 1/1990, pp. 105–8.
45. Ibid., pp. 109–12.
46. Ibid., pp. 112–13.
47. *Pravda*, 6 February, 1990.
48. Cf. V. Karavaev, 'Vostochnaia Evropa otkryvaetsia miru', *Mezhdunarodnaia zhizn'*, 3/1990, pp. 39–49.
49. E. Shevardnadze, 'Diplomatiia i nauka', *Kommunist*, 2/1990, pp. 17–18.
50. M. Gorbachev, 'Sotsialisticheskaia ideia i revoliutsionnaia perestroika', *Kommunist*, 18/1989, pp. 11–12.
51. Interview by L. Pleshakov with Shevardnadze, op. cit. (note 4).

8 The Soviet Union confronted with the German problem

SOVIET RELATIONS WITH WEST GERMANY IN THE
MID-EIGHTIES

Germany has always loomed large in Soviet policymaking. Lenin
believed that the world revolution he sought would make its
breakthrough as soon as the German proletariat threw off the
'bourgeois yoke' and thus joined the common cause. After Stalin had
extended his power into Central Europe in 1944–5, he felt he could
advance further West after the United States withdrew from the
Continent. Then the defeated German people's support would be
essential. The perceived need to woo the Germans became even more
imperative when the Soviet leader saw his hopes for American
disengagement from Europe frustrated and decided to wage a
sustained political struggle against the West.

With regard to Germany, Stalin drew two practical conclusions.
On the one hand, he made a sustained effort to mobilize the German
people under reunification slogans. On the other, he transformed the
Soviet Zone into a bulwark of communist power which was to
provide the nucleus for a future pan-German state. When the
German Democratic Republic (GDR) was officially proclaimed in
October 1949, Stalin hailed it as the nascent 'united, democratic, and
peaceloving Germany' within the Soviet sphere of influence and
expressed the hope that it would bring about a 'turn in the history of
Europe'.[1] Such high expectations however, were disappointed. The
East German uprising of 17 June 1953 was the last event in a long
series of frustrations which led the Soviet leaders to conclude that
there was little chance of making the Germans side with them for a
long time to come.

In the summer of 1953, the Kremlin embarked upon a two-states
policy. Strengthening the GDR and making it a useful member of the
'Socialist Community' became the prime imperative. To be sure,
German unity propaganda continued until the second half of the
sixties. But when the West Germans began to demand practical
action in 1966–70, both the Soviet Union and the GDR gradually
retreated from the position they had verbally taken. From then on,

the two states in Germany were portrayed as the final outcome of World War II which must not be jeopardized. The East German leaders went even as far as to say that there was no German nation any longer. Two nations, a 'socialist' and a 'capitalist' one, had developed.

The shift of the Soviet orientation did not mean that the Kremlin had finally accepted the Federal Republic's integration into the community of Western nations. In particular, West German NATO membership was not acceptable. The Soviet Union's effort to make the West Germans opt out of the Atlantic alliance received a new impetus when Gaullist France left NATO's military organization at the end of 1966. From then on, the decisionmakers in Moscow felt that NATO would be unable to continue if the Federal Republic were no longer a member. To make this possibility come true, the Soviet leadership attempted again and again to effect West German withdrawl from NATO by either enticement or pressure. This political strategy was modified in the late seventies and early eighties. The Western alliance was to be hit fatally by being prevented from deploying medium-range missiles in Europe. To achieve this, the Kremlin sought particularly to make the West Germans oppose and resist the projected measure. The underlying assessment was that if the Federal Republic would not take the missiles, no other country would. Soviet policies would prevail and NATO would be in shambles.[2]

When Gorbachev came to power in March 1985, relations with Bonn were at a very low ebb. The Kremlin had decided to punish the ruling Christian and Free Democrats for not having yielded to the peace movement and to the demand that the missiles be kept out. At the same time, the West German Social Democrats were viewed with sympathy in Moscow for having ultimately sided with the anti-missile opposition. As a result, the ruling Christian Democrats and Free Democrats were snubbed and the Social Democrats courted. Intergovernmental relations between Bonn and Moscow were restricted to a minimum of formal routine.

For a number of years, the Soviet decisionmakers felt they could invest their political hopes in the Social Democrats who were likely to win the next federal elections in January 1987. One year before that, however, they realized that they had greatly overestimated the political chances of their favorites in West Germany. Since then, they began to seek a better relationship with the official circles in Bonn. It was, however, not before spring 1987 that the new trend gained momentum. After a year, the Gorbachev leadership decided that it was in need of a substantial West German contribution to the economic and technological buildup of the Soviet Union. The result was Chancellor Kohl's October 1988 visit to Moscow and

Gorbachev's travel to Bonn in June 1989.

It was in this context that the Soviet decisionmakers had to readjust their view on the German problem. Until then, they had always been careful not to encourage West German hopes in *rapprochement*, let alone unification, with the GDR — a line which had even been pursued when, during the missile controversy, a maximum effort had been made to appeal to the West German sentiment. What was more, the Kremlin had taken the view that the intra-German border had to be recognized unconditionally as a permanent divide. Every one who had voiced reservations had been labeled a 'revanchist'. This stance was a barrier to improving relations with the Federal Republic which, after all, had always claimed that relations with the GDR were 'intra-German' in character and that the German people had the right of national self-determination in a European framework. Given the overriding Soviet interest in economic and technological cooperation with the Federal Republic, the Kremlin could not stick to its demand that advocacy of German unity be ignored. There was a compelling need to tolerate their envisaged partner's position. With some reluctance, the Gorbachev leadership accepted the inevitable. As a result, the West German view that the German problem continued to be open and had to be resolved, could not be declared illegitimate any longer. This did not mean, of course, that Moscow adopted Bonn's view, but it allowed this view to be made the basis of discussion. This was the first step towards bringing the German problem back on the international agenda.

At the same time, there was a growing awareness among some policy experts in Moscow that the German problem was likely to emerge as an acute issue soon. As early as in April 1989, the Ministry of Foreign Affairs was advised that the East–West relationship should be fundamentally restructured. Crucially important in this context would be a new approach to the issue of German unity. Both security relations and a new economic cooperation with the Federal Republic would require formation of a consensus on the other side's national future as well. The author, Viacheslav Dashichev, also argued that comprehensive reform along the lines of both Western democracy and a Western market economy was necessary in the East European countries allied to the Soviet Union. The region had to open up to the West, particularly to West Germany. The process of fundamental change would not leave out the GDR, Honecker's adherence to communist orthodoxy notwithstanding.

The change foreseen could be used to serve the Soviet interest. A reformed GDR could act as an important intermediary when economic and scientific–technological cooperation between the Federal Republic and Eastern Europe and the Soviet Union would be established. Simultaneously, the division of Germany would have to be gradually overcome. This did not necessarily mean that the two states would unite. But it was indispensable that the border in Germany was gradually opened, that the two states cooperated with each other on a comprehensive basis and that free contact was permitted between the Germans. In a second phase, 'formation of a voluntary confederation of the two German states', 'other forms of merger' or 'close cooperation between the FRG and the GDR' had to be envisaged. This development was to take place 'under conditions of domestic and external stability' and had to be 'linked to a gradual transformation of the two opposed blocs into pan-European organizations'. Underlying these recommendations was an awareness that an increasingly critical situation was emerging in the GDR.[3]

In spring 1989, the Soviet leaders did not yet feel that the German problem was likely to become acute soon. But accepting that the West Germans were free to advocate unity entailed a more benign portrayal of the issue. Gorbachev himself took the lead by saying that history would essentially decide what solution there would be to the German problem. The formula was non-committal with regard to the kind of solution which would emerge and to the time when it would occur and even to whether it would happen at all. But Gorbachev's phrase had the appearance of an affirmative ring and clearly contradicted previous statements wherein German unity had already been ruled out by history. Soviet rhetoric generally gave the impression that the Kremlin was considering a more flexible attitude and might even change its policy.

DEVELOPMENT OF THE SOVIET ATTITUDE TOWARD GERMAN UNITY: SPRING–AUTUMN 1989

During Gorbachev's Bonn visit in June 1989, the Soviet leader expressed himself on the German problem with much reserve. At a reception on 12 June he avoided any kind of statement on the issue and rather emphasized 'the GDR's characteristic awareness of its particular responsibility for the fate of peace and progress in the centre of our continent'.[4] He also skirted the German problem on the following day when he spoke instead of the need to overcome 'military confrontation' between NATO and the Warsaw Pact and to create 'new structures and new norms of interaction between our peoples'. In order to dispel any suspicion that he was seeking to lure his hosts out of NATO, he assured them that he did not advocate a dissolution of the Atlantic alliance. He added that both the Soviet Union and West Germany would remain 'loyal to its obligations vis-à-vis its allies'. However, he attached a condition to this: 'as long as they [the alliance obligations on either side] serve European stability'.[5]

During the press conference on 15 June 1989 at the end of his visit, Gorbachev was asked about the Berlin Wall. His answer was basically identical to remarks which had been made by the East German leader Honecker a few months before who had concluded that the Wall could still last for a hundred years.[6] The Wall could be torn down when the 'conditions' which had made its construction necessary no longer existed. He added, though, that this was 'no great problem'. Asked about the prospects for German unification, the Soviet leader said that the present situation had emerged over time — 'those are the realities'. But he went on to express his hope that 'time will take care of the rest', given the general trend toward cooperation and *détente*.[7]

By that time, lower-level Soviet spokesmen had already been more positive on German unity when they addressed Western audiences. For example, the head of the Central Committee's International Department, Valentin Falin, had given an interview which was published in Britain under the heading 'One Germany Would Not Worry Moscow'.[8] Statements of this kind, however, were exceptional rather than normal. The Soviet media generally displayed a negative attitude toward German unity, and Gorbachev did his best to underline that scepticism about the short- and medium-term prospects for unification reflected the official attitude. At a joint press conference with President Mitterrand in Paris on 5 July 1989, he bluntly stated that hopes for German unification were unrealistic. The division, he went on, was 'so decreed' as a consequence following from the last war. He felt that 'one does not reverse history simply for a hope's sake, however pleasant that hope might be'. However, with the vague suggestion that the Germans should help construct the 'common European home' Gorbachev sought to suggest to the West German public that a positive solution of the German problem might be found within the pan-European framework he advocated.[9]

In essence, the Soviet leader's statements contained very little that altered the previous position on the German problem, but it was clear that the tone had lost its previous intransigence. This was noticed in East Berlin with increasing concern. Soviet willingness to enter into a broad dialogue with the Federal Republic and to respect the West German view raised the question of what would come out of it in the end. The East German leader began to feel that the dialogue between Moscow and Bonn would ultimately be at the expense of East German interests. The West Germans noted with satisfaction that Soviet statements on the Berlin Wall implied that it was an East German affair for which the Soviet Union no longer took responsibility. The comments from Moscow were seen as a product of the Kremlin's inclination not to be politically and morally burdened with that dreadful monument of repression. Wouldn't that result, it was asked, in a more general Soviet detachment from the GDR's policies of seclusion from the West?

The East German leaders' apprehensions must have been aggravated further by unofficial Soviet statements opposing the central European status quo. In an interview with the West German radio network Deutschlandfunk, Viacheslav Dashichev, who was introduced as an adviser to Gorbachev, said the division of Germany was 'not normal' and that the Soviet Union acknowledged the 'right of the German people to self-determination'. He also pointed out that there were 'prospects for a new form of cooperation between the two German states' when the political development currently being initiated would eventually make the two military blocs superfluous.[10]

It was the dynamism of change in Eastern Europe which led the Soviet leaders to think more carefully about the situation in Germany. Honecker's overthrow in the GDR in mid-October 1989 was, of course, the key event. The subsequent revolutionary upswing at first shattered the foundations of the communist regime and then put the country's existence as a separate state into jeopardy. In the beginning, the Soviet policymakers tried to cope with the problem by ignoring it. The report presented by the Ministry of Foreign Affairs to the Supreme Soviet on 23 October 1989 did not refer to the German development at all.[11] Several days later, a statement from the Warsaw Pact emphasized the 'right of each people to national self-determination and to a free choice of its social, political, and economic path of development with no intervention from abroad'. It added, however, a warning against 'any attempts to destabilize the situation, to put the postwar boundaries into question, and to resume discussion about these issues'. These phrases implied that national self-determination could be accepted only to the extent that borders were not affected. East Germany had to provide for an orderly transition to a new regime, with all thoughts about elimination of the intra-German boundary, ie unification with the Federal Republic, being left aside. Hints at the alleged 'danger of neo-Nazism and revanchism' in 'some countries of Western Europe' were intended as a warning against West German demands for a reversal of the status quo of German partition.[12]

Despite such warnings, the Kremlin was cautious in expressing its negative attitude toward German unification. This became clear when Honecker's successor Egon Krenz paid a visit to Moscow on 1 November 1989. The East German leader made a plea for unification not to be put on the political agenda. 'There is nothing which might be reunited, for socialism and capitalism have never stood side by side in this fashion, and there is equally nothing which might be reunited for the reason that these two German states belong to different alliances which have formed in the postwar period.' Krenz also felt that the existence of two German states was a crucial 'element of stability in Europe'.[13] These violent diatribes were not included in the report which *Pravda* published on the visit. Only Krenz's commitment to 'friendship and cooperation with the USSR' was mentioned as the 'fundamental factor of the existence and the development of the German socialist state'. Gorbachev was quoted as calling the GDR 'our reliable friend and ally' and as emphasizing the SED's 'vanguard role' in the current 'process of renewal'.[14]

The subsequent period was characterized by the Kremlin taking the position that domestic change in East Germany was admissible, but that unification with the Federal Republic could not be permitted. Consideration of the 'possibility of revising the borderlines existing in Europe' was stigmatized as being contrary to the 'clear obligation concerning the inviolability of frontiers' in Europe.[15] The existence of two German states was an established fact which had been 'internationally acknowledged' and was, therefore, the 'reality' on which all considerations had to be based.[16] All peoples were seen to have the right to exercise their 'free choice', but in this instance this right had a 'specific trait' which resulted from World War II and the realities subsequently established: The 'existence of the two German states and of two military–political alliances' had to be respected. It was this basis on which 'the security and the stability of Europe' rested. However, the Soviet policymakers left a small loophole for change. While realities could not be altered unilaterally, there was such a possibility 'in mutual agreement'. The Soviet Union was not 'against any change', it did not want to 'preserve all European realities'. Europe had entered a period of change which, however, had to be agreed upon within the framework of the Conference on Security and Cooperation in Europe (CSCE).[17]

On occasion, it was made clear that their negative attitude toward German unification was contingent on the current situation. Movement toward German unity would be possible if the 'real situation of two sovereign German states and their position in Europe's political system' were to be taken into due account. Either state was 'not free of international obligations'. But if the military danger were to be reduced, the situation could be looked at 'in another way'. In particular, the United States would have to be willing to participate in the 'pan-European process' and to live in the 'European home' proposed by the Soviet Union. This would imply both the elimination of weaponry and the dissolution of the two blocs' military organizations by the year 2000.[18] These ideas were not intended as a policy guide for the present but as a perspective for a more distant future.[19] For the time being, some kind of static 'contractual community' between the two states was recommended to the Germans. West German Chancellor Kohl adopted this term when he put forward his Ten Points on 28 November 1989, but in contrast to what the Soviet leaders postulated, he proposed a dynamic contractual relationship between the two German states. The Ten Points were a concrete program of phased *rapprochement* which would gradually result in confederation and ultimately unification. This was not at all what the Soviet leaders wanted. Therefore, their reaction to Kohl's concept was predominantly negative. When the West German Foreign Minister went to Moscow in early December, he was told that both restraint and responsibility were required in the current situation and that East Germany continued to be the Soviet Union's crucial ally and an important guarantor of peace and stability in Europe.[20]

Speaking to European Parliamentarians in Brussels on 19 December 1989, Foreign Minister Shevardnadze reiterated the Soviet view that exercise of national self-determination must not infringe upon the territorial and political status quo. He therefore advocated 'further peaceful cooperation between the GDR and the FRG according to the principles of respect for the quality and the sovereignty of the two German states'. At the same time, he emphasized that the Soviet Union did not exclude change in some undefined future. History might set new processes into motion which, he warned, had to keep within the 'framework of development of the pan-European process'. Particularly if the two alliances were eventually to cease to be necessary, German unification might become feasible. The 'road to this goal', however, would be 'not easy'. To illustrate this point, Shevardnadze posed a number of tricky questions to which he claimed an answer had to be found before unification could be a realistic prospect.[21]

For the time being, a united Germany was viewed in Moscow as being inconceivable, particularly if it were proposed in the form of East Germany being incorporated into West Germany. A united German state would greatly change the correlation of forces in Europe and had, for this reason, 'nothing in common with a Europe of peace and cooperation'. As could be gauged from relevant official statements, the anticipated speed of the German unification process was a major cause of concern. If the development took a long time, it might be so channelled as to create less apprehension.[22]

SOVIET ACQUIESCENCE IN GERMAN UNIFICATION

Soviet opposition to German unification rested on the premise that the GDR was both willing and able to continue as a state on its own.

But precisely this became increasingly doubtful after the Wall had been opened and both travel and emigration to the Federal Republic became freely available to the East Germans. Despite all the information which had previously been transmitted to the GDR through West German television, large parts of the population began to realize only then the full extent of their poverty compared to their compatriots in the West when they saw for themselves the shops and the warehouses on the other side of the border. Every weekend, millions went West and returned with a sharp feeling that they had been cheated. 'For forty years, we have lived for nothing', was a standard phrase used again and again. The reaction took two forms. On the one hand, the exodus to the Federal Republic, which had destabilized the GDR prior to the political change of October 1989 and had continued ever since, increased to unprecedented proportions. The country was confronted with the prospect of 'bleeding out' as the expression was at the time. That is, the very foundations of the already ailing economy and the strained social services were jeopardized by people leaving. On the other hand, the political direction of the opposition movement changed. Until then, the central demand had been for democratic restructuring. The slogan 'We are the people!' had been shouted during the demonstrations. Now people increasingly focused on the postulate that Germany be united. The new slogan was: 'We are one people!'

At the end of the year, a superficial observer might have seen signs of a political stabilization. Protest in the streets had receded. But in reality, the situation had greatly destabilized. Morale was deteriorating not only among the population but also in the apparatuses of party and state. The communist government of Modrow added to the trend when, in January 1990, it sought to provide a basis for some continuation of the hated secret police Stasi and built up the bogey of neo-Nazism to justify its future existence. As a result, there was a public outcry. The Stasi headquarters were raided. Simultaneously, emigration to the Federal Republic increased to unheard of dimensions. The East German army began to feel that it had no future and to show signs of falling apart. Modrow appealed to the opposition to join his government in a common effort to stem the tide of destabilization.

It was at this point that both East and West Germans began to realize that the situation could be saved only by rapid unification. If the people in the GDR were given a clear prospect of economic and social improvement by a merger with the Federal Republic within a short period of time, unification would take place on West German soil. Chancellor Kohl concluded that the gradualism he had proposed in the Ten Points did not meet the needs of the situation any longer. Quick action was needed. The economic and currency union of the two states which had been envisaged as the result of a long process of *rapprochement* had to be established soon in order to make the East Germans regain hope and stay where they were. Therefore, the unification schedule was reversed and the economic and currency union put first.

Reluctantly, the Soviet leaders eventually realized that their rejection of German unification was becoming untenable. The GDR was simply not capable of existing as a separate entity any longer. Therefore, the Kremlin decided in the second half of January 1990 that it had no choice but to acquiesce in the two German states uniting with each other. In contrast to Chancellor Kohl, however, they saw unification as a process which had to be slow and gradual. This appeared indispensable for the sake of allowing the German process and the European one to be synchronized. As the Kremlin saw it, a future united Germany had to be embedded into a pan-European order, particularly as far as security was concerned. Germany must not unite before the conditions of this arrangement had been worked out and agreed upon.

Soviet change of attitude became publicly known when Modrow met Gorbachev in Moscow on 30 January 1990. *Pravda* quoted the East German President as saying that he saw an overriding need to get his country out of the current 'socio-political and economic crisis' which, as he appeared to imply, had to be solved in cooperation with the Soviet Union. For his part, Gorbachev emphasized that the present changes in the GDR had to be seen as a part of the liberation process which was taking place in all of Eastern Europe. This process, however, was being jeopardized by 'a spontaneity of nihilism, a diktat of the masses and attempts at social and ideological revenge'. The two politicians agreed that foreign interference with East German affairs and destabilization of the GDR must not be permitted. They also advocated a 'qualitative restructuring of the security system in Europe in such a fashion that the possibility of military confrontation is excluded and very deep cuts of the military potentials of the Warsaw Pact and NATO are concluded'.[23]

On this basis, Gorbachev declared his willingness to sympathize with 'the interests of the Germans in the GDR and the FRG' and with 'their aspiration to intensify their mutual commonality, cooperation and interaction'. Just like the Germans, the Soviet people wanted an assurance that peace would not be disturbed. Mutual awareness of the responsibility for peace would 'allow for finding correct solutions' and also 'universally acceptable methods to implement them'.[24] According to a Western press report, the Soviet leader stressed that the German process would have to be a 'realistic' one and added that history which had to decide about the German question was already adding corrections.[25]

Gorbachev had expressed himself only vaguely on both the internal modalities and the international guarantees which would provide 'correct solutions' to the German problem. Modrow sought to fill this gap. The next day, he expounded the idea that only such a confederation between the two German states would be acceptable which, creation of common institutions not withstanding, would leave the GDR intact as a state of its own. The resulting German tandem would have to leave the military blocs and to accept a neutralized status.[26] Clearly, the communist leader of the GDR wanted to limit unification with the Federal Republic as much as possible and to exact a maximum concession from NATO. The latter tendency surfaced again when East Germany's leading communist paper subsequently advocated that Soviet and Western troops be evacuated from both East and West Germany.[27] There was an obvious difference between the Kremlin's position and Modrow's. Whereas Gorbachev had left open to what extent Germany might be united and what form its inclusion into a European framework would take, the GDR's communist leader displayed a most restrictive attitude on both.

Soviet acceptance of German unification implied that the Kremlin had a number of reservations about the process and the results envisaged by the Federal Republic and the Western powers. The principal issue was over Germany's membership in NATO. The Western side felt that West Germany had to remain part of the Atlantic alliance, while a guarantee might be given about the East German territory's non-inclusion into the Western defence system. West Germany's continuing contribution to NATO was clearly essential for the Western governments. If the Federal Republic were to be out of the alliance, the key country on the European continent would not be available any longer. NATO would then be unlikely to continue. It was also felt, particularly in West Germany, that Western integration was needed for the enlarged German state to be compatible with European security and to be spared the risk of international isolation. After all, Germany's historical dilemma of having been either anvil or hammer relative to its European neighbours had been solved by postwar integration into the West which had allowed for a relationship of mutual obligations and mutual utilities in the field of security. Neither the West Germans nor their Western partners were willing to abandon this achievement. The Soviet leadership, on the other hand, felt that it had to exact a price for allowing its 'strategic ally' the GDR to opt out of the Warsaw Pact — a solution which was also bound to entail Soviet troop withdrawal from there sooner or later.

Opposing the Western demand for Germany's inclusion into NATO, the Kremlin had to face two problems. On the one hand, its political position was rather weak. The Soviet forces were already in a process of being evacuated from Czechoslovakia and Hungary. Their leaving Poland and also East Germany was but a question of time. Simultaneously, the Warsaw Pact showed clear signs of military and political disintegration. As a result of all this, the Soviet Union had little to offer which it was not losing anyhow. On the other hand, Moscow was unable to propose a convincing alternative to German membership in NATO. The idea that the Germans had to be somehow included into some kind of European security framework was no solution to the task which Shevardnadze had defined as the creation of a 'European Germany'. It was very likely that the practical result would be a militarily independent German state — which nobody wanted. Semi-official and even official voices in Moscow which advocated a neutral Germany clearly implied that this would actually be the result. The only way to avoid this consequence on the basis of the Soviet idea was to treat the Germans as a defeated nation again and to impose unilateral controls on their military establishment, as some statements from Moscow appeared to suggest.[28] Also, the Soviet demand for a German peace treaty to be concluded posited that the 1945 relationship of victors and vanquished had to be re-established.

Such a pattern was not really feasible forty-five years after the war during which the Federal Republic had become a reliable partner in the Western world and an economic power on whose willingness to cooperate with the European Community, the Group of Seven and, not least, both Eastern Europe and the Soviet Union depended. Under the conditions of equality which the situation required, however, the Kremlin's proposal could only result in creating an independent German army. In view of this, it was logical that the Soviet Union was isolated from its allies. At the Prague meeting of the Warsaw Pact in April 1990, the representatives of Poland, Czechoslovakia and Hungary made clear that they supported Germany's membership in NATO. The Kremlin was caught between two fires. On the other hand, it had a clear interest in creating the impression that it firmly opposed Germany's inclusion into NATO. On the other, it sought to avoid an irrevocable commitment given that it might be forced to give in.

At first, the desire to maintain flexibility prevailed. When Chancellor Kohl came to Moscow on 9/10 February, Gorbachev used the flexible formula that German unification 'must not destroy the European balance' and that the Germans were entitled to a 'new place in the European and the global structure'.[29] When his interlocutor stated the view that Germany must not be neutralized and demilitarized but remain in the Atlantic alliance, the Soviet leader's response was, as the Chancellor subsequently stated, no outright rejection.[30] East Germany's Modrow, however, claimed that, in a subsequent telephone conversation, Gorbachev had assured him that he would not accept a united Germany in NATO.[31] A number of public statements followed. Shevardnadze said that the idea of neutralizing Germany was a 'good and benign' one. As to Germany's staying in NATO, one had to keep in mind that it was the 'common interest of all peoples' to preserve 'stability in Europe'. Also, the interests of the member countries of both NATO and the Warsaw Pact had to be considered. The Soviet foreign minister also expressed his sympathy with the Modrow proposal, but he stopped short of stating unequivocally that the Soviet Union would reject the idea of Germany being in NATO.[32] Only lower-level Soviet spokesmen expounded the view that German membership in NATO was definitely unacceptable and that the country had to be neutralized and to remain outside the alliances.[33]

This pattern of caution continued until another Modrow visit to Moscow. Talking with the communist leader of the GDR on 6 March, Gorbachev emphasized 'with all resolve' that inclusion of the future Germany in NATO was 'unacceptable'.[34] He reaffirmed this stand saying to a TASS correspondent that it was 'absolutely excluded' for the Soviet Union to agree to a united Germany being in NATO. This seemed to be unambiguous at last, but the Soviet President himself softened his stand when he added that the political transformations which were taking place in Europe might eventually make the current bargaining over Germany's status pointless.[35]

Shevardnadze, who had generally taken a somewhat harder position on Germany, subsequently sought to restore some vagueness and ambiguity. When asked by an East German journalist whether he could imagine a united Germany as a member of NATO, he avoided a clear answer. This was, he explained, one of those questions which had to be discussed in the forthcoming negotiations on Germany. He criticized the 'rash statements of some Western politicians that a united Germany had to belong unconditionally to NATO' which were 'at least tactless'. Such a 'prediction' did not correspond to the Soviet Union's 'idea about its national interests and about a firm structure of a peaceful "pan-European home"'. Hence it was 'necessary to look for a solution' which would be 'adequate to the complexity and the importance of this problem'. Germany, he conceded, need not be totally demilitarized. The crucial point was that 'aggression from the territory of Germany' had to be rendered impossible.[36] The willingness to allow for compromise was expressed most clearly at lower levels. Referring to Gorbachev's rejection of Germany's NATO membership, the head of the International Department of the CPSU Central Committee explained that no military asymmetry detrimental to the Soviet Union must emerge in central Europe. He implied that this was the crucial Soviet demand to be met.[37] In the second half of March, flexibility was again displayed in the highest quarters as well. The foreign minister stated directly that, given the controversy about the 'military–political status of a united Germany', more than one variant had to be taken into account.[38]

None the less, the Soviet leaders continued to stick to the position that German membership in NATO was unacceptable. It was not only Modrow's advice which influenced the Kremlin. More important still, conservative and other right-wing criticism of Gorbachev's policies toward the Warsaw Pact allies, and particularly with regard to Germany, had an increasing impact. What was more, the military leaders appear to have issued a clear warning to the Soviet leader that their tolerance was in the process of being exhausted. As a Soviet source has stated in a conversation with a NATO official on 25 February 1990, Gorbachev was confronted with a demonstration of willingness to resist him if he were to continue at the same pace to give up positions in Central Europe and to pursue his intentions regarding a Soviet military run down.[39]

The essential elements of the evolving stance were continued in a detailed Shevardnadze statement published by a NATO periodical in May 1990. The crucial point made was that synchronization of the intra-German and the European aspects of unification was no longer seen to be necessary. The two states might unite before a solution to the problem of Germany's eventual inclusion into an international security system were found. The Soviet foreign minister also suggested that the Western desire for German membership in NATO was acceptable if the Germans would simultaneously join the Warsaw Pact. Such a solution would be a positive step toward a pan-European future, since it would initiate both a political transformation of the two alliances and their future merger into a single common security system.[40]

The common denominator of the two proposals submitted by Shevardnadze was to establish Soviet co-control over united Germany until the West would acquiesce in the Kremlin's demands. The idea of decoupling the intra-German and the European aspects of unification was linked to insistence that the four occupying powers of 1945 retain their rights and responsibilities in Germany and exercise them commonly as long as the problem of the country's international status remained open. During this interim period of undetermined length, the Germans would have to accept the troop presence of the four powers as an imposed obligation which, together with reasserted quadripartite control rights, would not be lifted until the Soviet Union was satisfied with the kind of security arrangement it would be offered in return. The dual alliance membership proposal had similar implications: it was to give the Soviet Union the right both to keep its troops in East Germany — against German will — and to extend the GDR's alliance obligations to the emerging united German state.

Such provisions were clearly unacceptable to the Western capitals and Bonn. Germany was not to be under four-power tutelage, and for an unlimited period of time at that. Nor was it in the Western interest to concede a veto to the Soviet Union on Germany's international status thus providing it with a power position making it possible for the Kremlin to exact in the future what it was incapable of getting at present — Germany's exclusion from NATO. The Soviet leaders, however, doggedly pursued the line they had taken. When — after the article in the NATO journal had already become known to the Western governments — Shevardnadze visited Bonn in April, he sought to persuade the West German government that desynchronization of the unification's two aspects was a good thing.

Shortly afterwards, Moscow announced that it had stopped troop reductions in the GDR, as announced by Gorbachev on 7 December 1988, pending agreement on the security implications of German unity. In fact the reductions, which had been below those promised in 1989, had been discontinued a number of weeks before. It was difficult, though, to imagine that the Soviet Union could really afford to keep massive forces in what was going to be an increasingly isolated outpost for an indefinite period of time. The future of both Soviet military deployment and the indigenous communist military cadres in the GDR were bleak after the 18 March 1990 elections had brought a non-communist government to power in East Berlin at last.

THE DOMESTIC MODALITIES OF GERMAN UNIFICATION

When the Soviet leaders had decided not to oppose German unification any longer, they accepted that the Germans were to be given full leeway with regard to decisions on the intra-German aspect. They would themselves have to solve the 'problems of the German nation' and to 'make their choice on the kind of state, the schedule, the speed and the conditions which will put their unity into practice'.[41] During the following weeks, however, the Soviet leaders began to feel that Chancellor Kohl was pressing for consummation of unification in too short a period of time. This appeared to imply an acute danger that the Germans would create a *de facto* situation which would leave the Soviet Union without any influence on both the process and its result. The four powers (which, according to the agreement reached in Ottawa in mid-February 1990, would have to negotiate the international framework with the Germans) might simply have to ratify a merger which had already taken place. On such a basis, there would be no possibility for confronting the Germans with international requirements for unification. Germany would be united without having paid much attention to what the Soviet Union and other countries thought. As it appears, such apprehensions were greatly fuelled by the assessments which Modrow, the GDR's communist head of government until early April 1990, transmitted to Moscow. Modrow, who had been a Soviet confidant for a long time, had previously been opposed to unification and then acquiesced in it only on Soviet advice. He continued to have reservations about unity and was inclined to do what he could to slow down the process and to reduce its implications for East Germany.

The Kremlin thus began to take a keen interest in the procedures of German unification and in some of the domestic issues which had to be decided in the process. On his way back from Ottawa to Moscow, Shevardnadze expressed his conviction that it was very important just how German unity would come about. This did not pertain, as one might have thought, to the plans for merging currency and economy soon. The foreign minister stated that the Soviet Union would profit from this, since trade with East Germany would then be handled according to world market conditions.[42] Apparently, it was the prospect that joint political institutions, including a joint government and a joint parliament, might be rapidly created which haunted the Kremlin. On 6 March 1990, Gorbachev emphasized that it was 'certainly not a matter of indifference in which fashion the *rapprochement* between the two German states proceeds and how the international obligations will be fulfilled'.[43]

Soviet attention increasingly concentrated on the legal aspects of the unification process. Under the Basic Law of the Federal Republic, two possible procedures for uniting Germany were available. The authors of the West German constitution had seen West Germany as a provisional political entity which would soon be replaced by a pan-German state. Therefore, German unification might be consummated through a pan-German national assembly expressing the will of the whole German people and drafting a new constitution on this basis. According to this idea, article 146 envisaged that the 'temporary arrangement' (as the Federal Republic was seen at the time) would give way to a fundamentally new state. The Basic Law also contained article 23 which provided for the possibility that German territories could apply for 'accession' to the Federal Republic. This procedure, which had been used when the Saarland joined West Germany in the late 1950s, implied acceptance of both the current constitution and the political order based on it as the foundation of the greater Germany.

Weighty reasons of expediency made all parties in the Federal Republic, except the Greens, and all political groups in the GDR, except the communists and a few leftists, feel that article 23 had to provide the basis for uniting the two German states. It was not only that more than four decades had elapsed since article 146 had been written — a very long period during which the Federal Republic had grown beyond a 'temporary arrangement' that needed replacement by a more permanent political order. It was also hardly conceivable in practical terms that all the domestic and international regulations which had been created by the West Germans over a very long period of time might be null and void and be replaced by another set of functionally equivalent regulations. While total revision of all the previous order was suitable for the GDR which was on the verge of collapse and could not hope for salvation except through total abandonment of its old ways and through massive West German assistance, the Federal Republic was a political and economic success and could only lose by jeopardizing its fundamental structure. At the same time, it appeared imperative to maintain continuity. If the constitutional order of Germany was open to revision, a long period of uncertainty in both domestic and international relations would ensue, since nobody would know which rules would obtain in the future.

With respect to German unification on the basis of either article 23 or article 146, the GDR's Modrow again appears to have played the role of a troublemaker. Soviet commentators, spokesmen and politicians adopted his view that application of article 23 would result in an 'Anschluss'. Just as Austria had been annexed and subjugated by Hitler's Germany in 1938, the GDR would be 'devoured' by the Federal Republic. Accession to West Germany was portrayed as being tantamount to acceptance of Bonn's diktat by the East Germans who would be deprived of any opportunity to have any say in determining the procedures and the results of unification. Also, unification would be consummated in one single step. Everything would be done in a moment — a prospect which particularly terrified the Soviet leaders. All this, however, was a total misrepresentation of the actual implications. While the Basic Law would in fact have to be adopted by the GDR, the conditions of unification were open to negotiation. *Rapprochement* between the two parts of Germany would certainly be a long process in the course of which numerous problems would have to be discussed and decided. This might also include agreement on modifications and changes of the Basic Law.

Whatever the real situation, Soviet suspicion had been aroused with regard to article 23. As a result of Modrow's talks with Gorbachev and Soviet Minister President Ryzhkov on 6 March 1990, the East German government spokesmen stated in public that the three leaders had reached agreement that German unification was to be sought only gradually, in stages, and on a basis other than article 23.[44] A few days later, the Soviet Foreign Ministry issued a declaration saying that Bonn wanted to use article 23 as a weapon to deprive other countries of the opportunity to exert any influence on German unification. At the same time, use of article 23 would deny 'sovereign prerogatives' to the GDR, eliminate the possibility of East German 'socialist achievements' to be maintained, prejudice Germany's 'military–political status' to Western advantage and create a basis for future territorial claims (against Poland as could be easily guessed). Consequently, German unification must not pursue this line.[45] As it appears, there was concern in Moscow that the international process which was part of German unification would be determined by the Germans as well and that the Soviet Union would be marginalized as a result. The underlying logic (which again seems to have been transmitted to the Kremlin by Modrow) was that West Germany's commitments, particularly NATO membership, would be then automatically extended to the united state. Moscow saw a need to raise objections in both East Berlin and Bonn against a possible use of article 23 after a freely elected government had taken over in the GDR in mid-April 1990.[46]

Interestingly enough, there was little concern in Moscow about economic losses as a result of German unification. In one of his interviews, Shevardnadze went even so far as to say that the Soviet Union would actually benefit from German unity in economic respects. Once the West German currency were introduced in the GDR, the Soviet Union would be able to exchange goods and commodities under more profitable world market conditions.[47] It can be surmised that, in addition, the Soviet leaders realized that the new relationship which would result from unification was quite likely to make Bonn more forthcoming with regard to satisfaction of the Soviet Union's economic and technological needs.

CONCLUSIONS

The Gorbachev leadership was far from playing the 'German card' against the West, as had been expected for years by many Western observers. There was no effort to take the political initiative and offensive by appealing to the Germans to seek unification and to side with the Soviet Union for this purpose. The political development which resulted in putting the German problem on the international agenda was not due to Soviet encouragement and promotion. On the contrary, the Kremlin was always the most reluctant actor in the game. The Soviet leaders, it is true, had been sympathetic toward those forces in the GDR who combatted the old Honecker regime and eventually toppled it. The underlying expectation was, however, that a newly reformed East German state would result. Neither the sudden opening of the GDR's borders to West Germany nor the ensuing drive toward unification had been envisaged, let alone sought, in Moscow. For some time, the Soviet leaders still tried to stem the tide. Only when they had realized at the end that this was a hopeless venture, did they give up at last.

The Kremlin was being driven and not driving. Consequently, it found itself in a position which opened few opportunities for obtaining a German unification that was seen to be in the Soviet interest. Both the Western governments and the government in Bonn began to press for the future Germany to be in NATO as the Federal Republic had been for three and a half decades. The Soviet Union which was losing its military and political influence in East and Central Europe, was in a difficult situation. The problem was aggravated by Moscow's failure even to indicate a viable alternative. Under these conditions, the Soviet decisionmakers seized upon the opportunity suggested to them by the East German communist government (which was in office until mid-April 1990) to raise objections to unification on the basis of article 23 — apparently in the hope that this would provide a suitable means to make the Germans and the Western powers heed the Soviet interest. It was doubtful, however, whether this could provide an appropriate means to make the Federal Republic withdraw from NATO or to give satisfaction to the Soviet need for both a symmetrical solution of the German problem and for making a start with a future pan-European security network.

Subsequent Soviet decisionmaking focused on the issue of German membership in NATO. The Kremlin emphasized its share in the four-power rights regarding Berlin and Germany as a whole — a remarkable shift of attitude given that it had tended to ignore these rights for a long period. After the Ottawa East–West conference in February 1990, a 'two plus four' negotiation team, consisting of the foreign ministers of the two Germanies and the four powers — the United States, Britain, France and the Soviet Union – was to seek agreement on the external aspects of German unification once free elections were held and a democratic government installed in the GDR. It was in this forum, which started its activities with a session in Bonn early in May, that the international framework for a united Germany had to be hammered out.

The Soviet attitude was influenced by domestic factors in two respects. First Gorbachev had to respond to the weakening of his position in internal power politics. From early 1989, he was increasingly losing his dominant role in domestic affairs as a result of his failure to steer a fruitful course of reform and thus to make a success of *perestroika*. The Soviet Union had entered a stage when the old order ceased to work, but a new one had not really been introduced. There was a lot of talk devoted to 'radical reform', it is true, but in practical terms what had remained functioning under the old repressive system began to fall apart as well. Second, Gorbachev's previous and natural allies, the reformers, were increasingly estranged. They felt that the president shrank back when necessary steps had to be taken both to create a new mould and to make the Soviet Union a viable society. They also began to realize that their leader lacked adequate insight into what a democratic order and a market economy really were. Therefore, he stuck to old principles when it came to practical action and aligned himself with the orthodox–conservative forces in the CPSU who were loath to lose their privileged positions. Gorbachev's indecisiveness meant that the democratic reformers increasingly constituted themselves as a separate political force, the elected soviets being their principal forum for influence. Starting in winter 1989–90, the orthodox communists responded by asserting themselves as a group as well and using the apparatus, particularly of the party, as their asset in the struggle for power. Consequently, power centres of both left and right emerged and Gorbachev had to adapt himself to these policies. Despite a wave of right-wing criticism against official policies towards Eastern Europe and Germany, the president and his government continued to have considerable freedom of action in foreign affairs.

The hardening of the Soviet stand in early March 1990 regarding Germany's NATO membership is clearly reflective of rightist pressure on Gorbachev not to acquiesce in what was portrayed as a crushing defeat of the Soviet Union and to insure such gains as had been made as a result of World War II. Both by the public at large and in the CPSU Central Committee in particular, Gorbachev and his foreign minister were accused of selling out the empire and of betraying Soviet security interests. What is more, evidence points to Gorbachev having been 'warned' by leading military figures not to overstep the line of concessions beyond which they would be forced to take decisive action. This political impact gradually evaporated, however, when the democratic opposition displayed increasing strength. A crucial event in this respect was that, after both Moscow and Leningrad had elected reformist mayors, the Russian Union Republic was taken over by this group as well. The new Russian President Ieltsin and his government proposed to their soviet that it declare Russia a sovereign state, claim priority of the Republic's legislation over that of the Union and side with the Baltic Republics in their struggle for national independence — motions which were passed almost unanimously. It should also be noted that Ieltsin received foreign policy advice from liberal experts who were favourably inclined toward German unification and advocated German membership in NATO. Since Russia is the Soviet Union's indispensable heartland, Gorbachev could not afford to ignore the shift of power which had taken place there. At the same time, informed Soviet observers tended to conclude that the threat of a rightist coup was less serious than it had appeared. They had increasing doubts that the *apparatchiki*, including the conservatives among the military, were still in sufficient control of the security forces to manage a coup. And if indeed they were, they would win no more than a Pyrrhic victory comparable to what Jaruzelski achieved with martial law in December 1981.

The domestic power scene was not the only factor to result in a relaxed Soviet stand on German NATO membership. There were also economic imperatives which made concessions highly desirable. In June 1990, the Kremlin leadership realized that, within one or two months, the Soviet Union would be unable to honour its financial obligations to other countries unless it received massive assistance from the West — for which the Federal Republic was an obvious candidate. Moscow had a very strong incentive for avoiding a declaration on its inability to pay since this was likely to entail far-reaching negative consequences. This was not the only aspect of the problem which the leaders of the country were facing. Food shortages had already become endemic. In the first half of 1990, it became clear that the situation might deteriorate to a point where the political survival of Gorbachev and his followers would be jeopardized. The president sent urgent pleas to the West asking for interim help in support of the economic reform which he said would be started in earnest at last. Inescapably there would be a period of time during which things were bound to deteriorate still further before — after an estimated three years — the reform effort's success would bear fruit. Again, West Germany was willing both to advocate and to provide large-scale help once political conflict had been overcome and a cooperative relationship had been established.

In the field of foreign policy, the Soviet position *vis-à-vis* the NATO countries continued to weaken. A principal factor in this was what can be rightfully called the waning of the Warsaw Pact. Not only were Soviet representatives isolated when, at the Pact meeting of April 1990, they advocated the opposition of Germany's NATO membership, but the Polish, Czechoslovak and Hungarian representatives openly stood up for the very solution that the Soviet Union did not want. After that, Moscow tried to preserve some appearance that although the Warsaw Pact was breaking apart as a military organization at least it continued to exist, whatever its shape might be. At the meeting in early June, therefore, the Soviet Union dropped any formal membership requirement and offered any concessions regarding the Pact's structures and functions, if only the members stayed in until the envisaged pan-European security had been agreed. But even so, the Eastern alliance had no future. Immediately after the meeting, Hungarian Prime Minister Antall made it clear that his country would seek to opt out as soon as possible, albeit in a regulated manner.

To be sure, the Soviet leadership made a sustained effort to exploit whatever political assets it had in the 'two plus four' negotiations, particularly the Soviet forces deployed in East Germany and the four-power rights with regard to Berlin and Germany as a whole. But the West German government and its Western allies did not allow themselves to be impressed. Shevardnadze's repeated attempts to use these two assets as a lever to enforce fulfilment of Soviet wishes such as, in particular, a prolongation of the German unification process and a Soviet voice in German affairs, were firmly rejected. The concomitant threat that otherwise the Soviet forces might remain in place was not felt to be very impressive in Western capitals. The West's scepticism was justified. After all, Soviet experts clearly realized that an extension of their country's military stay on German soil was not a viable option since no military commander could be happy with his troops being in such an exposed position. Also, it was doubtful how the Soviet soldiers would respond to living in what was expected to become an increasingly thriving Western societal environment.

In this difficult situation, Gorbachev once again displayed the political courage he had shown since 1986–7 when he decided to break the mould of the old order in the Soviet Union and Eastern Europe. He realized that there was no chance of avoiding German membership in NATO. He therefore made up his mind to make this concession soon and on a voluntary basis rather than being eventually forced to do so later. At this stage, he could, and did, still ask for substantial concessions in return. In the course of an extended secret negotiating process, he received the assurance that the strength of Germany's forces would be reduced to 370,000 men, that the Soviet Union would be integrated into Europe and thus retain influence in European affairs and that Soviet troops would remain in East Germany until they could be absorbed by their homeland, ie for an interim period of approximately three years. Also, the concession which had already been publicly offered by the West, that NATO would not extend its structures to East Germany, was reaffirmed. A most crucial point for the Soviet leaders was that Bonn was willing to enter a broad cooperative relationship with the

Soviet Union, furthering both the maintenance of minimum living standards and the introduction of economic reform. The prospect of having Germany as a partner in the process of *rapprochement* with the West, that is with Europe, was highly valued in Moscow.

Both NATO and the European Community were satisfied with the arrangement which was finally worked out during the Gorbachev–Kohl meeting on 15–16 July 1990. The Atlantic alliance would thus provide the basis for the future security system in Europe. Both Western groups had greatly contributed to the agreement which had resulted by displaying a clear willingness to make cooperation rather than confrontation the basis of relations with a democratizing Soviet Union. For Gorbachev, this meant that his idea of Europe's transformation into a zone of common security was coming into being at least to some extent. To be sure, his original concepts — to create a pan-European security system either on a totally new basis or as a result of the two alliances transforming themselves and merging with each other — had failed. But he could reasonably expect, and he explicitly did so, that NATO would not continue as an alliance directed against the Soviet Union but change into an integrative framework in the interests of the whole of Europe.

On balance, Gorbachev had successfully pursued *'realpolitik'*, using this German term directly in his Russian language. He had given in where he had no chance of succeeding, and had exacted crucial concessions in return. In the complicated and difficult domestic situation which he experienced, he had won what he needed most: a sympathetic and helpful Western environment. In the five and a quarter years which had elapsed since his takeover in the Kremlin, he had gone a long way from antagonistically challenging the West, as he had done at first. The overriding needs created in the course of domestic restructuring which had become ever more far-reaching and difficult in the process had gradually led him to seek the West's assistance. This became an essential without which he would clearly be unable to cope with the problems which had piled up in the past. But it is equally evident that the new relationship with Western countries will not automatically eliminate current difficulties at home: there are domestic competitors who feel that they know better what the country needs (some of whom may well be correct), and no amount of Western assistance can conceivably provide the insight and self-help with which the Soviets themselves will have to meet their domestic challenges.

NOTES

1. Congratulatory telegram from Stalin to the leaders of the GDR, 13 October 1949, *Dokumente zur sowjetischen Deutschlandpolitik,*

vol. 1, Berlin (East), Ruetten & Loening, 1957, p. 238.
2. Cf. for example V. Shaposhnikov, 'Nekotorye problemy sovremennogo antivoennogo dvizheniia', *Mirovaia ekonomika i mezhdunarodnye othnosheniia*, 12/1981, p. 23.
3. For a slightly abridged text of Dashichev's April 1989 memorandum see *Der Spiegel*, 6/1990, pp. 142–58.
4. *Pravda*, 13 June 1989.
5. *Pravda*, 14 June 1989.
6. *Neues Deutschland*, 20 January 1989.
7. *Pravda*, 16 June 1989.
8. *The Independent*, 13 May 1989.
9. *Pravda*, 6 July 1989.
10. *Deutschlandfunk*, 2 July 1989.
11. *Mezhdunarodnaia zhizn'*, 12/1989, pp. 7–138.
12. *Izvestiia*, 27 October 1989.
13. *Neues Deutschland*, 2 November 1989.
14. 'Druzheskaia vstrecha', *Pravda*, 2 November 1989.
15. Statement by Soviet Foreign Ministry spokesman Gerasimov during an international press conference in Moscow on 10 November 1989, *TASS*, (in Russian), 10 November 1989.
16. Statement by Gorbachev in a Soviet TV discussion on 16 November 1989 as reported by *Neues Deutschland*, 18 November 1989.
17. Statement by Foreign Minister Shevardnadze before the Supreme Soviet on 17 November 1989, *Pravda*, 18 November 1989.
18. Deputy Foreign Minister Viktor Karpov in the West German magazine *Bunte*, 19 November 1989.
19. Cf. Gorbachev's explanations during his joint press conference with President Andreotti in Milan on 2 December 1989, *Pravda*, 3 December 1989, and during his joint press conference with President Mitterrand in Kiev on 6 December 1989, *Pravda*, 8 December 1989.
20. See the reports on Genscher's talks with Gorbachev and Shevardnadze in *Pravda*, 6 December 1989, and in *Frankfurter Allgemeine*, 7 December 1989. Similarly Gorbachev's address to the Central Committee Plenum of the CPSU on 9 December 1989, *Pravda*, 10 December 1989.
21. *Pravda*, 20 December 1989.
22. E. Shevardnadze, 'Evropa ot raskola k edinstvu', *Izvestiia*, 18 January 1990.
23. 'Druzheskaia vstrecha', *Pravda*, 31 January 1990.
24. Ibid.
25. Manfred Rowold, 'Gorbatschow: Niemand zweifelt an Vereinigung der Deutschen', *Die Welt*, 31 January 1990.
26. For the text of this 'Modrow Plan' see *Frankfurter Allgemeine*, 2 February 1990.
27. 'UdSSR bereit zu sofortigem Truppenabzug aus der DDR', *Neues Deutschland*, 5 February 1990.
28. This idea was also reflected in Shevardnadze's variant of decoupling the German problem's international aspect from the domestic one: four-power-control would have to be re-established in Germany (see his statement at the 'two plus four' conference in Bonn on 5 May 1990 as reported verbatim by TASS, 5 May 1990).
29. 'Vstrecha M. S. Gorbacheva i G. Kolia', *Izvestiia*, 11 February 1990.
30. Chancellor Kohl in his Bundestag speech of 15 February 1990 as printed in *Bulletin* the Federal Press and Information Office (eds), Nr. 26/1990,

16 February 1990, pp. 201–8.
31. 'Zeigen, dass Lehren aus der Geschichte gezogen wurden', *Neues Deutschland*, 13 February 1990.
32. Shevardnadze at a Moscow press conference on 10 February, *Pravda*, 11 February 1990.
33. See for example the statement made by the spokesman of the Soviet Foreign Ministry, Gerasimov, as reported by Uwe Engelbrecht, 'Irritation in Moskau ueber die deutsche NATO-Mitgliedschaft, *General-Anzeiger*', 14 February 1990, and the interview given by V. Falin to *Der Spiegel*, 8/1990, p. 169.
34. 'Vstrecha M. S. Gorbacheva s pravitel'stvennoi delegatsiei GDR', *Pravda*, 7 March 1990.
35. 'Neobkhodimo poetapnyi podkhod', *Pravda*, 7 March 1990.
36. *Neue Berliner Illustrierte* (East Berlin), 9 March 1990.
37. See Falin's contribution to a discussion on the German problem which was printed under the heading: 'Dve Germanii, odna Evropa?' ('Two Germanies, one Europe?') in *Pravda*, 12 March 1990.
38. 'UdSSR-BRD ueber Militaerstatus der Deutschen uneinig', *Neues Deutschland*, 23 March 1990.
39. Andrew McEwen, 'Troops Handed Arms in Warning of Gorbachev', *The Times*, 4 May 1990.
40. Eduard Shevardnadze, 'Towards a Greater Europe — The Warsaw Treaty Organization and NATO in a Renewing Europe', *NATO's Sixteen Nations*, April–June 1990, vol. 35, no. 3, pp. 18–22.
41. Gorbachev in his conversation with Chancellor Kohl on 10 February 1990 as reported in *Pravda*, 11 February 1990.
42. Shevardnadze in an interview with the Soviet journalist M. Iusin, *Izvestiia*, 19 February 1990.
43. *Pravda*, 7 March 1990.
44. See 'Moskau gegen Beitritt nach Artikel 23', *Frankfurter Allgemeine*, 7 March 1990.
45. *Pravda*, 14 March 1990. Similar concerns were voiced by Shevardnadze in the interview published by *Neue Berliner Illustrierte* (East Berlin), 9 March 1990.
46. AP report from East Berlin, 18 April 1990.
47. *Izvestiia*, 19 February 1990.

9 Conclusions

GORBACHEV'S DRIVE FOR POLITICAL CHANGE

Western analysts have always noted that the Soviet Union's economic and technological potential was inferior to that of the United States and other Western countries. For a long time, however, this lower level of development was explained as resulting from the past. The Soviet leaders have traditionally felt that they had the task of catching up but that their system was superior in achieving this end. From the fifties to the sixties, Khrushchev was confident in predicting that the gap would be closed within two decades and that then the Soviet Union would emerge as a power economically superior to the West. In this context, the old Marxist–Leninist prophesy of capitalism's progressive crisis and the eventual world-wide takeover of socialism would come true. There was also a widespread feeling in the West that the Soviet system was particularly well suited for the rapid industrialization and hence modernization of less developed countries. It was on this basis that, for a while, socialism was seen to be historically in the ascent.

The great promise was, however, deceptive. The Soviet system did not move forward but increasingly displayed signs of decline. The goal set by Khrushchev became ever more embarrassing as the target date approached. Worse still, the extent to which the Soviet Union was lagging behind was becoming bigger with the course of time. Also, a new industrial revolution began with the socialist countries essentially unable to follow suit. Instead, the spectre of progressive backwardness and inefficiency loomed before the Soviet Union and the socialist camp. This historical trend was obscured from the public by the immense military strength the Soviet Union and its allies could muster and exploit in relations with the outside world. Seen in retrospect, the Euro-missile controversy of 1979–83 was the watershed. The Kremlin made a sustained effort to use its military potency as its crucial asset in the ongoing political struggle, seeking desperately to turn the tide against the West and to gain the upperhand at last. The 'general crisis of capitalism' which had been expected for so long, would thus have been effected, if artificially.

The design did not only fail; it also brought home the lesson to the Soviet leaders that the avenue of action they had chosen was leading toward eventual disaster. The Soviet Union's 1979–83 effort made the United States embark on both military counterarmament and political confrontation. A competition was initiated which the Soviet Union could not hope to sustain for long, given the other side's superior economic and technological resources. The argument, which was to become conventional wisdom in Moscow later, clearly expressed this: Reagan was allegedly seeking to exhaust the Soviet Union by forcing excessive armament upon it, and the Kremlin did its best to make the American effort succeed by making a bid for arms superiority. As a result, the Soviet Union deepened its economic and technological failure. The situation became so critical that the latent problem could no longer be ignored.

Underlying the emerging crisis was the Soviet system's inherent inability to provide economic efficiency and to generate technological innovation. Of course, there had been various attempts to cope with this age-old weakness. On the one hand, all Soviet leaders after Stalin had sought help from the West — either in the form of cooperation limited to the economic and technological spheres or by systematic illegal acquisition of Western know-how through the KGB. On the other, the Kremlin used what it felt was its system's fundamental superiority in order to compensate, and even to overcompensate, for its economic–technological weakness: that is, the available resources were concentrated on the regime's priorities such as, in particular, arms and astronautics. The underlying logic was that although the West possessed superior resources the Soviet Union could direct more resources to where they were really needed. This idea became doubtful as farsighted Soviet experts began to realize that only an economy which was developed in every respect would be successful in the future. The superiority of the Western system's capacity to generate resources was emerging as crucial. The Soviet Union's handicap as a military superpower possessing little else to make its influence felt in the world was becoming ever more important. The Soviet leaders were confronted with the prospect that their country's underdevelopment was deepening and that its military power would be of declining relevance. Furthermore, military strength itself would not be sustainable in the long run. Necessarily, this posed questions about the underlying system. The Western system became increasingly relevant as an alternative not associated with the failures inherent in the Soviet system.

Gorbachev was the first Soviet leader who realized that his country could not continue as before and who had the courage to draw the practical consequences. From the very beginning the road he took was not easy. All kinds of vested interests had to be challenged.

Within two years, it also became clear that the very essentials of the Soviet system would have to be changed. The bases of power had to be restructured which implied their being put into jeopardy. Political change was set in train — something which the Brezhnev regime had always avoided. To be sure, Gorbachev was not aware of most of the far-reaching consequences that the change would entail. None the less, the obstacles which he had to face in the immediate future were already formidable indeed. To embark upon a new policy was a courageous decision even though the difficulties ahead were clearly underestimated. Despite the objective fact that the Soviet situation imperatively required political action, it took Gorbachev's decisions as a politician as well to allow history to move forward. Otherwise, a total breakdown, with catastrophic consequences, would have resulted later.

In what the Soviet leaders have always seen as their 'historical struggle against the West', the economic and technological inefficiency of socialism thus turned out to be the crucial Western asset. The determining factor was the security insurance provided to the West by NATO. The Atlantic alliance prevented the Soviet Union from exploiting its military power. Once the military factor was neutralized in East–West relations, the two systems' relative capacity to satisfy people's material needs could not but become crucial in the long run.

The often voiced concern that a regime's weakness at home can result in expansion against the outside world is certainly not ill-founded *per se*. The Soviet leaders might have moved in such a direction if the West had not created a convincing deterrent against war and applied pressure. The lesson of the past also applies to the future. Gorbachev's adherence to demilitarization of interstate relations alone will not permanently guarantee peace and security. It must be underpinned with a continuing deterrence from war, if only to provide a safeguard for situations when Soviet decisions will be shaped by persons other than Gorbachev. In a historic period which is likely to be unstable and at the same time frustrating for quite a few groups inside and outside the Soviet Union, enthusiasm about political progress should not obscure the continuing need for security. After all, the Soviet Union will remain a superpower with a sophisticated arsenal of nuclear weapons, a most powerful geostrategic position in Europe and conventional forces whose strength has not thus far been much reduced. The decisive shift in the correlation of forces essentially lies in the Soviet Union's loss of political control over the other Warsaw Pact countries. But even if the Soviet Union had to withdraw to its own boundaries it would still retain a potentially predominant position on the European continent.

At present, however, turmoil not only in the Warsaw Pact but also in the Soviet homeland absorbs available energies to the extent that the Soviet Union cannot afford to challenge the outside world. Additionally, the current effort to introduce economic and political reform requires both friendly relations and large-scale cooperation with Western countries. Gorbachev is clearly in a weak position internationally, but he is a master at turning such weakness into political strength. A deliberate effort is being directed at persuading Western audiences that the Soviet Union, weak and disunited as it is, can't possibly be a threat to any one. Therefore, NATO must reciprocate by eliminating the threat it allegedly poses to the Soviet Union. There are continuous appeals to the Western countries that they abandon the military strategy and the defence system of the Atlantic Alliance and transform it into a mere political organization which in turn will gradually merge with the Warsaw Pact into some pan-European security system. Such an outcome would result in a reconsolidation of the wavering Eastern alliance and in Western renunciation of its basic security system.

There are three options for shaping European security after East–West confrontation has subsided:

1. The postwar dualism of NATO and Warsaw Pact can be restored. Modifications would have to be added to ensure that henceforth the two coexisting alliances would direct their efforts at creating a war-preventing equilibrium rather than renewing the previous power-political and/or ideological confrontation. Irrespective of whether this is seen as an attractive option, this may no longer be a practical possibility given the process of decomposition in the Warsaw Pact and the concomitant feeling of the Western public that NATO's previous anti-Soviet mission has become anachronistic.

2. As an alternative, the Gorbachev leadership tries to sell the idea of a pan-European security system to the West. Soviet official explanations about such a system's structure have been comparatively scanty and sometimes contradictory. There has been occasional reference to the idea of collective security. The group of thirty-five nations comprising the CSCE would provide the framework within which common institutions for verification of arms control agreements, for implementation of military confidence-building measures and for political crisis management could be created. Such a security structure may be useful to some extent if it were supplementary in character. Were it to be espoused as the very basis of European security, it is likely to be destabilizing in the long run, since its effectiveness in providing international security is open to doubt.

3. The Western governments have little confidence in such a system.

They therefore advocate continuation of NATO as a framework for security integration in Europe. Some Western experts feel that eventually the European Community might take over security responsibilities from the Atlantic Alliance. If the Warsaw Pact were to fall apart, the only security system to remain would be on the Western side. This would mean that the model of political/ military integration which has provided a solid basis for reconciliation and peace among Western nations in the last four decades would henceforth affect all of Europe. This would apply also if NATO and a European Community with added security responsibilities, were to recruit new members in Eastern Europe eventually including the Soviet Union as well.

The most concrete vision of a Soviet-type security system for Europe is the idea of collective security. The underlying fundamental principle is that any member state that was the victim of aggression would receive the other member states' support against the aggressor. Seemingly, the arrangement provides for a majority to side with any participant which became the target of attack. In practice, however, things are different. No state has taken such a concrete obligation. If aggression were to occur, each country is free to say which side it chooses to regard as the originator and as the victim. That is, an arbitrary definition could be put forward if a government wanted to take a line other than helping the side under attack. As a result, the promise to support the victim of aggression may not mean anything when practical action is required. Therefore, it is not by coincidence that systems of collective security have failed in the past. The League of Nations of the twenties and the thirties was unsuccessful in preventing not only lesser aggressions such as Mussolini's invasion of Ethiopia but also the global disaster of World War II.

In contrast to this, the system of two alliances has worked remarkably well in the postwar period. Situations of extreme tension and outright crisis in East–West relations have been safely handled. While there has been much war on other continents, Europe has been spared any larger military conflict. When armed power was applied or projected in the European theatre, it was not between the opposing alliances but inside the Warsaw Pact. The reason war prevention has worked is that both sides have had a clear definition of the potential opponent and the participating states were committed to preparations against it. Thus both alliances induced their members to make a joint effort to neutralize the other side's war-waging capability. Mutual deterrence from war resulted.

The third model, military integration, has provided the political framework which has allowed old enmities such as, most notably, French–German antagonism to be coped with. It has proved, however, less than completely successful in cases when two adversaries failed to make a sustained effort to overcome their differences. The relationship between Greece and Turkey can illustrate the point. The severest conflict between the two countries is over Cyprus, which is inhabited by both Greeks and Turks. NATO has mediated between the two sides and has prevented an all-out conflict between them on various occasions, but it was unable to make the two sides overcome their differences generally and seek permanent reconciliation. In the autumn of 1974, Turky — after having been much frustrated by Greece — even resorted to armed action in Cyprus. While this did not amount to a direct clash with Greece, it was certainly felt by the Greeks as violating their vital national interests. The Atlantic alliance was successful in making the Turkish action a short episode, but the display of military power had none the less been sufficient to allow the Turks to achieve crucial goals. The example makes clear that although military integration, if effective, can greatly restrain military hostility among member states, it does not provide a panacea for overcoming conflict under any conditions. However, substantial benefit can be expected to result as subsequent Greek–Turkish political interaction demonstrates. This makes most European politicians feel that military integration can make a vital contribution to containing both nationalistic antagonism in Eastern Europe and prospects of excessive strength from a united Germany.

German unification has posed a question as to what role this central European country is to take in the context of European security. That Hitler's Germany drew the continent and the whole world into a disastrous war of unprecedented dimensions still looms large in the minds of Europeans. In an historical perspective, the problem is more fundamental than a war-prone dictator seizing control over the Germans and using their potential for his purpose. The Germans are a great and talented nation; their country is strategically located in the centre of Europe. Therefore, what happens in Germany is bound to be relevant for the other Europeans as well. From the Thirty Years War onwards, European neighbours recognized that Germany had to be weak and divided so as to be susceptible to foreign influence and responsive to foreign security needs. European security was thus bought at German expense, with many European wars being fought on German soil. When the Germans reasserted their strength and unity in the late nineteenth century, they naturally changed this situation. This time security was sought under German conditions and at the expense of the other Europeans. The logical consequence was that Germany was increasingly exposed and became the target of international hostility.

Neither imposition of a European peace order on the Germans nor imposition of a German peace order on the Europeans was a good solution to the problem. In the postwar years, military integration was developed as a means to overcome the German security dilemma. The Western countries and West Germany entered a mutually binding security relationship with obligations and rights, costs and benefits being equally distributed among the participating states. The old problem of which side — the Germans or the other Europeans — would make it at the expense of the other one was solved. It is this capacity to solve the German problem which, *inter alia*, makes NATO appear as an indispensable element of a future European security system in the eyes of not only Westerners but also of Easterners such as the Poles, the Czechs, the Hungarians, and even a number of Soviet experts. For there is no Eastern substitute for NATO integration: the Warsaw Pact was never an integrating framework since it only served as an instrument of military subordination.

IMPLICATIONS OF THE POLITICAL SHIFT IN EASTERN AND CENTRAL EUROPE

The impending unification of Germany has made a long-term decision regarding Europe's future security order both possible and imperative. Until now, Germany's division has been the crucial element in East-West confrontation. Its being overcome entails that the previous structures of confrontation can give way to a new European order. New problems emerge. Has the challenge to the European countries' security gone? Or has it transformed into a new challenge resulting from current political destabilization in Eastern Europe and in the Soviet Union? At the same time, unification of Germany entails the need to make a decision on what role the united country should play in the context of European security. If the greater Germany is included in NATO, this would mean either the continuation of the dualism of two pacts or the extension of Atlantic integration to all of Europe. If, on the other hand, Germany were taken out of NATO or given dual membership in the two alliances (as Shevardnadze and Gorbachev suggested on repeated occasions), the road toward a pan-European security system along Soviet lines would be implicitly taken. This is why the issue of German membership in NATO has been the hard core of both the German problem and the European security issue.

In the past, Western analysts have often voiced the expectation that the Kremlin would play the 'German card' against the West when the time came. The Western countries would then have been put into a very embarrassing situation: Soviet expansionism and German nationalism would unite to challenge the West's position in

Europe. None of this has happened. The Soviet leaders, not the Western governments, were ill-prepared to cope with the German problem once it was put on the international agenda — against their will, to be sure. They are currently far from able to seek expansionist goals, and there is certainly no German nationalism to support them against the West.

The Kremlin is predominantly on the political defensive. Its primary policy motive is to save the last remnants of its previous influence in Eastern and central Europe. Apart from the fact that the fluid situation in the continent does not permit maintenance of the status quo, there are also offensive policy elements. The Gorbachev leadership has reluctantly acquiesced in East Germany leaving the Warsaw Pact for unification. Thus it became inevitable that Moscow would insist on some other security arrangement if NATO is not to take over all of Germany.

Such a solution would have resulted in a political victory over NATO, since the Western alliance would have hardly been able to continue for long if the Federal Republic of Germany, its very backbone on the European continent, had been taken out. It was clear, therefore, that the Western powers including the Federal Republic itself were determined not to allow for such an arrangement. Western willingness to stick to NATO was motivated less by adherence to previous attitudes of confrontation and suspicion than by a keen sense of emerging new challenges to European security. To be sure, the positive change of Soviet policy towards the West which had been initiated by Gorbachev and which gained further momentum in the course of 1990, was seen as a crucial but still fragile achievement in Western capitals, and hence appeared to require precautions in case the Kremlin's policy line might change for the worse again. After all, there was a rising wave of opposition to both Westernizing domestic reform and political cooperation with Western countries – a situation of active intra-Soviet contest in which Gorbachev's stand often seemed ambiguous. But what impressed Western leaders even more than that, was the progressive realization that, once East–West confrontation weakened and appeared to come to an end at last, new threatening conflicts were bound to emerge. In particular, Eastern Europe and, possibly even more so, the Soviet Union were in a process of destabilization and thus entering a period of potentially violent upheaval which in turn might invite armed struggle and brutal repression.

This prospect called for a security structure which provided both political cohesion in Europe and, in the event of need, also sufficient military might so as hopefully to deter or, at minimum, to contain armed action. Not only Western governments saw this need. Gorbachev was equally aware of it when, during the stormy East European events of autumn 1989, he sought an alliance of stability between the Warsaw Pact and NATO, particularly the United States. His design did not work for long, however, since the Warsaw Pact broke down to such an extent that it became a liability rather than an asset to the Soviet Union. As a result, the USSR's concept of gradually developing a pan-European security system through approximation and merger of the two opposing alliances became inoperative. At this point, Soviet international relations experts began to realize that a collective security system for Europe was not in their country's interest even if its creation might be affected by some miracle. Such a system would be structurally unable to cope with the security challenges of impending German unification and with the challenges of destabilization in what used to be the Kremlin's power sphere. So what purpose would it serve the Soviet Union? A recurrence of the international situation of the thirties was the least thing that responsible people in Moscow wanted.

It seems doubtful whether Gorbachev took this advice pure and simple. As the Soviet Union's supreme leader, he was confronted with a rising tide of pressing needs which were bound to take most of his attention. *Perestroika* was on the verge of resulting in failure both economically and politically. The national product and living standards were clearly on a downward trend from what was already a very poor point of departure. Public life got increasingly disorganized; discipline, authority and morals broke down; Gorbachev was blamed for the failure by radical democrats and reactionary apparatchiks alike. For a while, the president appeared willing to give in to the foreign policy pressures of the *ancien régime* cadres taking an intransigent stand on the crucial European security issue of German NATO membership. But he must have sensed that this was no way out of his problems both abroad and at home. *Vis-à-vis* the Western countries, Soviet rejection was an untenable position from the very beginning. The only asset which Moscow could use was to withdraw agreement to German unification – a stance which would alienate the Germans, seen to be crucial both economically and with regard to security, and which might be overrun by the innate dynamics of the German unification process. It was in May 1990 that the policy makers in Moscow concluded that they had nothing to win – and everything to lose – if they continued to exploit their power to withhold German unification. Sooner or later, they felt, they would have to give in without, however, being able to exact the present price. From this moment, the Kremlin began to seek an early rather than a late solution of the German problem.

Domestic considerations reinforced the foreign policy conclusions. Gorbachev realized that the best hope he had of coping with the downward trend within his country was economic, technological, political and other cooperation with the West, not only relieving the Soviet Union of its confrontation burden but also promising positive support in his effort to solve domestic problems. So the Soviet president had no choice but to come to terms with NATO. The Federal Republic of Germany was seen in Moscow as the prime source of potential help. This was another motive to seek accommodation with the Western alliance. Gorbachev did not behave as a petty salesman. To be sure, Bonn had already displayed willingness to help him out by providing credits which saved the Soviet Union from severe payment problems. When, on 16 July 1990, he met the press together with German Chancellor Kohl to publicize their agreement on German NATO membership, it became clear that the price had not been a fixed sum of money but initiation of a broad cooperative relationship between the two countries. Another part of the deal was that NATO was to take a cooperative rather than a confrontationist line (an orientation which the Western alliance had already adopted) and that CSCE institutions would provide permanent links between the West and the Soviet Union (so that the USSR would have reliable guarantees to be included in Europe and not run the risk of staying outside).

When one looks back to the development which has eventually resulted in both German unification and an emerging European security framework largely centred around a modified NATO, it is quite clear that this was certainly not the Kremlin's original choice. The Soviet leaders were obviously caught by surprise when, in the second half of 1989, the German problem became an acute issue in East–West politics. While it can be argued that Gorbachev's new policy line was the ultimate cause of the situation which made German unification inevitable, the Soviet leadership definitely did not want the issue to come up. It was the political change in Hungary and Poland which, among other unforeseen consequences, entailed at first a fundamental political change in East Germany and then an almost irresistible trend toward German unification. Thus the most crucial thing, the re-emergence of a united Germany outside the Soviet sphere of influence, was an unintended by-product of Eastern Europe's 'Finlandization'.

It is an irony of history that the very 'Finlandization' which has haunted Western politicians and analysts for decades as a perceived threatening prospect for Western Europe's independence *vis-à-vis* the Soviet Union, has eventually been put into practice as a process of East European emancipation from the Soviet Union. The Soviet allies which had previously been generally dependent (domestically and ideologically), were allowed to be free and only needed to consider a few rather limited Soviet security interests. The drive for liberty throughout the Warsaw Pact region was strong enough to make Gorbachev and his peers yield once again when the emerging trend toward German unification ran into conflict with Soviet security imperatives. And the Kremlin was willing to jump over its shadow in this crucial issue at last.

GORBACHEV AND THE FUTURE

During a time span of little more than five years, Gorbachev has already reshaped Soviet and European history. Political change, artificially constrained by his predecessors, has been allowed to take its course at last. Gorbachev's courageous decision to act, however, was bound to be both costly and risky. The longer that adaptation to reality had been postponed, the more forceful the negative repercussions were bound to be. What Alexis de Tocqueville had concluded 150 years ago, analysing the French Revolution, is equally valid for today's Soviet Union: nothing is as dangerous for a bad regime than its eventual effort to introduce reform. All the sins of the past are then held against those who seek to overcome the heritage.

Gorbachev has the historical merit in that he has initiated the political change which was inevitable both in the Soviet Union and in Eastern Europe. The Soviet leader has followed a clear vision that the old line could not be pursued any longer and that it had to be replaced by something else, but he was much less clear in recognizing what the problems were and how they could be solved. He also often shrank back from practical action which differed too sharply from traditional wisdom or else seemed too unpopular in the political context. Gorbachev's favorite approach was to act on the principle of trial and error. This was beneficial in that pragmatism, not dogmatism, was introduced as the yardstick of decisionmaking, but it also meant that many zigzags were made at the expense of decisiveness and continuity.

On this basis, the Soviet leader has largely failed to cope with the three crucial problems facing his country:

— the situation resulting from the decline of authority which the discredited CPSU is suffering;
— the increasing ineffectiveness of the economic system; and
— the need to restructure the relations between the different peoples of the Soviet Union.

Regarding the inter-ethnic problem, Gorbachev has already missed the chance to federalize. His protracted insistence that 'democratic centralism' be exercised as before through what was in fact a malfunctioning party could only alienate the forces of national emancipation and make them seek more radical solutions. At the time of writing, he also appears likely to miss the opportunity for a more modest confederalization. There is a general pattern wherein Gorbachev takes up crucial problems but fails to solve them. Much of what he has done has been too late and too little. The inevitable result has been that problems become more acute and pressing. Also, potential allies of reform tend to be alienated in the process.

When one takes a look at recent Soviet policies toward Eastern and central Europe, a similar pattern can be observed. Gorbachev has initiated necessary political change. The ensuing results, however, often came as a surprise to him and did not correspond to his desires. It must be acknowledged that the Soviet leader has gone very far in accepting what he originally had not wanted, but in a number of cases, particularly the development toward German unity, he was late in doing so and hence missed the chance to shape events rather than simply rubberstamping them. Future generations will give credit to Gorbachev for having avoided the use of armed force outside the Soviet Union and also, with some rather minor exceptions thus far, on Soviet territory. But since the problemsolving capacity does not match the resolve to renounce force, fields of intensifying conflict are emerging in the Soviet Union all the time.

What is going to result from this? Will unresolved conflicts allow for a third possibility besides chaos and violence? The time when Gorbachev played a progressive role in history may be nearing its end. The political change which he has initiated may turn out to be manageable only by other persons who adhere to more coherent concepts. At present, the rightist opposition to the Soviet leader attracts much attention, saying that the problems of both domestic and foreign policy are mishandled. It is doubtful, however, whether the conservatives and nationalists alone or in conjunction with the military have any other concept to offer but a renewal of repressive policy. Such a course might lead to armed pacification in some situations and to more violent conflict in others, but it would certainly not provide solutions to the problems that have emerged. Genuine problemsolving can be expected only from reformers who have a clear vision of what is needed. In late spring of 1990, the democratic reform groups in the Soviet Union made substantial political gains when they took control over the Russian Republic. From then on, Gorbachev's political discretion was much restricted with regard to foreign affairs. The capacity to exert pressure on the Soviet president shifted from the conservatives to the radicals, favoring *rapprochement* and accommodation with the West.

Despite all his massive legal powers, Gorbachev frequently appears to be incapable of doing what is necessary. Will he catch up with the pace of events through learning by doing? Or will he increasingly move towards aligning himself with the forces of the past and alienating the reformers? Or will the conservatives succeed in making his reformist spirit prevail again? Will a political alternative to Gorbachev, on either right or left, emerge as a result of current democratization? The answers to these questions will also be crucial for foreign policy decisions.

Index